The Education
of a Mississippian

The Education of a Mississippian

The Early Life of
E. WILSON LYON
Sixth President of Pomona College
1941–1969

Based on letters and personal reflections
compiled and edited by
ELIZABETH LYON WEBB

POMONA COLLEGE
Claremont
2009

ISBN 978-0-9818955-1-2

This book has been designed and produced in an edition of
five hundred copies by the Arion Press in San Francisco.
Copyright © 2009 by Elizabeth Lyon Webb.

For Wilson Lyon's grandchildren
Sarah and Allen Webb, Philip and Julia Lyon

CONTENTS

PREFACE

Historians know the value of the written word in capturing their immediate impressions of events. When they sense that they are in the midst of a life-changing experience, these written records assume special importance for them. It is therefore not surprising that my father, Elijah Wilson Lyon (1904–1989), carefully saved the letters recording his three years in Oxford, England (1925–1928) where he studied modern European history while in residence as a Rhodes Scholar from Mississippi. The scholarship became the pivotal stepping stone in a career path that led him eventually to the presidency of Pomona College in Claremont, California (1941–1969). It also led him away from Heidelberg, his rural Mississippi home, and away from the farming life of his father, grandfathers, and their forebears. He was intensely aware that he was in the midst of this life-changing personal journey when he appended a postscript to a letter to his mother from Hungary on August 20, 1926. "I think it would be a good idea if you would save my European letters," he wrote. "They might prove of interest and perhaps of value. Perhaps you have already saved them."

Wilson Lyon's Oxford letters offer a window on both his three years abroad and on the Mississippi home that he left behind. It was within the broad framework of those two worlds that he came of age. Both worlds shaped his education and both provided a context that helped define his personal identity. In editing them, my goal has been to bring both worlds to life. This volume, a biography of his youth, is the result of that effort. Its first three chapters cover as much as I have been able to discover about Wilson Lyon's life and education in Mississippi. I have been greatly helped in this task by *The Education of a Mississippian*, an unfinished and, regrettably, very partial autobiography that he began shortly before his death. My reading of the 1923-24 *Mississippian*, the weekly campus newspaper that he edited when he was a junior at Ole Miss, has provided me with additional insight into his thinking as an undergraduate and student leader.

His Oxford letters, in Chapters Four, Five, and Six, are a fitting climax to the Mississippi educational experiences which his unfinished autobiography sketches. They document the youthful determination and enthusiasm with which he prepared himself for membership in the academic communities of the English-speaking world. With them we follow young Wilson Lyon through three years of student life, watching him adjust to the Oxford tutorial system, study for exams, and do research for a B. Litt. thesis. The letters reveal fundamental qualities of character that shaped both his personal and professional life: persistence in pursuit of a worthy goal, optimism, realism, and deep love of family and friends.

Equally important, they offer historical commentary on contemporary events both at home and abroad. In the spring of 1926, he watches a Fascist parade in Naples and reports later that spring on the British General Strike. During the summer of 1926, he visits Geneva and the League of Nations. In the spring of 1927, the great Mississippi River flood leads him to speculate on a possible role for the federal government in preventing future disasters. That fall he attends the dedication of the battlefield at Verdun on September 18, 1927, and comments on the tragic legacy of war. As his thoughts turn increasingly toward home in the winter of 1928, he notes with alarm the battles between Mississippi's governor Theodore G. Bilbo and the University of Mississippi regarding the future of the university.

Chapter Seven, which follows the letters, describes what happened to my father personally in the months immediately after his return home, and also presents briefly the additional professional steps he took that led him to the presidency of Pomona College in the fall of 1941. Included is his own description of his coming to Pomona College. Finally, the concluding chapter looks at events that shaped major changes in both Heidelberg and the state of Mississippi, making both his home and his state dramatically different from the places that they were when he was a young man. I hope that readers will come away with a sense of the way history intersected both the life of Wilson Lyon and the life of his community, as he made his own personal and professional journey to Pomona College.

The gulf, between the world where my father grew up and the world where he "came of age" as a Rhodes Scholar during his years abroad, was wide and deep. His Oxford years, which were years of growth and self-discovery, also required him to redefine his relationship to all he had known before. His letters document the challenges, and at times the tensions, that such growth entailed.

Several key motifs emerge from these letters and give shape to our understanding of the importance of his Rhodes Scholar experience for him. Probably the most important of these is his conscious sense that he is literally making himself into a scholar and teacher, worthy to take his place in American academia. In 1921, when he enrolled at the University of Mississippi, he was still a farm boy, albeit one who knew he did not want to follow in his farming father's footsteps. He also knew, in 1921, that he loved learning, and that he had been at the top of his class when he graduated from the Jones County Agricultural High School that spring. He had no clear idea, however, how he would translate that love of learning into a professional choice. When his Ole Miss Latin instructor Alexander Bondurant suggested to him during his freshman year that he had the potential to become a Rhodes Scholar, he single-mindedly set his eye on achieving this goal. College for him became serious business, the gateway to the wider world of academia in which, he increasingly felt, he would find his true home.

It took courage, however, to make the transition from Oxford, Mississippi to Oxford, England. We sense from reading his letters home that adjustment during the first year abroad was not always easy, probably much more difficult than he imagined it would be. His academic self-confidence, buoyed by being selected a Rhodes Scholar and by four years of outstanding student leadership on the Ole Miss campus, was temporarily shaken by the newness of the Oxford tutorial system. Adjustment was made even more difficult because he had decided to "read" modern European history, even though English had been his major at Ole Miss. He therefore struggled to acquaint himself with a somewhat unfamiliar field of study, as well as a new type of academic system. As a result, he was homesick during those first few months, eagerly awaiting the arrival of letters from home and the *Jackson Daily News*, to which he subscribed during his first year at Oxford.

Uncomfortable academically during his early months in England, he was also somewhat uncomfortable socially. Always a Beau Brummell on the Ole Miss campus, he now worried because he did not have a tuxedo and hurried to purchase one. Money was another constant concern for him, never more so than when he first arrived in England. He worried that his Rhodes stipend would not carry him through the year when he discovered that £50 (half of the £100 he expected to receive on arrival) was being withheld until the end of his time at Oxford, to protect the university's coffers in case he left in poor standing, with fees still owed.

However, through travel, friendships with fellow Oxonians, American, English, and European, and his own increasing familiarity with the field of modern European history, he developed increasing intellectual and social maturity during his second and third years abroad. Letters written during those years show us again that Wilson Lyon was a young man consciously working to glean as much as possible from his Oxford years in preparation for a life in academia. He began to purchase books for a professional library, and was thrilled in the winter of 1927 when he won £5 in a history essay contest for the purchase of additional books that he would otherwise not have been able to afford. He worked hard to learn foreign languages, particularly French, which he had studied for only two years as an Ole Miss undergraduate. Now he needed to read the language for research, and wanted to learn to speak French so that he could travel with greater ease on the continent. There is no record that he audited any French classes at Oxford. Instead, he immersed himself in the language during vacation periods in Rouen, Nancy, Paris, and Brussels, living in student *pensions* and boarding houses and taking supplementary French lessons from private tutors whom he found.

As he matured intellectually, he became less and less tolerant of what he saw as weaknesses in Mississippi's educational system. He had harsh words for those whom he did not feel were intellectually competent teachers or administrators. He particularly singled out for criticism institutions which he felt had been infiltrated by religious fundamentalism. These institutions included the Presbyterian church, of which he and his family were members, and which he continued to attend, at least sporadically, during his Rhodes Scholar years.

His Oxford education was training him to see how philosophical biases affected one's understanding and interpretation of historical events. His tutors were helping him realize how important it was to view the past from a broad perspective. By the time he embarked on writing his B. Litt. thesis during his third year in England, he had become a scholar who could approach historical research with objectivity, willing to shine new light on the events of the past as a result of the discovery of new sources of information. As he looked toward his future in academia, he realized all too well that his education had over-prepared him to teach in many of America's, and particularly the South's, second-tier colleges and universities. This realization led to occasional outbursts in his letters both to his parents and to his Ole Miss roommate, Girault Jones. They reflect part of the process through which he was pulling away from provincialism, and working hard to make himself into a scholar and teacher who could become qualified to be a part of America's first-tier academic communities.

As his intellectual confidence grew, his social confidence also grew. Oxford, at first a place with strange ways, became his home. Writing to his mother on January 28, 1927 he commented that, "After all, whatever we may say about the food, this is more home than any other place in Europe. It is our one recourse when all others fail, the base of supplies and the retreat when all other helps fail. One learns to love it very much and to feel quite at home in the Oxford atmosphere."

With Oxford as his home base he entered a world of social sophistication beyond anything he had ever known or imagined. And he recognized that being able to move easily in that world would be one of the things that would mark him as an educated man. A house party at the home of his friend Girault Jones, which had been the social high point of his undergraduate years at Ole Miss, was replaced by London balls and dinners where Rhodes Scholars met the Prince of Wales and young women who were members of the British aristocracy. Tennis on a home-drawn court at his home in Heidelberg became the prelude to play on courts in England, France, and Hungary. His enjoyment of the game led to a trip to Wimbledon in June of 1926. Although he had barely learned to swim in the Mississippi creek near his home, he joined a group who rented a punt on the Cherwell in the spring of 1926, and enjoyed the sport throughout his three years at Oxford. His personal habits also changed. On the continent he enjoyed a glass of wine with his meals, a pleasure not legally available in the United States during the Prohibition era.

He began to learn about, and enjoy, art, music, and theater, which were a central part of the more highly sophisticated world that he entered. London and Paris became beacons of culture for him. He viewed great works of art that some of his Ole Miss professors had discussed, and then went on, particularly in the summer of 1927, to educate himself further by reading in the Home University Library series, which he described at length in a letter that he wrote to Girault Jones from Amsterdam on August 18, 1927: "I've bought the volumes in the Home University library on Russian Literature, German Literature, some aspects of French Literature, Drama, Painters and Painting, Architecture, Music, and Communism. Do you know the series? The volumes are small—rather extended essays for the person with limited knowledge on the subject. They are written by experts and I find them very good. The price here is 50¢ but I think 75¢ at home. Anyhow, Henry Holt and Co. publishes the whole series in New York—in case you are interested."

Those letters to Jones, however, are most noteworthy for their discussion of "the ladies", a subject always very close to Wilson Lyon's heart throughout his three years at Oxford. When he sailed for England, he left behind his Ole Miss sweetheart, Hattie May Benjamin. For two years they corresponded, sent gifts at Christmas, and even planned for a possible European reunion. But distance and practicality gradually led the relationship to change from romance to friendship. Neither of them had ever considered that they were engaged to each other, and from the beginning of his time abroad Wilson Lyon had dates with many of Oxford's young women students. He particularly enjoyed attending organized tea dances, which seem to have been very much a part of the Oxford social scene.

By the time his relationship ended with Hattie May, he found himself increasingly drawn to Marjorie Dance, an Oxford undergraduate with whom he spent many happy hours until he sailed home to the United States in the summer of 1928. There is no evidence, however, that he attempted to continue the relationship. The increasing objectivity that had developed in his thinking about home was also reflected in his ability to recognize the problems that might arise if he attempted to transplant an Oxford romance in American soil. As he packed his bags to return to the United States, it was clear that his Oxford education had included the education of his heart as well as his mind. It was also clear, however, that finding a woman to share his life was a central part of the future that young Wilson Lyon hoped to create for himself in the world of American academia.

Although often critical of the South and southern education during his three years abroad, Wilson Lyon was even more compellingly drawn to it because it was home. Within the context of its limitations, which he sensed all too clearly, his parents had recognized his abilities, encouraged his education, and sacrificed financially so that he could take up his Rhodes Scholarship. He recognized this sacrifice and expressed gratitude for it in the first letter he wrote them on the ship as he sailed toward England. At that time, however, he had no clear sense of what study abroad would truly mean to him. Far more significant is the thanks he sent to them in a letter written from Oxford on August 8, 1927, the day he took his *viva*, the oral exam in modern European history that determined that he would indeed receive his B. A. 2nd class and thus be qualified to go on to take a B. Litt. during his third year in Oxford: "You know, mother, I myself can hardly realize how much I have learned here. My travels and Oxford have fitted me to take a place with credit in almost any intellectual society one meets here. When I think of what all my education has meant and will mean to me, I feel more and more grateful to you and father who have made it possible for me to move into that fuller world so far removed from anything any of my schoolmates will ever know. When I think what might have been my fate had I not had sacrificing parents like you and father, I am unable to thank you enough. You have given me advantages better than those enjoyed by boys of far richer parents. I have had the best that the world affords, and I hope I can in some way repay you."

This devotion to family, which Wilson Lyon retained throughout his life, did not, however, prevent him from urging them to do all they could to improve their own standard of living. He was embarrassed that his home had no indoor bathroom when he left for Oxford in the fall of 1925, feeling that he could not invite friends to visit because of this fact. He therefore applauded his father's decision to fix up the house, even suggesting in some of his correspondence with Girault Jones that he himself had had some influence in their decision to do so. He wanted them to become more urbane, and urged them to get a car, spurred on by the fact that his mother's sister, Vera, had one.

Most significantly, he recognized that his career choice would draw him far away from them physically, and intellectually, and articulated this in a letter to them written from Oxford on February 24, 1927, even citing a car as a way of ameliorating the inevitable physical separation that he foresaw between himself and his family during the future: "It has seemed to me more and more a tragedy the older I've grown that we have never had much society in the family between us all. Every year has tended to draw us apart rather than throw us into a common society. My friends have all been found in a different order of life from our own, and forces have tended to separate our interests. I do not refer to our love and affections which are as strong as could be, but to the fact that we have never had a real family society like so many other people have. I, unfortunately, can never spend much more time at home, but the car would help tremendously for the rest."

His letters indicate all the ways he attempted to reassure his parents of his deep love for them, even though he knew he would be drawn away from them physically for the rest of his life. He constantly inquired about the state of their cotton crop, asked them to send a family picture, felt guilty that he had not fixed the fence around his mother's kitchen garden before he went abroad, and expressed interest in all their community activities. He worried relentlessly about his younger sister Josephine, partially deaf, and with limited vision as a result of a childhood illness. He wrote repeatedly to her, distressed when she did not respond, as was often the case, and elated when she did.

He also retained genuine nostalgia for the South, commenting in a February 10, 1927 letter to his mother that there was no spring anywhere as lovely as a Mississippi spring. He followed Ole Miss football and basketball avidly and was delighted when the university team defeated its arch-rival A&M—today's Mississippi State—at Starkville.

However, just as time brought him objectivity about his emotional life, so it allowed him increasingly to look at his community and home state and comment on essential improvements that he felt needed to be made. He was incredulous that electric power did not arrive in Heidelberg until the end of 1927. He felt that it was imperative that the state spend more money on the University of Mississippi in order for it to become a first-class institution. During his final year at Oxford, he was highly critical of Governor Bilbo's attempts to politicize higher education in Mississippi, particularly at Ole Miss, even writing letters to his state legislators to express his concern. Just as his education had led him to be intolerant of the narrow-minded constraints of intellectual and religious fundamentalism, so it had also led him to be intolerant of narrow-minded and self-interested politics.

Despite the existence of the autobiographical sources that I have described earlier, this project's historical scope would never have been possible without the help of many other individuals and sources. Primary among these is the late Girault Jones (1904–1998), who was my father's roommate at Ole Miss and one of his closest friends. Jones served as the seventh Episcopal bishop of Louisiana from 1948 to 1969. The depth of their friendship is illustrated by the fact that he saved a number of the letters that my father wrote him from abroad, and was very helpful in providing information about many of the Ole Miss classmates that my father mentions in his letters. Even more important, he provided me with critical biographical data, based on his reflections on his college friendship with my father. We know Wilson Lyon better because of the stories that Girault Jones shared with me. He and his wife Kathleen welcomed me to their home in Sewanee, Tennessee in 1989 and in Nashville, in 1997.

The late A. B. Lewis (1901–2000) was very gracious in showing me and my son, Allen Webb, the Ole Miss campus in the spring of 1989, as well as in reminiscing about some of the faculty members he and my father knew during their student days together at Ole Miss. My father greatly valued his friendship. Lewis' long association with Ole Miss, culminating in his being named dean of the College of Liberal Arts in 1957, gave my father a sense of ongoing connection to the university throughout his life. I am most grateful for his willingness to share campus history with me. I am also grateful to his son, Arthur Lewis, for the biographical material about his father that I have included in the Directory of Names at the end of this volume.

Residents of Heidelberg, Mississippi have also provided me with memories of my father and his family. Lanie Huddleston Edmonds, former Heidelberg postmistress, recreated for me a picture of the home where my father grew up and gave me a sense of what it was like to live in Heidelberg before the town had home phones, paved roads, electricity, and clean water. Annie Bell Porter, who helped care for my father's sister Josephine during the final years of her life, described what Heidelberg's rural farm life was like in the '20s and '30s. I am grateful for her ongoing friendship and the endless ways in which she has supported the Lyon family.

Another invaluable source of information about my father's family was my father's first cousin, Murray Smith (1909-2007). He and his younger sister, Orline Smith Zagger, were the children of Vera Wilson Smith (1881-1933), a younger sister of my father's mother, and were close friends of my father and his sister Josephine. He recreated for me the scene in December, 1924, when my father learned he had received a Rhodes Scholarship, and verified many details about the life of Rufus Lyon, my father's father.

I cannot deeply enough express my gratitude to the staff of the Mississippi Department of Archives and History. In 1997 a staff member directed me to the *Jasper County News*, which provided me with much of the central historical information about Heidelberg and the activities of my father's family that I used in editing these letters. With no letters remaining that my father's family wrote to him, I am grateful that the weekly *Jasper County News* (1925-1928) contains so much information about the activities of their daily life, allowing me to see both my father's parents taking on a variety of roles in the Heidelberg community. My thanks goes to the staff of Mississippi Power and Light who prepared a report for me that included all the legal agreements that finally turned on the lights in Heidelberg at the end of 1927.

Members of the faculty and staff at the University of Mississippi have been endlessly patient and obliging when I have turned to them for help in identifying some of the faculty and students that were part of my father's years at Ole Miss. In particular, I wish to thank Provost Emeritus Gerald Walton; Brenda West, project manager, Office of University Relations; Barbara Lago, director of Media and Public Relations; Sandra Kennedy, graduate assistant, Registrar's Office; and Pam Shelton, supervisor, Alumni Records. At the Jones County Junior College, which was Jones County Agricultural High School during my father's years as a student there, Tracy Stites was an able guide to the campus and its past.

I am also grateful to the staff of Special Collections of the Honnold/Mudd Library of the Claremont Colleges in Claremont, California where my father's papers detailing his years as president of Pomona College are deposited. Special thanks to Jean Beckner, formerly head of Special Collections, who coordinated cataloguing these papers, and to the staff members who assisted her. This careful cataloguing made it possible for me to easily reference some Mississippi sources, including a description of the Confederate service of Wilson Lyon's maternal grandfather, Thomas Wilson.

Carrie Marsh, currently head of Special Collections, Lisa L. Crane, Special Collections digital production librarian, and Jennifer Bidwell, curatorial associate, have been most helpful in facilitating my research and providing copies of some of the photographs reproduced in this volume. Pauline Nash in the Office of Communications at Pomona College assisted with photo location and identification. My gratitude also goes to Dr. Wanda Finney, archivist at Wilson College in Chambersburg, Pennsylvania, who provided the picture of Paul Havens, the Rhodes Scholar friend who submitted my father's name as a possible candidate for the presidency of Pomona College.

Special thanks to my sister-in-law, Rosemary Lyon, whose research in the applications for Union pensions on file at the National Archives led to the discovery of the first person narrative of Wilson Lyon's paternal grandfather, Elijah Washington Lyon, detailing his Civil War service in both the Confederate and Union armies.

I am grateful to Sherrill Pinney, assistant to Dr. David Alexander, during the years he served as American secretary for the Rhodes Trust (1981-1998). It was she who provided me with documentation explaining the requirements of the Rhodes Scholarship as it was administered in 1925.

In the summer of 1926, Wilson Lyon and his Rhodes Scholar friend Frank Gray spent a month in Gyon, Hungary, at the country estate of the family of Michael Halasz, a young Hungarian who was studying at Oxford. I am grateful to Ellen Gray, daughter of my father's Rhodes Scholar friend Frank Gray, for providing me with information supplementing my own knowledge of the visit.

My thanks also to Cara Downes and Clare Button, assistant keepers of the Oxford University Archives. They were able to send me information that Michael Halasz, my father's Hungarian friend; George Fearnley, his English St. John's classmate; and Marjorie Dance, his English girlfriend, provided the university on their matriculation forms. In George Fearnley's case, this information was supplemented by Michael Riordan, archivist for St. John's and The Queen's Colleges at Oxford University.

For decades, my father's Oxford letters were hidden away in the back of a drawer in the desk that had been in his study when he taught at Colgate University in Hamilton, New York (1929-1941), prior to coming to Pomona College. It was a special moment for me when I found the letters while cleaning out the desk after my father's death. Beneath the pile of letters were his parents' certificate of marriage, an invitation to their wedding, a newspaper account of the wedding and reception, and a list of wedding gifts, written on lined note paper and held together with a now-rusted straight pin. The fact that the letters were originally stored with these wedding documents suggests to me how important they were to the whole family.

Much of the stationery that my father used, and at times the color of the ink on his typewriter ribbon, illustrates his oft-expressed determination to live as frugally as possible so that he could stretch his annual Rhodes stipend as far as possible. Letterhead stationery from Cunard's RMS *Lancastria* was replaced by stationery from the St. John's College Common Room once he arrived in Oxford. His European and British travels were documented on stationery from the hotels and *pensions* in which he stayed. The letters themselves were sometimes handwritten, though frequently typed, particularly when he wrote from Oxford.

He even appears to have taken a typewriter on vacation with him on a number of occasions: there are typed letters written from Italy in the spring of 1926, and typed letters detailing his travels in Hungary and France in the summer and early fall of 1926. On several occasions, when the black part of his typewriter ribbon wore out, he typed a letter in red.

A total of ninety-nine Oxford letters exist, eighty-seven written to his parents and sister, and twelve written to his Ole Miss friend, Girault Jones. Forty-nine are included in this volume. Many of the editorial decisions I have made in presenting them have been governed by the fact that I want to make them as easily accessible to the reader as possible. I have consciously not wanted to turn letters from my father to his family into scholarly documents and have therefore not footnoted references in the letters. Instead I have attempted to set the stage for reading each individual letter with a brief introduction, placing it in the context of the time and events occurring when it was written, and explaining any information the reader needs to know to understand references in the letter. These introductory paragraphs are to some degree designed to stand on their own, as mini-essays. They reflect my editorial judgment regarding the significance of particular events or people that the letter may mention. Factual information in these essays was obtained from online sources referenced through Google.

In cases where the biographical information I wish to provide would be disruptive if it appeared in commentary at the head of a letter, I have placed it in the Directory of Names. If an individual is referenced in the Directory of Names, there is an asterisk by the name when it first appears. The information provided in the Directory of Names enriches my father's story for those who wish to pursue it.

In transcribing the letters, I have corrected occasional English spelling errors, as well as errors in French or Spanish. My father loved inserting French into his letters to Girault Jones. It is clear, from reading his letters, that improving his French was one of the personal goals he set for himself during his three years abroad. However, his early efforts at written French were often less than fully accurate, with accents omitted from typed letters, either because he didn't know where they belonged, or because he was rushing to get his letter into the mail and did not want to bother to put them in. This is most dramatically illustrated in his September 8, 1926 typed letter to Jones where no French accents at all appear. As he improved, he automatically corrected his French as he wrote, another sign of his growing intellectual maturity and his desire to express himself accurately.

For the most part, the letters selected for this volume are reproduced in their entirety. Deleted material usually repeats information given in another letter, or references a person whom it has been impossible for me to trace. Unfortunately, my father apparently saved no letters from anyone who wrote to him. If he had, it would have facilitated tracing some of these references. Articles in the *Jasper County News* have only partially made it possible for me to fill what is obviously a huge gap left by the absence of such a large body of correspondence.

A number of individuals have been helpful in reading drafts of this volume. I am particularly indebted to three of them. The first of these is Herbert Smith, professor emeritus of history at Pomona College, who helped me bring much more objectivity and conciseness to the presentation of my subject in the early stages of this project, and thus helped me find a focus for my work.

I am also deeply indebted to Beverly Wilson Palmer, documentary editor, Pomona College, and Dr. Gerald Walton, provost emeritus of the University of Mississippi. Their reading of my manuscript and their editorial suggestions proved invaluable in shaping my writing to bring Wilson Lyon fully alive during the formative educational years that eventually led him to the presidency of Pomona College.

Other helpful readers of much earlier drafts have been Elliot Gerson, American secretary of the Rhodes Trust (1999-), and David Alexander, president emeritus of Pomona College and American secretary of the Rhodes Trust (1981-98). Mr. Gerson was helpful in answering many of my queries about the Rhodes Trust and in directing me to *The History of the Rhodes Trust 1902-1999*, edited by Anthony Kenny and published by Oxford University Press in 2001. Dr. Alexander helped keep me historically accurate when discussing details of the Rhodes Scholarship. John Hawkes Napier III, Lt. Colonel U. S. Air Force (retired), an Ole

Miss graduate (1949) who spent his freshman year (1942-43) at Pomona College and knew my father during the early years of his presidency there, graciously reviewed a very rough draft of this text and offered helpful suggestions from the perspective of a Southerner and a Mississippian.

The photographs in this book were prepared for publication by Jason Bimber of Lumiere Photo in Rochester, New York. My thanks to him and to Lumiere's owner, Bill Edwards, who helped me in the initial phases of the photo selection process. My gratitude also goes to Ann Stevens of East River Editorial in West Henrietta, New York. She has been my local guide through the intricacies of preparing this manuscript for publication in California. I take full responsibility for any errors that remain.

Publication of this biography would never have been possible without the encouragement and support of Andrew Hoyem, Pomona '57, and the Arion Press in San Francisco, which he directs. My deepest thanks to him and to Pomona College, especially President David Oxtoby, for his willingness to have Pomona College act as publisher for the book and to publicize it to alumni, faculty, and staff who knew Wilson Lyon. My heartfelt thanks go also to my brother, John Lyon, for his support of this publication.

In closing, I wish to express my deep gratitude to my husband, Pierce Webb, whose encouragement has kept me from abandoning this project when I did not feel I could find the time or strength to see it through. His computer expertise, assisted by the late Nelson Stiles, and his willingness to save early drafts of my writing have made it possible for me to bring disparate elements of my research together with an ease that would never have been possible otherwise. As always, his support has sustained me.

Pittsford, New York
November 2008

The Education
of a Mississippian

Wilson Lyon's
Mississippi

Memphis

Holly Springs

Oxford

Starkville

Meridian

Jackson

Newton

Garlandville ● Paulding

Heidelberg ● ● Shubuta

Collins ● ● Laurel
● Ellisville

Hattiesburg

McComb

Woodville

Map by John Kosboth.

New Orleans

CHAPTER ONE
Early Years in Jasper and Jones Counties
1904–1921

When RMS *Lancastria* sailed from New York on September 26, 1925, one of its passengers was Wilson Lyon. He was twenty-one, had just graduated from the University of Mississippi in Oxford, and was now embarking on the most important adventure of his life as he prepared for study as a Rhodes Scholar at "the other Oxford" in England. The Rhodes Scholarship would be for him the tangible first step toward achieving his dream of becoming a college teacher. The network of personal contacts made through his Rhodes experience would lead him to every job in his professional career from his first position at Louisiana Polytechnic Institute in Ruston, Louisiana, to the Department of History at Colgate University in Hamilton, New York, and finally to the presidency of Pomona College in Claremont, California, where he served from 1941 until his retirement in 1969.

As the ship eased out of its harbor berth and sailed past the Statue of Liberty, twenty-two of the thirty-two young Americans who would be his classmates were also on board. When they reached Oxford, they would join the class of 1925, sixty-three Rhodes Scholars representing all of Canada's provinces, Australia, New Zealand, the Union of South Africa, Rhodesia, Jamaica and Bermuda, as well as the United States.

All the members of the American class of 1925 were male, single, and white. Oxford had four colleges for women in 1925, but the first female Rhodes Scholars would not arrive until 1977 after the Rhodes trustees broke the terms of Rhodes' will to make the selection of women possible.[1]

Although he specifically excluded women, Rhodes did not establish any racial qualifications for the scholarship. However, he had built a fortune in sub-Saharan Africa through racial exploitation

---

1. The colleges for women at Oxford when Wilson Lyon arrived were Lady Margaret Hall (1878), Somerville (1879), St. Hugh's (1886), and St. Hilda's (1893).

and manipulation and it is therefore fair to deduce that he implicitly assumed that at least all American scholars would be white.[2] Elliot Gerson, American secretary of the Rhodes Trust, reports that in 1907, just three years after the American Rhodes Scholarship had been inaugurated, an African American from Pennsylvania (Alain Locke, a Harvard graduate) was elected a Rhodes Scholar. The election caused consternation among some of those administering the program in Oxford, and raised fears that Southerners, whose colleges and universities were segregated, would fail to apply for Rhodes Scholarships if they were open to both black and white Americans. Although Locke did accept his scholarship and re-mained for three years, he was ostracized by many American Rhodes Scholars during his time in Oxford. It would be 1963 before another black American Rhodes Scholar was elected.[3]

The young Americans entering Oxford as Rhodes Scholars with Wilson Lyon were therefore a highly privileged class. They repre-sented the group, in both Britain's colonies and in America, from which Rhodes felt that leaders should be drawn. Writing to his solicitor in 1898 on his way back to the Cape from Britain, Rhodes noted that in awarding scholarships he wanted first consideration to "be given to those who have shewn during their school days that they have instincts to lead and will be likely in after life to esteem the performance of public duties as their highest aim".[4] Those who stood at the rail of the *Lancastria* with Wilson Lyon, heading for study at Oxford, had been selected because they had already demonstrated strong leadership abilities during their undergradu-ate college careers. The American portion of the Rhodes class of 1925 represented thiry-two states from California to Maine and their undergraduate educational experiences had been quite varied. Some were Ivy League graduates; others had attended the United States Military Academy. Still others, like Lyon, had been educated in their home states in public universities. The family backgrounds

2. Robert L. Rotberg, *The Founder. Cecil Rhodes and the Pursuit of Power* (Oxford: Oxford University Press, 1988) p. 668.
3. An excellent discussion of this topic is included in David Alexander's chapter, "The American Scholarships" in *The History of the Rhodes Trust 1902-1999*, Anthony Kenny, ed. (Oxford: Oxford University Press, 2001), pp. 108-113.
4. Rotberg, p. 666.

of this group of young men also differed widely. Though many members of the class of 1925 were sons of professionals, others were first generation college students.

Lyon was one of these. His father, Rufus Lyon, was a cotton farmer in south Mississippi's rural Jasper County, and was himself the grandson of one of the area's pioneering families. Those pioneers, Nicholas Lyon, and his bride, Nancy Cox, entered Mississippi from their home near Abbeville, South Carolina in the fall of 1834 and purchased farm land in Jasper County from the federal government in January, 1835 at $1.25 per acre. They were drawn by the lure of new land for growing cotton, which at that time was a very profitable crop.

The Lyons were part of a major influx of settlers into Mississippi that took place in the early 1830s after the Chickasaw and Choctaw Indians, who held large tracts of land in the northern and eastern parts of the state, had been moved west by the federal government to Indian Territory, later known as Oklahoma. At the time they arrived, Mississippi had been a state just seventeen years. Jasper County itself was only a year old in 1834. Because many of its settlers had come from South Carolina, they named the county for Sergeant William Jasper, a South Carolina hero of the American Revolution.[5] Like his great grandfather, Wilson Lyon was entering new territory as he sailed for England. The next three years would take him physically, intellectually, and psychologically into places as uncharted for him as the Mississippi wilderness that had beckoned to Nicholas Lyon.

Wilson Lyon had made all the educational and personal preparation for the life adventure on which he was embarking in his home state, where he was born June 6, 1904, in Jasper County, near the town of Heidelberg. Both his father, Rufus Lyon, and his mother, Willia Wilson, were Jasper County natives, and had grown up in the years just after the Civil War. Born July 16, 1867, in Claiborne, Mississippi, his father was the only child of Elijah Washington

5. E. Wilson Lyon, *The Education of a Mississippian*, pp. 3-4. Personal papers, Elizabeth L. Webb. Written about 1980, this is an extended essay about Wilson Lyon's education in Mississippi, with brief discussion of his study in Oxford, and teaching experiences at Louisiana Tech and Colgate University.

Lyon and Frances Morgan, and spent his childhood and youth on his father's farm, outside what would become the town of Heidelberg. Heidelberg itself was not laid out as a community until 1882, when Rufus Lyon was fifteen. That was the year that Washington Irving Heidelberg, an early settler, gave the right of way over his land to the New Orleans and Northeastern Railroad. Incorporation of the town followed in 1884.[6]

The education that Rufus Lyon encouraged his son Wilson to pursue represented opportunities inaccessible to him. After attending several different rural schools during his childhood, Rufus Lyon had completed his formal education at the Oak Bowery School, which had also been attended by his own father, Elijah Washington Lyon. A tuition bill found in Elijah Lyon's account book seems to document that in the fall term, in 1886, Rufus Lyon was taking a course of study listed as "public school" at a cost of $2.00 a month, with Latin added for an additional $1.00 a month.

There is no indication, however, that Rufus Lyon ever had any plans for a professional career, unlike his own father who, in 1860, had enrolled, at age twenty-one, at the Medical College of Alabama in Mobile, just before the outbreak of the Civil War. By the time Rufus Lyon was twenty, he was working full time, helping run the family farm. His doing so allowed his father to give fuller attention to his medical practice, with the assurance that his son was taking charge of farm operations.

About 1900 Rufus Lyon began his courtship of Willia Wilson. She was a native of Garlandville in northern Jasper County where her father, Thomas Wilson, was a farmer. Born in 1874, the fourth of eight children, she was seven years younger than Rufus Lyon. After completing her education at the Garlandville Academy, she had become an elementary school teacher. One of her teaching assignments was in the Claiborne community, near the Lyon family home. Wilson Lyon reports in his unpublished autobiography that in Claiborne, Rufus Lyon renewed an earlier acquaintance with her.[7] On Thursday, May 14, 1903, at 8:30 pm, they were married in the Presbyterian Church of Garlandville.

6. Information drawn from *Heidelberg Centennial 1884–1984*, a cookbook and local history produced for the Heidelberg Centennial celebration in 1984.
7. *The Education of a Mississippian*, p. 5.

When Rufus Lyon married Willia Wilson, he married into a family that was part of a community in some ways very different from his own. Unlike Heidelberg, which was still a relatively raw frontier town in 1903, Garlandville was the oldest settlement in Jasper County, dating from 1833. Its original settlers were prosperous planters, who had built beautiful homes prior to the Civil War. The devastation of the war, however, had left its prosperity shattered, with many of its antebellum homes only faintly suggesting their former splendor by the time Rufus Lyon and Willia Wilson were married.[8]

The background differences that the bride and groom brought to their union extended far beyond differences in the communities where they were raised. Perhaps the most significant differences were those between the Civil War experiences of Rufus Lyon's father, Elijah Washington Lyon, and his new father-in-law, Thomas Eugene Wilson. Elijah Washington Lyon had initially enlisted with the Confederacy, but after an almost fatal bout with typhoid deserted the Confederate cause. He went north where he enlisted in the Ohio cavalry in 1863 and served in a military hospital with the Union army in Colorado. Thomas Wilson had fought for the Confederacy and survived unwounded against incredible odds in battles in Mississippi, Georgia, and Tennessee, finally surrendering at the battle of Nashville and being imprisoned in Chicago until after the war was over.

Despite these facts, there is no indication that Elijah Washington Lyon's Union service caused tension between the two families, probably because he was never in combat against Confederate forces in the South. However, the differences in the Civil War experiences of their fathers certainly meant that Rufus Lyon had grown up with a perspective on the war that was entirely different from Willia Wilson's.

After a New Orleans honeymoon, Rufus Lyon and his bride returned to the country outside of Heidelberg to live on the Lyon family farm with his parents. The farm house "was an ample one story building, which incorporated an earlier log house. The entire

8. WPA file on Jasper County housed at the Mississippi Department of Archives and History, Jackson, Mississippi.

structure stood on strong pillars which guaranteed protection in a rainy country". The Lyon farm had about one hundred acres under cultivation, with farm operations carried out by four black tenant families.[9]

For Willia Wilson, this move to the country was a dramatic change from the life she had known. Although her own father was also a farmer, she and her large family of brothers and sisters had always lived in the town of Garlandville. Now she found herself alone in the country, with no women her own age to talk with, and a mother-in-law who was in poor health. On October 22, 1903, Rufus Lyon's mother, Frances Morgan Lyon, died.[10] Willia Lyon's sense of loneliness was compounded, and quite probably was tinged with apprehension, as soon as she realized that she was expecting her first child. She would have no woman in the house to share her feelings and questions with in the months ahead.

In his unfinished autobiography, Wilson Lyon provides a glimpse of what Jasper County was like at the time of his birth, a description that makes his mother's country loneliness very understandable. "Jasper County . . . resembled in many ways the earlier settlements of the American people west of the Appalachians. Its economy was based on agriculture, and the products of the forest. The roads were all dirt, and almost impassable in winter. Cross-county travel was largely by horseback. The only communication with the outside world was by the New Orleans and North Eastern Railroad." The racial make-up of the county reflected its slave heritage. About half its 15,000 residents were black, about half were white.[11]

Fortunately Willia Lyon did not experience any complications at the time her son was born. She and her husband, Rufus, named him Elijah Wilson Lyon, thus tying him to both their families. Elijah

9. Wilson Lyon's personal notes not included in his unpublished autobiography. *E. Wilson Lyon Papers*, Box 1, File 8, Special Collections, Honnold/Mudd Library, Claremont, California.

10. Only sixty years old at the time of her death, Frances Morgan was the granddaughter of Mahlon and Mary Jane Morgan. Her grandfather and Nicholas Lyon had been close friends and their families had entered Mississippi from South Carolina together in 1834.

11. *The Education of a Mississippian*, p. 3.

was the name of his grandfather Lyon; Wilson was his mother's maiden name. Wilson Lyon loved his paternal grandfather, but he did not like the name Elijah. Throughout his life he was known to everyone simply as Wilson. Even on the most formal occasions, he hid "Elijah" behind the letter "E" and was known then as E. Wilson Lyon.

A year after Wilson Lyon's birth, in 1905, Willia Lyon persuaded her husband to leave the house in the country and move into the town of Heidelberg, still a relatively new community, with a population of less than 400.[12] Their first home stood at the end of Heidelberg's single commercial street. The move to town mitigated Willia Lyon's loneliness to some degree, but did not relieve much of the drudgery of daily living. There was no electricity in town. She and her husband drew water from a well in their backyard; they had no indoor toilet. There were no paved streets, and few dirt roads leading to other communities. For the Lyon family, and many other area residents, the daily *Laurel Leader* from nearby Jones County and the weekly *Jasper County News* were therefore lifelines of information about the world beyond Heidelberg.

Only one story remains about young Wilson Lyon's earliest years. Because it was just steps from their house to Heidelberg's general store, Rufus Lyon often took his young son with him, and would give Wilson, by the time he was three, a penny to buy a piece of candy. According to a story passed through the family, Wilson put a biscuit in his pocket one morning before leaving for the store with his father. When he arrived, he put the biscuit on the counter and said, "Candy". It's doubtful that the storekeeper could refuse the exchange![13]

Two years after the family moved to town, Wilson Lyon's sister, Alice Josephine, was born at home, on August 24, 1907. Within a year of her birth, the Lyons moved again, this time to the home

12. Census figures show Heidelberg's population was 228 in 1900, and 477 in 1910. Mississippi Power and Light Company, Economic Research Department, *Mississippi Statistical Summary of Population 1800-1980*, Bay Springs, Paulding, Ellisville, and Jackson (February, 1983).

13. Letter from Clifford Lyon to Wilson Lyon, July 24, 1967. Clifford Lyon's grandfather, Rufus Lyon, was a younger brother of Wilson Lyon's grandfather, Elijah Washington Lyon. *E. Wilson Lyon Papers*, Box 1, File 7.

where they would remain for almost fifty years. That house no longer exists, but Lanie Huddleston Edmonds, former Heidelberg postmistress, longtime community resident, and Lyon family friend, describes it as a "pretty" home, set by itself in a grove of trees slightly away from "downtown", but still within easy walking distance of Heidelberg's stores, bank, and post office. The front door had a glass panel and opened onto a central hall, with rooms on each side that had dark beaded wooden ceilings.[14] In hot summer months, after supper, the family might gather on the wide gallery (what Northerners call a porch) that encircled both the front and side of the house; in winter, they might gather around the dinner table after the dishes were cleared away, perhaps reading by the light of a kerosene lamp in the early evening darkness.

Wilson Lyon attended the Heidelberg school through the eighth grade. Like all other institutions of his Southern childhood, it was racially segregated. Statistics paint a bleak picture of white schools during this period, and a desperately tragic picture of black education. During the 1913-14 school year, when he was in the fourth grade, Mississippians spent annually only $8.20 to educate each white pupil and just $1.53 for each black student. The money came from a combination of state allocations and local levies.[15]

Despite these facts, Lyon's own early educational experience was a very positive one. The white Heidelberg school was built in 1908, and was therefore new when he entered in 1910. It was a two-story wood frame building with four classrooms, two on each floor. He and his young classmates gathered around a wood stove on cold days to eat the lunches they brought in lunch boxes from home. Often, he remembered, that lunch included a cold yam. A deep well in the school yard provided water; sanitary toilets were located outside the building.[16] All of Heidelberg's white children went back to

14. Interview with Elizabeth Webb in her home in Heidelberg, Mississippi, November, 1997.

15. These statistics are drawn from a table of Mississippi School Expenditures per Pupil and by Race, 1913-1914 to 1949-1950, created by Neil McMillen, and found in his book *Dark Journey: Black Mississippians in the Age of Jim Crow*, (Urbana: Illinois, 1989), p. 73.

16. State of Mississippi, Department of Education, *High School Report to State Accrediting Commission, 1927-28*, pp. 1-2.

school each fall in early September, with schools closing by mid-April. Because September was cotton picking time, the black elementary school opened approximately a month later than the white school, allowing black children to work in the fields.[17]

At school, Wilson Lyon's classes were small, with several grades taught in a single room.[18] He attended elementary school long before Heidelberg had consolidated its school with those of neighboring districts, thus guaranteeing him more individualized instruction than would be possible in most public schools anywhere in America today. Reflecting on his early schooling, he commented particularly on the devotion of his teachers. "I look back upon them with admiration and affection. They were interested in us, encouraging us, and seeing that we acquired the fundamentals."[19] When one adds his mother's nightly lesson review sessions with him, it is not hard to see how he got off to a wonderful start in school.

His mother, known fondly to her friends as "Miss Willie", continued to teach in Claiborne, near Heidelberg during much of his childhood. Throughout his life he remembered her active encouragement as one of the most important things contributing to his academic success: "Until I had completed the fourth grade, she went over all my lessons with me the evening before they were to

17. Dual school calendars for whites and blacks continued to be the legally accepted practice for decades. A brief article in the September 6, 1928 issue of the *Jasper County News* announced that the white grammar schools had opened on September 4 and that "all colored schools in the county will open the first Monday in October." Black schools also closed earlier in the spring so that children could help with spring planting.

18. The United States Census reported a total population of only 477 for Heidelberg in 1910, both black and white. Although no numbers are available for class sizes in the white school, they must have been very small. Proof of this is documented by the fact that in the 1926-27 school year, when the town had grown by approximately 200 but still before school consolidation, there were only 59 white students at all grade levels (first through tenth) enrolled, according to the annual report to the state accrediting commission filed by the Heidelberg High School. In contrast to the small group in attendance at the white school in 1926-27, the state reported 176 black children in Heidelberg who were eligible by age for school attendance. *Biennial Report and Recommendation of the State Superintendent of Public Education To the Legislature of Mississippi for the Scholastic Years 1927-28 and 1928-29*, p. 91.

19. *The Education of a Mississippian*, p. 5.

be heard. We sat at the dining room table, and subject by subject I studied and recited my lessons. After I had finished the fourth grade, she discontinued this practice and told me that henceforth I was on my own."[20]

In the summer, while school was out, young Wilson Lyon and his friends enjoyed going to nearby Beaver Creek, where they learned to swim (his own swimming never progressed beyond dog paddling) and caught crawfish. There was also the annual family trip to Garlandville, probably at least a half day journey by horse and wagon. Wilson and Josephine loved being with their maternal grandparents, aunts, uncles, and cousins for an extended stay. Recalled Lyon near the end of his life: "Annual summer visits to Garlandville were the height of our year, and our only family vacation."[21]

Although the influence of his mother and her extended family were central parts of Wilson Lyon's childhood, the influence of his paternal grandfather was equally important. After his wife, Frances Morgan Lyon died in 1903, Elijah Lyon lived with Rufus and Willia Lyon and their children until his own death on March 22, 1918. It was his wide range of interests and his independent spirit that drew Wilson Lyon to him. In his later years when he was no longer farming or practicing medicine, he had the leisure to talk with his young grandson in the afternoons when he returned home from school.

It was through him that young Wilson Lyon first developed an interest in history, as his grandfather spoke of events described in Gibbon's *Rise and Fall of the Roman Empire*. He recalls that his grandfather "subscribed to magazines and bought books on many aspects of history". As he and his grandfather read and talked together, they shared the excitement of learning about new worlds and new ideas.

Natural history, however, was Elijah Lyon's particular interest. In many ways, he was a man ahead of his time; he owned a copy of Darwin's *On the Origin of Species*, unusual in Mississippi, where religious conservatism became so strong that the legislature would

20. Ibid., p. 6.
21. Wilson Lyon's personal notes, not included in his unpublished autobiography. *E. Wilson Lyon Papers*, Box 1, File 8.

outlaw the teaching of evolution in the public schools in 1926.[22] Tucked away among his medical book receipts was a description of Greensand Marl from nearby Garland's Creek which he copied from Hilgard's *Geology of Mississippi*, a reflection of his insatiable curiosity about the world around him.

Remembering his grandfather, Lyon noted that he "experimented with new plants and trees, testing whether they would thrive in Jasper County".[23] With a grandfather who opened nature's fascinating complexity to him, he developed an interest in all growing things, which remained with him throughout his life. His letters written to his family during his three years abroad as a Rhodes Scholar are filled with descriptions of the natural settings and plants of the places where he lived or visited.

In a small Southern community like Heidelberg at the dawn of the twentieth century, Wilson Lyon also learned the lessons of history, reflected in the memories of the adults of his community, in particular his mother. From earliest childhood, he was taught to honor and remember the Confederacy. He may have heard Confederate battle stories from his Grandfather Thomas Wilson and most certainly heard his mother talk of Thomas Wilson's participation in some of the most difficult engagements of the war: Corinth, the three month battle for Atlanta, and the disastrous Confederate defeat at Nashville, which had led to his capture and imprisonment in Chicago. From her father's stories, Willia Wilson Lyon knew first-hand about the suffering, tenacity, and unrecognized heroism that for him, and many thousands of young Southerners, had marked their coming of age. Given her father's valiant Confederate service, it is not hard to understand Willia Lyon's ongoing involvement in the United Daughters of the Confederacy. Throughout her son's childhood, she was a very active member of the UDC's Heidelberg chapter.

Wilson Lyon cannot fail to have appreciated the importance of his mother's UDC activities. Before his seventh birthday she had begun working hard to raise funds for a Confederate monument for Heidelberg. These monuments, still found in almost every town in

---

22. *Jasper County News*, 11 March 1926.
23. *The Education of a Mississippian*, pp. 4–5.

Mississippi, honor the Confederacy with the statue, at least thirty-five feet high, of a young soldier, whose figure stands on a pedestal. They dominate the landscape, making it impossible to forget the sacrifices of those whom they honor. Heidelberg's monument cost $2,900.

Willia Lyon delivered the welcoming address to the Confederate veterans present when the monument was unveiled on September 27, 1911. A picture taken on dedication day shows seven-year-old Wilson Lyon in the front row of a large group comprised of townspeople and veterans. He is dressed in short light pants and a long-sleeved shirt. Black stockings and shoes complete the outfit. One of the veterans stands on crutches, his left trouser leg pinned up at the knee of his amputated leg. It is a hot day and some people hold umbrellas to protect themselves from the sun. Eleven little girls, each of whom holds one letter spelling out "Confederacy", are dressed in white. For young Wilson Lyon, the day was undoubtedly especially exciting because his thirty-seven year old Mother gave a speech. It marked an important moment in his childhood, one that he never forgot. The story of his mother's speech at the monument's dedication was one he passed on to his own children as they were growing up.

Church going was also part of life in the Lyon household. His mother, in particular, was active in Heidelberg's Presbyterian church, providing room and board for the minister when he came into town to preach.[24] Late in her life, Josephine Lyon recalled taking buckets of water to the church to wash the pews, a chore made very difficult since the town had no running water. It is not hard to imagine the sense of satisfaction that Willia Lyon experienced when her family put on their best clothes and sat on those freshly washed pews for Sunday services.

The daily structure of the Lyon family's life, however, was shaped by the work required to run their home and cotton farm, and to find additional ways to supplement the family income. Many factors affecting the farm's annual profit were outside Rufus Lyon's control: weather, disease, and cotton's market price, in itself influenced by the complex factors of supply and demand

24. *Heidelberg Centennial,* p. XI.

originating far away from Heidelberg's fields. Though the town was isolated by poor roads and no electric power during Wilson Lyon's childhood, and through most of the 1920s, Heidelberg's cotton farms linked the tiny community to the fortunes of one of the largest commodity markets in the United States. The Lyon family's income, and that of other Jasper County farmers, fluctuated with the price of cotton. This fact is clearly evident by the constant references to the cycles of the growing season and to cotton prices which appear in the letters that Lyon wrote to his Mississippi family from abroad.

In 1995, less than two years before her death, Josephine Lyon talked about the Lyon family farm. It was located west of Heidelberg in what she referred to as the Philadelphia area. Tax records from 1917-18 indicate that at that time Rufus Lyon had 100 acres of cultivated land and 420 acres of uncultivated land. There were also 180 acres inherited from his mother, Frances Morgan Lyon, and referred to as the Morgan Place in family documents. By the late 1930s he would own 740 acres, distributed among three farms ranging in size from 520 acres at Tallahatta to 40 acres at Tallahalie, near Paulding.

Rufus Lyon operated the cultivated land on these farms with the help of black tenant families, who rented land from him and lived in housing he provided. They paid rent at the end of the growing season, sometimes in cash, sometimes with a percentage of their crop. A farming accident left Rufus blind in one eye during Wilson Lyon's childhood. After that accident, he stopped doing manual farm labor.[25] Finding and retaining reliable tenants therefore became critical to the success of his farming. New tenant housing that he constructed while his son was abroad offered prospective tenants, whose help was essential to the operation of his farm, clean and adequate living arrangements, and made him a desirable employer.

As a child, young Wilson sometimes accompanied his father to the cotton fields. In later years, he reminisced about farming by telling his family the story of the mule who ate his lunch when he

25. Telephone conversation with Murray Smith, Wilson Lyon's first cousin, November 30, 2000.

failed to tie it high enough in a bush. The cotton farmer's way of life was one of the implicitly understood facts of his childhood; to him, its details seemed as endlessly repetitive and inevitable as the act of breathing. But he never worked in the field chopping cotton or hung a cotton sack over his shoulder. Because of this, he always stood a step away from really understanding the process in a visceral sense.[26]

Cotton's growing cycle defined the pattern of life in Heidelberg annually from April until September. Annie Bell Porter, born in 1918, recalls farming during her childhood with her grandfather, a tenant farmer, who lived on a farm near the Lyon family farm. The methods she describes were documented in the 1930s when WPA interviewers traveled to every county in Mississippi, creating a portrait of daily life. Her description, which follows, gives a picture of the cotton growing season as Wilson Lyon would have observed it.[27]

Lyon's first trips to the cotton fields each spring probably took place during late April or early May, when he and his father watched cotton being planted. Mules pulled all the machinery that was used. A disk prepared the land for planting, and a distributor spread fertilizer evenly over the prepared land. Next a cotton planter, attached to the back of the plow, dropped seed at regular intervals. The planter was like a round bucket, with a device on the bottom to make a furrow.

---

26. Throughout Wilson Lyon's youth and college years, the price of cotton gyrated wildly. During 1922-28, while he was studying at Ole Miss and abroad, cotton prices steadily declined from the heights (35.34 cents a pound in 1919) they had achieved at the end of World War I, with the decline becoming disastrously precipitous after the Depression set in. The numbers tell a story of growing struggle for Mississippi farmers—black and white—with cotton at 17.98 cents a pound when Lyon returned from Oxford in 1928, dropping to only 5.66 cents a pound by 1931. It is not difficult to see why he began the practice of sending money home monthly to his family in Heidelberg after he began teaching at Louisiana Polytechnic in Ruston in the fall of 1928. Even with his son's help, Rufus Lyon was forced to mortgage his farm in 1934. Statistics cited are from Saloutos, *Farmer Movements in the South*, 255 and are quoted in William D. McCain, "The Triumph of Democracy", in *A History of Mississippi*, 2, Richard Aubrey McLemore, ed. (Hattiesburg: University and College Press of Mississippi, 1973), p. 94.
27. Interview with Elizabeth Webb at her home in Heidelberg, Mississippi, November, 1997.

As the weather became warmer, the activities required for a good cotton crop became more and more arduous. Wilson Lyon was undoubtedly grateful that his family had tenants to do these jobs. Chopping and picking cotton were done completely by hand. Annie Bell remembers chopping cotton with a hoe on Saturdays when the cotton was about a foot high, leaving only two or three strong plants in each group and removing grass and weeds growing around the plants. It was hot work, done in late May or early June.

Cotton picking usually began in late August, when summer was at its hottest. Annie Bell notes that she began picking cotton when she was about seven; three of her brothers and sisters also picked. She describes putting a strap on the cotton sack to hang it from her shoulder and remembers how heavy the sack felt. If it got unbearably hot, her grandfather sent the children out of the field in the middle of the day, and had them wait until 3:00 pm to return. In a rare article headlined "News for Negroes", the *Jasper County News* empathized with the plight of black cotton pickers when it announced, on April 5, 1928, that a newly invented cotton picker was being extensively tested in Leland, Mississippi in the Delta, and touted the machine as a hope for relieving "tired black backs of nightly aches during fall months".

A wagon, pulled by mules, took cotton to the gin after it was picked. Ginning removed the seeds from the cotton, which was then made into 480-pound bales. Prior to the arrival of electricity in Heidelberg at the end of 1927, the gin was powered by a steam engine. Agents at the gin purchased the cotton after it was processed.

Both Annie Bell Porter's grandfather and Rufus Lyon sold their cotton at the gin owned by Allen Lyon, Rufus Lyon's first cousin. It seems very likely that Wilson Lyon spent time at the gin in the fall, when cotton was being processed, sold, and shipped by rail to market. Allen Lyon was a favorite cousin of Rufus Lyon and a friend of the whole family.

Fortunately, throughout Wilson Lyon's youth, cotton was not his family's only source of income. With farm earnings unpredictable, Rufus Lyon was able to fall back on another income resource from his uncultivated land: timber. Mississippi is heavily forested in many areas, including Jasper County, where there are stands of long-leaf pine. Heidelberg had two lumber mills, with good rail connections to the rest of the state and beyond. The lumber business thus provided a potentially significant additional source of income for Rufus Lyon, who had extensive stands of timber on some of his uncultivated acreage. He had the option of either selling this timber outright to lumber companies or of selling the right to remove timber for a specified number of years in the future. In years when cotton prices were low, selling timber interests was a way of supplementing the income of the Lyon household. For Rufus Lyon, buying and selling forested land was therefore a hedge against the financial risks inherent in raising cotton.[28]

A further source of income for Rufus Lyon came from his activities as a cattle dealer. Periodically local farmers paid him to supervise the shipping and sale of their cattle. New Orleans was the point of shipping and sale and Rufus Lyon traveled there by train whenever he had a large enough shipment to make the trip profitable.

Once, when Wilson Lyon was probably about ten or eleven, his father invited him to accompany him. That trip was one of the highlights of his childhood. In handwritten notes on file in the Pomona College archives, he describes it in detail.

"It was the custom for the shipper of the cattle to ride in the caboose of the freight train to which the cattle car was attached. In the city we stayed in a boarding house frequented by shippers. The street cars made quite a noise as they rounded the curve in the street. As we sat on the porch of the boarding house, I was fascinated by the cars as they came down the street with their distinctive noise.

---

28. In Jones County, just twenty miles from Heidelberg, William Mason patented a method for making hard board from the crushed particles of trees. The process used small young pines, previously thought unmarketable. Landowners began planting second growth pines when they realized that they could get a quick return from their investment. In 1937, Rufus Lyon profited from Mason's invention when he sold 240 acres to the Masonite Corporation in Laurel for $900. Depression cotton prices made the land sale dramatic proof of the value of timber in hard times. For more discussion of the timber interest see Nollie W. Hickman, "Mississippi Forests", in *A History of Mississippi*, 2, pp. 212-232.

"We went down to the wharves where cargo was being unloaded. I was fascinated by a cargo of bunches of bananas being unloaded from the great ships onto the shoulders of the workmen who transferred the bananas to freight cars in which they would be transferred for shipping to towns in Louisiana and Mississippi. The bunches were brought off on a moving belt and grasped by the workmen for loading in a car. Ripe bananas were removed and shared with everyone standing by. This was real excitement for a small boy.

"After several days, and when our cattle had been sold, we returned by a local passenger train from New Orleans to Heidelberg. I carried with me the exciting memory of a great city. When father and I returned to Heidelberg, I had something really interesting for my playmates!"[29]

Back in rural Heidelberg, Wilson Lyon's mother coped throughout his childhood with the difficulties of homemaking. Those tasks were arduous and time-consuming. Cooking and baking required that the fire in the kitchen wood stove be maintained at the right temperature. Laundry, rubbed clean on a scrub board by a black washer woman, was done in the backyard after a huge cauldron of water drawn from the well was heated over an open fire. In the house, Willia Lyon swept the floor with a broom. The family's large home garden kept her busy in the fall, canning vegetables to carry the family through the winter. Records in the back of her cookbook list beans, tomatoes, squash, cabbage, peas, and cucumbers—undoubtedly pickles—as well as peaches and berries. She was also concerned about the welfare of her black tenant families, checking on them if there was illness, sometimes taking them food. All these tasks, combined with her teaching, left her little time for leisure.

In the Heidelberg of Wilson Lyon's childhood, where residents worked hard, both in the fields and at home, education was a luxury. The limited resources of many rural Mississippi communities made it impossible for them to provide much more than a basic eighth-grade education even for young white people. At the time Lyon was ready for high school, Heidelberg had no accredited high

29. Wilson Lyon's personal notes not included in his unpublished autobiography. E. *Wilson Lyon Papers*, Box 1, File 8.

school program.[30] His family therefore decided to send him to the Jones County Agricultural High School, twenty-five miles south of Heidelberg in Ellisville. He was a boarding student, traveling between home and school by train. In September, 1918, six months after the death of his grandfather Lyon, he left home at the age of fourteen to continue his education.

Jones County Agricultural High School, which admitted its first class in 1911, was one of fifty agricultural high schools organized in Mississippi between 1908 and 1919 under the Agricultural High School Law of 1908. Its purpose was to provide high school training in rural parts of the state, combining academic courses with courses in agriculture and home economics. Its course of study involved only three years of work beyond the eighth grade. The agricultural courses were designed to instruct students in farming practices that could lead to maximizing yield per acre on the family farms that some of them would return home to cultivate after high school graduation.[31]

Most of the students were boarding students, since there was an established high school in Ellisville serving those who lived in the community. Monthly tuition in 1916, two years before Wilson Lyon entered, was $7.50 a month. The students raised most of the food they ate, with all students participating in farm work. In 1913-14, the Jones County Agricultural High School farm produced 2,000 pounds of hog meat, 200 bushels of corn, 250 bushels of

30. The Heidelberg school was not accredited for high school work until 1924, and even then only work through the tenth grade was offered. The accreditation announcement was reported in the April 17, 1924 issue of the *Jasper County News*, and came at the conclusion of high school graduation ceremonies. At the time of accreditation the high school offered work in English, Latin, History, and Mathematics (Algebra and Geometry). No science was taught, no home economics or manual training, no music or drawing, though all were offered in some of the urban high schools in the state. There was no separate room for a school library, but the school did have between 150-200 uncatalogued books in a "library space" set aside for student use. This is the high school program from which Lyon's sister Josephine graduated in the spring of 1926. (Information found in the report filed with the State Accrediting Commission by the Heidelberg High School for the 1927-28 school year).

31. Reuben W. Griffith, "The Public School 1890-1970", in *A History of Mississippi*, 2, pp. 395-96.

sweet potatoes, 100 gallons of syrup and 2,500 gallons of milk. So much pork was served in the dining room during Lyon's years at Ellisville that he never wanted to eat it again. As a result, pork hardly ever appeared on the dinner table after he married and established his own home.

All boys enrolled in the Jones County Agricultural High School did more than merely till the soil. They were taught to vaccinate livestock, terrace land, and spray fruit trees. After learning these agricultural skills, some students, at the request of the farmer, provided these services to Jones County farmers at no cost beyond the cost of materials required for a given project. As part of his own agricultural training, Wilson Lyon raised a pig, Black Prince, who won prizes in local 4H fairs—and probably ended his days on the dinner table.

The campus expanded rapidly during the school's early years. When Lyon arrived in the fall of 1918, there were three modern brick buildings on campus, which had opened in 1912: an administration building with offices and four classrooms downstairs and an auditorium on the second floor, a boys' dormitory that also contained faculty housing, and a multi-purpose building that included a girls' dormitory, the principal's home, and the dining hall. By the end of the 1912-13 school year the school had built a new barn, with four horse stalls, two cow stalls, a tool shed, a harness room, and a loft. By the end of the next year a new forge shop for the agriculture department had been set up. Academic buildings, however, were not neglected. A new chemistry lab was installed in 1914, and the school soon began charging a matriculation fee, at least part of which was designated for the support of the library.[32]

Despite the school's agricultural emphasis, teachers encouraged their students to continue their education beyond high school. Wilson Lyon felt that during his three years in Ellisville he received "excellent preparation in English, history, mathematics, and science" and was "well prepared for college work". He rose to the top of his class. In his unpublished autobiography, he notes that "the

32. Cecil "Boots" Jordan, *The Story of Jones County Agricultural High School 1911 to 1957*. Printed in 2001. Available through the offices of Jones County Junior College.

school had a practice of naming each six weeks the students who had outstanding averages for that period. To my surprise, I was in second place the first six weeks. Then, encouraged by my teachers, I held first place throughout my three years there. We saw our teachers in the dining hall and in social situations, as well as in class. There were only 200 of us, and the teachers could give us time. We were all urged to get further education beyond high school, and most of us went to college."[33]

These associations with faculty were particularly important to Lyon. Thinking back on his high school years near the end of his life, he noted that he was "deeply obligated to Mrs. J. T. Gantt, whose teaching gave me a love of history that ultimately was a determining factor in my professional life". Students also had more time to talk with and learn from their teachers, because the school had few extracurricular activities. "Athletics were restricted to basketball and baseball. (I never saw a football game until I entered college.) There was no student body organization and no student paper. To a large extent, we were restricted to our studies."[34]

Despite the lack of extracurricular activities, however, some of Lyon's most valuable high school experiences were not academic. Although he had never liked the work of farming, the love of gardening and plants that was first nurtured by his grandfather was developed further by his required courses in animal husbandry and agriculture. His agriculture teacher was Mr. A. C. L. Smith "who, with Mrs. Smith, presided over our table in the dining hall".[35] During his senior year he won a place on the school's 4H livestock judging team, which received first prize at the Mississippi State Fair in Jackson. The prize was a trip to the International Livestock Exhibition in Chicago. He and his Jones County AHS teammates rode north on a special Pullman car that they shared with other 4H Club winners. It was his first trip outside of the South.

His 4H experience extended into the summer and fall after his graduation from high school in 1921. That summer he attended a short summer course at Mississippi Agricultural and Mechanical College in Starkville. There he was named a member of the

33. *The Education of a Mississippian*, pp. 6-7.
34. Ibid., pp. 7-8.
35. Ibid., p. 7.

Mississippi state team that would compete in the fall with other state teams at the Southeastern Livestock Show in Atlanta for a first-prize trip to the International Livestock Show in London. During the month prior to the show, he and his teammates traveled and trained for the event by studying several major livestock exhibitions, including the Tri-State Fair in Memphis, the Illinois State Fair in Peoria, the National Dairy Show in Minneapolis and the National Livestock Show in Chicago.

Although the Mississippi team did not take first prize in Atlanta, participation on the team initiated what became a life-long friendship between Lyon and fellow teammate Myres McDougal*, from Booneville. Both he and McDougal subsequently were elected Rhodes Scholars from the University of Mississippi, Lyon in 1925 and McDougal in 1927.

Writing in his unpublished autobiography about his stock judging experiences, Wilson Lyon notes that preparation for the stock judging show in Atlanta required him to apply for a month-long leave of absence from the University of Mississippi just days after he had enrolled as a freshman. He marvels that he had the temerity to make the request so soon after arriving on campus—and that the request was accepted. "I have always wondered why Dean Milden* granted it. But he did so, only reprimanding me for misspelling 'absence'!" He notes parenthetically that though he was a month late enrolling in classes, he still received As in all his courses.[36]

36. Ibid., pp. 7-9.

* Asterisks denote names included in the Directory of Names.

CHAPTER TWO
Ole Miss
1921-1925

The decision that Wilson Lyon should attend the University of Mississippi in the first place had come after some deliberation between him and his parents during his senior year at Ellisville. "We considered the colleges of the Southern Presbyterian Church, to which we belonged, but these were more expensive than we could afford. From the first, my father had preferred the University of Mississippi at Oxford. Fortunately, the Commencement speaker when my class graduated in 1921 was Alfred W. Milden, Professor of Greek and Dean of the College of Liberal Arts at the University. I had an opportunity to talk with him, and he confirmed my view that I should go to Ole Miss. How simple and easy a matter was entering college in those days. All I had to do was to send my transcript and pay a five dollar application fee."[1] At the time of his acceptance, Lyon had just celebrated his seventeenth birthday.

Although his 4H travels had allowed Lyon to experience life beyond the insularity of his rural Mississippi home region for the first time, it was at Ole Miss that he, with the help of supportive faculty, began the development of a real plan for his future education that would lead him to places that he little dreamed of as he entered the university in the fall of 1921. Oxford, Mississippi was both geographically and culturally far removed from his home in Heidelberg. To get there he had to travel for two days over 300 miles by train, with an overnight stop in the state capital at Jackson. "The train was met by a welcoming committee of students and at once I felt at home."[2] When he arrived in Oxford, he was struck by its courthouse square, fine homes and tree-lined streets, in marked contrast to the newer towns of his South Mississippi home and the area surrounding it.[3]

1. *The Education of a Mississippian*, p. 7.
2. Wilson Lyon's personal notes not included in his unpublished autobiography. E. *Wilson Lyon Papers*, Box 1, File 8.
3. *The Education of a Mississippian*, p. 9.

In June, 1989, just three months after Lyon's death, A. B. Lewis*, a former dean at the university and Lyon's lifelong friend, showed his daughter, Elizabeth Webb and grandson, Allen Webb, the campus "as E. W. knew it."[4] They walked around the circle at the center of the campus which is dominated by the magnificent Ionic columns of the Lyceum Building, the original building of the university. Buildings on that circle face into an ancient grove of trees. A Confederate monument sits at the foot of the circle. When the Civil War began in 1861, the university, chartered in 1844, had been holding classes for only thirteen years. Almost immediately, most of its young men left the campus to take up arms for the Confederate cause, closing the university until after the war was over. The campus and its buildings were the site first of a Confederate military hospital and then a Union military hospital after Grant arrived in Oxford in early December, 1862.[5] Mississippi had not yet recovered, either economically or psychologically, from that war when Wilson Lyon entered Ole Miss in the fall of 1921.

Like all the other institutions of his youth, Ole Miss reflected the legalized patterns of segregation that at that time defined life for all Mississippians, black and white. These patterns grew out of a response to Civil War defeat and a subsequently defiant reassertion of white supremacy at the end of the nineteenth century that culminated in the adoption of the Mississippi Constitution of 1890. Although segregated schools were central to the maintenance of social inequity between blacks and whites, they were only one of Mississippi's many segregated facilities. The trains that Lyon rode back and forth to school, first to the Jones County Agricultural High School and then to Ole Miss, had separate cars for whites and blacks. In neighboring Jones County where he and his family

4. At the time of the trip, Allen Webb was twenty, and this was his first trip to Oxford. The trip, which had begun as a sentimental journey, suggested to this editor the possibility of reconstructing many of the details of Wilson Lyon's life as an Ole Miss undergraduate. After our stop in Oxford we traveled to Sewanee, Tennessee. There Girault Jones, Lyon's Ole Miss roommate, and his wife Kathleen, were wonderful hosts; as we visited together he began bringing to life a picture of Wilson Lyon, the Ole Miss undergraduate.
5. David G. Sansing, *The University of Mississippi: A Sesquicentennial History* (Jackson: University Press of Mississippi, 1999), pp. 110-115.

shopped during his youth, the city of Laurel did not allow blacks to drive automobiles within its city limits.[6] In Gordon Hall, the men's residence hall where he lived at the University of Mississippi "we enjoyed a service that is largely unknown today. Our rooms were cleaned and our beds made by black janitors, and our meals were served by black waiters. All of them gave us excellent service, and we had warm regards for them. Our comfortable living conditions were conducive to study."[7]

How revealing this quotation is about the world Wilson Lyon knew as a young man. This was a world where blacks and whites met each other daily and had cordial and friendly relations. As a condition of those cordial relations, however, blacks were to view themselves as second-class citizens in a white controlled society. The degree to which this was accepted as a normal state of affairs, even by caring and compassionate whites, is dramatically illustrated by Lyon's failure to comment on the inequities of educational opportunity that his lifestyle in Gordon Hall reflected, even when he wrote about it decades later. As an educator, he would come to champion education as an avenue to opportunity for all students able to work hard and achieve. How different this is from the concept of education as a privilege available only to some, a concept that was reflected in the social realities of his own education, both at home and later as a Rhodes Scholar.

In his unpublished autobiography, Wilson Lyon reflects on what Ole Miss was like when he entered in 1925. He notes that "(a)lthough the University embraced a Liberal Arts College and professional schools of Law, Medicine, Engineering, Pharmacy, and Education, the enrollment was small, and relations of faculty and students were very close. The entire enrollment of the University was approximately seven hundred when I entered, and it did not attain nine hundred until my senior year. Those of us who lived on the campus knew nearly everyone else. Tradition dictated that

6. Custom, not law, was the basis for many of Mississippi's segregation practices. Restrictions on black motorists exemplified this fact. "For a time following World War I, Jackson's Capitol Street, portions of Greenwood, the entire city of Laurel, and doubtless all or parts of many other communities were know to be open only to white motor traffic." McMillan, p. 11.

7. *The Education of a Mississippian*, pp. 9-10.

we speak to all who passed us. The post office was a genuine social center."[8]

When students went in to pick up their mail, they might encounter William Faulkner, their postmaster, who, according to stories Lyon later told, barely kept track of the letters and packages that arrived each day. No one was aware, certainly not Wilson Lyon, that Faulkner was an aspiring writer. He had yet to publish anything. At "Ole Miss, where everybody speaks", according to the campus motto, his taciturn disregard for order and convention won him few friends among the students.[9]

Shortly after arriving at Ole Miss, Lyon met fellow freshman Girault Jones*, who became his closest college friend, a friendship that continued throughout their lives. Jones went on to have a distinguished career of service to the Episcopal Church, serving as the seventh bishop of Louisiana from 1948 to 1969. The human sensitivity that marked Bishop Jones' life in the ministry also was the defining strength of his college friendship with Lyon.

Jones' recollections of the first months they spent becoming acquainted paint a picture of young Wilson Lyon with loving candor. Recalled Jones: "It was the custom in those days to shave the heads of men entering as freshmen. Early in the term, well before cool weather or for that matter six-weeks' tests, the upperclassmen would sweep through the dorms with their scissors. They did no more than mutilate our locks so as to require the service of a barber the next day. In twenty-four hours, two hundred bald heads were sporting beanies to avoid sunburn. Wilson had a superb head of honey-blond hair, and no one was more transformed by sudden baldness than he. From Apollo to Ichabod in five minutes! With my faithful Number Two Brownie, I snapped his picture on a Sunday afternoon standing on the site of the future chemistry building and with a pick-axe held overhead. In the next few years he would have paid any price for that picture; I kept it until it appeared in our senior yearbook for posterity's sake.

"However, that haircut was a turning point for Wilson. It marked a new beginning. As his hair grew, he restyled it using the beanie in

8. Ibid., p. 9.
9. A. B. Lewis conversation with Elizabeth Lyon Webb, June, 1989.

the retraining. It was to be distinctively his for the rest of his life.

"At the same time, Wilson began to discard those suits acquired at the Ellisville Men's Store and order tailored suits from an established haberdashery whose salesman came regularly to campus. We soon learned that Wilson had an eye for fabrics and a yen for style, and it was not long before Ichabod was the acknowledged Beau Brummel on campus, and especially at Ricks Hall, dormitory for women."[10]

Reflecting on his friendship with Wilson Lyon in 1989 and again in the fall of 1997, less than a year before his death, the late Bishop Jones noted that "(e)ach of us had more interest in academics than in athletics; each of us felt a compulsion to do well in class. While he was Presbyterian and I an Episcopalian, our parental training had set us in the matrix of a Christian behavior which the freedom of college did not destroy. When others reveled in a new-found liberty, we remembered our mothers' teaching and we respected each other for it. It was not long before we leaned on each other."[11] This "leaning", which began at Ole Miss, was an essential reason for many of the letters that Lyon wrote to Jones during his three years as a Rhodes Scholar. Jones was always a sympathetic listener, with whom Wilson Lyon could share his thoughts on any topic.

Lyon received a bachelor of arts degree at Ole Miss, which required him to take work in Latin, Greek and mathematics, as well as courses in English literature, history, chemistry and French. Although he would receive B. A. and B. Litt. degrees in modern history as a Rhodes Scholar, at Ole Miss he majored in English, and minored in Latin and Greek.

It was his Latin professor, Dr. Alexander Lee Bondurant*, who called Lyon aside one day after Roman history class during his freshman year and encouraged him to work toward a Rhodes Scholarship. This conversation had a tremendous impact on him. Girault Jones notes that by the end of his freshman year Lyon "was exploring all the ramifications of the Rhodes Scholarship selective

10. Personal recollections written for the Lyon family following Wilson Lyon's death in 1989. A copy of these reflections is included with the personal letters and papers of E. Wilson Lyon that may be found at the J. D. Williams Library on the campus of Ole Miss.
11. Ibid.

process. For most of us, building a class schedule was simple; we took what was required, or what some faculty adviser proposed. Wilson struggled with long-range goals. At a time when few of us did any such planning, he studied each course to make sure it was a dependable stepping stone. I used to tease him by saying that he was the only Presbyterian I knew who rejected predestination; he did not think anything was foreordained, for it was up to him to make it work."[12]

The friendship between Wilson Lyon and Dr. Bondurant extended beyond the classroom to the Latin Club, for which Bondurant was the advisor. Lyon was club president in the fall of 1923. Monthly meetings, as described in *The Mississippian*, the weekly college paper, included everything from singing in Latin to roasting marshmallows, wieners and toast at the Roman *castra*, "a delightful place in the woods where a gorgeous camp fire is always mysteriously found on exactly the right night."[13] Imagining Lyon presiding over informal meetings of the Latin Club, with Dr. Bondurant in attendance, it is easy to see how their friendship deepened each year, as Lyon responded to Dr. Bondurant's encouraging guidance while preparing himself to be a Rhodes candidate.

Girault Jones' remarks about Wilson Lyon's determination to pursue a college course that would lead to a Rhodes Scholarship are a reminder that some of his extracurricular activities at Ole Miss were chosen with an eye toward impressing the Rhodes selection committee. Never an athletic person, he must have been somewhat distressed to realize that "physical vigor, as shown by an interest in outdoor sports or other ways" was one of the criteria for selecting Rhodes Scholars.[14] Although freshmen were required to take physical education for an hour twice a week, he remembers that "the wooden gymnasium was inadequate."[15]

However, one sport, tennis, seems to have attracted his attention.

12. Remarks prepared for presentation by family members at Wilson Lyon's memorial service at the First Presbyterian Church in Heidelberg, Mississippi, June 24, 1989. Jones was unable to attend the service to deliver them in person.
13. *The Mississippian*, 12 October 1923, p. 2.
14. *Rhodes Scholarships Memorandum for the United States of America, 1924*. Material provided for use of the selection committee and candidates for the scholarship.
15. *The Education of a Mississippian*, pp. 10-11.

Although tennis does not appear to have been one of the options included in the required physical education program for freshmen, Ole Miss did have an intercollegiate tennis team. In addition, there was a tennis club for women students,[16] and it is possible that one of Lyon's female friends on campus introduced him to the game.

In any case, he came to love tennis. His cousin, Murray Smith*, recalls that in the summer of 1924, when he was fifteen, he drove to Heidelberg in a car that he had fitted with a truck body. No drivers' licenses were required in those days and Murray had been driving since he was twelve. "My cousin Wilson Lyon was home for the summer. The past year he had been a junior at Ole Miss. He had learned to play tennis and had a court marked out on his lawn (a net but no back stop). That was my first introduction to tennis. He could not drive, so I taught him using my car. The joke around the family afterwards was that Wilson taught me tennis and I taught Wilson to drive."[17] It is quite possible that Lyon discussed his love of tennis during his Rhodes interview. Certainly he derived great pleasure from playing the game during his three years at Oxford.

The only other indication of athletic participation, if not enthusiasm, that he could present to the Rhodes selection committee was a track team that one of Girault Jones' roommates formed after learning that Ole Miss had none. Jones recalls that "both Wilson and I were persuaded to 'go out for track.' There were less than a dozen of us altogether and since no two of us trained for the same event there was no real competition between us. No intercollegiate meets were anticipated, so our only claim for fame was a training table in the dining hall. But we did get our picture in the annual, and while the stream of athletic history was never at flood stage at Ole Miss, that picture is definitely the low-water mark."[18]

Aside from only modest athletic accomplishments, however, Wilson Lyon's extensive participation in campus activities and his outstanding academic achievement made him a strong candidate for the Rhodes Scholarship, which required of applicants both "literary

16. Sansing, pp. 166, 169.
17. Murray Wilson Smith, *Murray and Willie Mae: Their Life Story* (Raleigh, North Carolina. April, 2007), p. 8.
18. Memorial service remarks, June 24, 1989.

and scholastic ability and attainments" and "qualities of manhood, force of character, and leadership."[19]

He was able to demonstrate his "literary and scholastic ability and attainments" outside as well as inside the classroom. One avenue came through his participation in debating, a campus activity which he particularly enjoyed. On the Ole Miss campus there were two rival literary societies for men, Phi Sigma and Hermaean, that met each Monday evening after dinner to engage in competitive debate and public speaking. Lyon was active in Phi Sigma throughout his four years at the university. He notes that "Robert's Rules of Order were our text, and I learned how to preside and direct a meeting."[20] It was the perfect introduction to his future career in educational administration.

The most important of his campus activities, however, was his work on *The Mississippian*, the Ole Miss student newspaper whose staff he joined during his freshman year. In order to work more quickly and efficiently as a newspaperman, he took a course in typing at the Business School. By his sophomore year he was managing editor of the paper. His experiences gathering news of both student academic and extracurricular activities soon made him aware that there was a great deal going on at the university that was not being publicized. He recalls that during his sophomore year "I sought an appointment with the Chancellor* and told him I felt that steps could be taken to give greater publicity to the life and activities of the University. The Chancellor responded by asking me to act as a reporter for the University at a stipend of thirty dollars a month. He took me to Memphis and introduced me to the news editor of the *Commercial-Appeal*. This was the initiation of work for newspapers that would continue throughout my junior and senior years at the University."[21]

Encouraged by the chancellor's response, Lyon on his own also approached the Jackson *Clarion Ledger* and the *Meridian Star*. Both papers hired him to report university news. On at least one occasion (October 28, 1923) the *Jackson Daily News* reprinted his October 26, 1923 editorial from *The Mississippian*, which praised

19. *Rhodes Scholarship Memorandum*, 1924.
20. *The Education of a Mississippian*, p. 10.
21. Ibid., p. 11.

students at both Ole Miss and A&M for their sportsman-like behavior during the Ole Miss/A&M football game in Jackson. Sports reporting was an ongoing part of his job as campus reporter. He routinely telephoned final scores of campus athletic contests to the papers in Meridian, Jackson, and Memphis. Girault Jones pictures his friend Wilson at campus sporting events, "sitting in the press box or with the official scorers, filing the only reports sent in those days to the daily press."[22]

But sports were not the only area of campus life that Lyon covered for the Meridian, Jackson and Memphis papers. He included all campus news as potential subjects for articles, and Jones, who like Lyon reported news to papers in New Orleans and Jackson, recalls that Wilson was quite consumed by the job during their junior and senior years when they roomed together in West Gordon Hall. They were paid by the column inch. "I can still see Wilson, standing over a newspaper spread out on our center table, razor blade in hand, searching out and clipping his stories. These were pasted together, rolled up, and mailed in at the end of the month. That reportorial job got him access to and interviews with an extraordinary number of people."[23] Lyon notes that his income from the three papers was about $75.00 a month for the next two years, more than he needed for his college expenses.[24]

According to Girault Jones, the newspaper work Wilson Lyon initiated in 1922-23, reporting both sports and campus news for three daily Mississippi papers, so impressed students on the staff of *The Mississippian* that they made him editor in the fall of 1923, "an unusual achievement for a junior."[25] As editor of *The Mississippian*, he instituted changes. In his opening editorial, he announced that the paper would be expanded from six pages to eight, and that the annual subscription price would drop from $2.00 to $1.50. It proved to be a very effective marketing plan. The increase in news coverage, combined with a lower subscription cost and prudent business management, increased subscriptions and raised $2500.

22. Memorial service remarks, June 24, 1989.
23. Ibid.
24. *The Education of a Mississippian*, p. 11.
25. Memorial service remarks, June 24, 1989.

This covered all bills plus the purchase of a new Remington type-writer and left a small surplus for 1924-25.

Thirty issues of *The Mississippian* were published under Lyon's editorial guidance during the 1923-24 school year. His editorials reflect, even at this early point in his life, the "idea of a university" that would recur in his conversation and writing throughout his professional life. He saw the university as a real community of learners, and viewed collegial relationships among its students and faculty as the means for stimulating and encouraging academic achievement and personal growth. He encouraged his fellow students, as members of the university community, to participate fully in its life through extracurricular activities. And he certainly did not think college was the place for pranks, a view that became stronger throughout his life. His editorial in the November 11, 1923 issue of *The Mississippian* praised students for endorsing existing college regulations forbidding freshman head shaving, in a vote taken the day after the regulations had been ignored by some rowdy upperclassmen. It was a new regulation and one that Lyon, who had had his own head unceremoniously shaved when he was a freshman, thought should be respected.

He was also determined to publicize the university and its activities throughout the state and region. In an editorial published May 16, 1924 he asked "Is Ole Miss bashful?" He noted that the foot bridge leading from the railroad station to the campus was unmarked and suggested an arched sign over the railroad end of the foot-bridge, "proclaiming to the passing world that Mississippi's greatest educational institution lies just beyond. . . . Connected with the campus lighting system, such an announcement would . . . show that we who claim the university as OURS are proud to put it before the eyes of strangers."

The Rhodes Scholarship selection committee cannot fail to have been impressed by the initiative and ingenuity exemplified by Wilson Lyon's newspaper work. Nor can they fail to have noted his deep commitment to the idea of the university as a community of teachers and students supporting each other in the ongoing search for knowledge, a view repeatedly reflected in his campus newspaper editorials. Most important, however, as they read his recommendations they would have been impressed to read repeatedly that Wilson Lyon was a man of the highest character, a quality admired by friends and professors alike. It was a quality so marked that all who knew him throughout his life knew that they could rely on him absolutely, and that once committed to a task he would follow through.

His word was his bond. Notes his roommate Girault Jones, he "was a man of integrity, a man of moral stature. Despite his consuming desire to achieve, I never knew him to take any of the illicit shortcuts so often used by collegians: No cribbing, no pony in a language class, no skimping on assigned reading, no apple-polishing for faculty members. His academic acceptance on the part of faculty, like his social acceptance on the part of his friends, was earned. There was no pretense about him; his academic endeavors and his extracurricular life on campus simply rang true."[26] In him the Rhodes selection committee must have recognized a student whose character destined him for leadership and whose proven intellectual strength made him ideally suited to benefit from the Oxford University system of education, where individualized student/faculty tutorial sessions were supplemented by a wealth of lectures and activities held in the wider university community. In every way he showed the "qualities of manhood, force of character, and leadership" sought in scholarship applicants by Cecil Rhodes.

Lyon's faculty mentors nominated him for a Rhodes Scholarship in the fall of his junior year, even though they did not expect he would be selected, reasoning that the experience of being interviewed would provide invaluable preparation for his crucial Rhodes interview in the fall of 1924, at the beginning of his senior year. The October 19, 1923 issue of *The Mississippian*, which he was editing, announced that he and H. S. Lipscomb would represent the university as candidates for the Rhodes Scholarship to be awarded in Mississippi. Lipscomb was a 1921 graduate of Ole Miss and a first year law student who was also teaching several classes in the Oxford High School. In addition to his editorship of *The Mississippian*, the article noted that Wilson Lyon was "an intercollegiate debater, vice-president of the YMCA and an official in various student clubs."

26. Ibid.

When the Rhodes committee met on the Ole Miss campus on December 6, 1923, ten candidates from colleges throughout the state were interviewed. Neither Lyon nor Lipscomb was selected for the scholarship. Instead it was awarded to "Mack" Swearingen*, a native of Jackson with a B. A. from Millsaps and an M. A. from the University of Chicago. At the time of his appointment, Swearingen was teaching history at Emory University in Atlanta. The interview experience as well as the high calibre of the scholar selected cannot fail to have impressed Wilson Lyon. Filled with as much determination as ever to win a scholarship, he must also have been somewhat humbled by the competitive challenge that he faced in achieving his goal.

During his senior year, he served as president of the School of Liberal Arts at Ole Miss,[27] as well as serving as president of the campus YMCA These leadership positions further strengthened his qualifications as a Rhodes Scholarship candidate. On December 13, 1924 at interviews held in Jackson, he was chosen to represent Mississippi in the incoming Oxford class of 1925. The interview had occurred just before university classes adjourned for Christmas vacation. On his Christmas train trip home from Ole Miss to Heidelberg, he stopped at the home of his first cousin, Murray Smith, who lived in Collins, Mississippi. Smith recalls that it was the day when the results of the Rhodes interviews for Mississippi were to be announced. The Smiths had a phone and Lyon placed a call to Ole Miss where he was told of his selection. Smith says that the first person his cousin Wilson called after learning the news was Hattie May Benjamin*, a classmate at Ole Miss with whom Lyon was so deeply in love that he thought, erroneously as events would prove, that their romance could survive the separation that his study abroad would impose.[28]

To get the news to his family, however, he had to complete his train trip home to Heidelberg since they had no telephone. One can only imagine their excitement and the joyousness of their

27. Ole Miss Commencement Week Program 1925, *E. Wilson Lyon Papers*, Box 1, File 17.
28. Telephone conversation between Elizabeth Webb and Murray Smith, November 30, 2000.

Christmas celebration in 1924. With untutored charm, the *Jasper County News* spread the word to everyone in the county, reporting that "all of Heidelberg is rejoicing with Mr. and Mrs. R. Lyon as their son Wilson, has won the Rhodes Scholarship, which takes him to the University of England for three years, an honor that so few young men attain."[29]

He was the fourteenth Rhodes Scholar to be selected from the state since the scholarship's inception. Eleven of those fourteen had been graduates of Ole Miss. The six man selection committee, chaired by Alfred Hume*, chancellor of the University of Mississippi, included five Rhodes Scholars, including two Ole Miss graduates: Leonard Eugene Farley and Louis Meredith Jiggits*. Both Jiggits, who had entered Oxford University in 1919 and Drane Lester*, an Ole Miss graduate still completing his Oxford degree at the time of Wilson Lyon's Rhodes selection, had been members of St. John's College. Acting on their advice, notes Lyon, "I applied at St. John's too. I was to find it a happy choice."[30]

29. *Jasper County News*, 22 January 1925.
30. *The Education of a Mississippian*, p. 12.

CHAPTER THREE
Family Letter Readers at Home:
Reading Between the Lines
1925-1928

The results of this "happy choice" are recorded in the letters Wilson Lyon wrote to his family over the next three years. These letters trace the development of close friendships with fellow Rhodes Scholars, as together they "learn the ropes" of the university and explore Europe during extended vacations. By his third year, feeling totally at home, he welcomes fellow Mississippian Myres McDougal to St. John's, and continues a friendship begun when they were teammates on the Mississippi 4H stock judging team in 1921.

As we read these letters we can also imagine his parents reading them at home. The letters arrived in Heidelberg by train, dropped off in a mail bag that the train crew hooked on a post beside the track.[1] They were then taken to the post office, where his family picked them up at their postal box. Perhaps his mother eagerly opened a letter and shared its news with friends right away. The place to savor news, however, was at home, after the work of the day was completed.

The letters introduced Lyon's parents and sister to worlds of experience they had never known and never would know. Although Willia Wilson had had some teacher training, neither she nor her husband had a college degree. Their own role in preparing their son to be honored with a Rhodes Scholarship, however, had been a pivotal one. It was their early recognition of his academic interests, and their willingness to make financial sacrifices to continue his education, that had been essential elements in his success.

This being said, it must also be noted that they did not stand in their son's shadow. In Heidelberg and Jasper County both were respected leaders in their own right, involved in a variety of community activities. While their son studied abroad, these activities

1. Interview with Lanie Huddleston Edmonds in Heidelberg, Mississippi, November, 1997.

marked them as much more than merely the parents of a local Rhodes Scholar hero.

Rufus Lyon did not confine his activities to farming or to the buying and selling of timber interests during Wilson Lyon's Oxford years. He also worked for his community in a variety of other ways. Under contract with the Jasper County Board of Supervisors he supervised the building or replacement of wooden bridges over local creeks, part of an endless process necessary to keep the county's dirt roads open.[2] He was active in town government, serving as town tax collector,[3] and was elected Heidelberg's marshal on December 14, 1926.[4] His interest in education, reflected in his support for his son, Wilson, was also shared with his community. He was a member of the Board of Trustees of the Jasper County Agricultural High School in Bay Springs,[5] and on the committee that selected a site for a new consolidated school that would include Heidelberg High School.[6]

Rufus Lyon was most well known in his community, however, as a court watcher with a phenomenal memory. He loved going to circuit court in Paulding, the county seat, and tried to be there

2. Wooden bridges were built by county residents who bid for the job. With the arrival of cars and trucks, bridges had to carry increasingly heavy loads, and this, combined with the effect of weather and possible termite damage, meant they often needed to be replaced. The *Jasper County News* reported that Rufus Lyon was awarded bridge contracts in 1924, 1925, and 1927. Under the April, 1927 contract for a bridge on Little Bogahoma Creek, noted in the April 21, 1927 *Jasper County News* report of the monthly Proceedings of the Board of Supervisors, he was paid "$2.69 for 80 feet new bridge and 49 cents per foot for 80 feet old bridge". Mississippians' incredible reluctance to relinquish control of their roads to a state authority, preferring that control remain with the county supervisors, to whom responsibility for road maintenance was given in the 1890 Constitution, is well documented in Thomas D. Clark, "Changes in Transportation", in *A History of Mississippi*, 2, pp. 286-301.

3. See prefatory material to February 16, 1926 letter in Chapter Four.

4. The election date and candidates were listed in the December 9, 1926 issue of the *Jasper County News*. Wilson Lyon sent his congratulations to his father on being elected in a January 9, 1927 letter written from Nancy, and not included among the letters in this volume.

5. *Jasper County News*, 21 June 1928.

6. *Jasper County News*, 22 December 1927.

whenever possible.[7] He also took his turn on jury duty, as noted in court records printed in the *Jasper County News*.[8] The cases he heard as a juror would undoubtedly have included burglary, and violations of Mississippi's strictly enforced Prohibition statutes, both common crimes in the 1920s in Jasper County. He spent so much time over the years in court as an observer, and remembered so accurately what had taken place on a given day, that after the Paulding courthouse burned in 1932 a court stenographer and interviewer were sent to his home in an effort to reconstruct as accurately as possible both land records and the information contained in the records of court proceedings that had been destroyed.

One learns a great deal about character—both Wilson Lyon's and his own father's—in the comments about money that mark his Oxford correspondence. In their mutual desire to sacrifice financially for each other, each reflects a deep respect for the needs of the other. Rufus Lyon always was willing to share his limited resources with his son. He provided money to pay his passage on the *Lancastria* in the fall of 1925, since there were no funds available from his Rhodes Scholarship until he reached England. He sent him with several signed blank checks to tide him through possible emergencies.[9] A year later, in the fall of 1926, and knowing his son's finances were severely strained, he decided not to cash a £10 check Wilson sent him to pay for a life insurance premium. Reading the financial references in many of the younger Lyon's Oxford letters, it is possible to sense Rufus Lyon standing quietly behind his son, supporting him every step of the way in a journey that he knows will lead him to a profession and way of life that may take him far from his Mississippi home.

Like her husband, Willia Lyon, who had been her son's encouraging teacher since childhood, was also a leader in community affairs during his years of study abroad. Although she had retired from teaching by the time he left for England, education was still a central concern for her. In the fall of 1925, she was the high school PTA vice president, explaining the school budget at the opening

7. Telephone conversation with Murray Smith, November 30, 2000.
8. *Jasper County News*, 16 February 1928.
9. See reference in October 9, 1925 letter from Wilson Lyon to his family.

meeting.[10] She was also chair of the district PTA and spoke at the district meeting in Stringer in October, 1925.[11] A year later, at a similar district PTA meeting, she spoke on "What Mothers Can Do in Education." Her speech was reprinted in the November 18, 1926 issue of the *Jasper County News*.

Willia Lyon was a person who loved meetings and working within organizations to get things done. In every aspect of her life, she was a doer rather than a passive participant. Her activities with the United Daughters of the Confederacy were extensive in the years after she helped raise money for the Confederate monument that was dedicated in Heidelberg in the fall of 1911. As president of the Heidelberg chapter of the UDC, she organized an Old Soldiers Reunion in the summer of 1926.[12] In the spring of 1927, she attended the state UDC convention in Jackson.[13]

The relationship between Wilson Lyon and his mother that one gathers from his correspondence was a close and complex one. She is the one to whom most of his letters are addressed, and it is from

10. *Jasper County News*, 24 September 1925.

11. *Jasper County News*, 8 October 1925.

12. Willia Lyon's published letter to county residents shows how much she was looking forward to the event. Because the weather failed to cooperate, the reunion was not as well attended as she had hoped. The Civil War had been over for sixty-one years in the summer of 1926, so the veterans would have been in their eighties.

Jasper County News, August 19, 1926
Soldiers Reunion

The Jasper County Old Soldiers' Reunion will convene in Heidelberg on August 25. We are asking that the people of the county turn out and participate in the occasion and help to make this a day of pleasure to the few remaining veterans. We want to see a large crowd out to pay honor to these fast-passing heroes. The United Daughters of the Confederacy are making special arrangements for the entertainment of the Heroes of Gray, but we feel that all will want a part so we are asking that all who come will bring well-filled baskets so that the crowd too will be entertained and provided dinner for.

Our town is too small to do all, so please co-operate with us in this perhaps the last reunion of the men of Gray. Arrangements for the day's entertainment is being made and lets all come and have a good day together. Respectfully,

Mrs. R. Lyon,
Pres. of U. D. C.

13. *Jasper County News*, 12 May 1927.

her perspective that he received most of his news from home. Throughout his stay in Oxford, he retained a deep sense of home not only through her letters, but also through the things she sent, often at his request. Mississippi pecans and a fruitcake arrived at Christmas, and throughout the year her letters were supplemented with newspaper clippings. Because he had reported Ole Miss sports news to Memphis and Jackson papers while he was an undergraduate, he was especially eager to receive the sports section, so he could keep track of intercollegiate rivalries. She even tried her own hand at publicizing community activities, and submitted primarily social events to the *Jackson Daily News* where they received occasional publication. The idea of doing newspaper work to earn a little extra money was probably inspired by her son's own success as a newspaper writer. It was another bond between them.

Though Willia Lyon was a strong woman, she did not always feel strong when dealing with the problems of Wilson's sister, Josephine. When she was four or five, Josephine had an illness, probably meningitis, that left her with seriously impaired vision and hearing. These handicaps made her withdrawn and reclusive, a situation her energetic, outgoing mother found very hard to cope with. Josephine was not strong enough to go to school until she was eight years old. However, she was a good student, and in the winter of 1925 she was Heidelberg's entrant for 2nd year Latin in the District Field Meet held at Vossburg.[14] Nevertheless, she was almost nineteen when she graduated from Heidelberg's newly accredited high school in the spring of 1926, still without enough course work to qualify her for college.

In both the spring of 1926, and the spring of 1927 Willia Lyon sought Wilson's advice about the appropriate "next step" in Josephine's education. His responses suggest that at times he was both more objective and somewhat more optimistic about these matters than his mother was. He wrote from Hungary on August 10, 1926 giving his mother a series of reasons why the Jones County Agricultural High School would probably be the best place for his sister to take an additional year of work so that she could be prepared for college. He cited teachers that he thought were

14. *Jasper County News*, 5 March 1925.

excellent, particularly Mrs. Gantt who taught history. He thought it would do her good to live in a dormitory, making her "self-reliant", something that one notes it would be hard for her to become in the presence of a strong mother.

A concern for his sister and her future is one of the dominant themes that emerges from his letters. Unfortunately, Josephine Lyon never achieved the kind of independence that her brother Wilson, and no doubt her parents, longed for her to have. After graduating from the Mississippi Synodical College in Holly Springs, Mississippi in 1929, she returned to Heidelberg and lived at home with her parents. She never held a job.

Willia Lyon taught her son Wilson that only education would open the future to him, and lack of interest in farming made him listen to her advice from the time he was very young. He had only to look at his own father to know that intelligence alone would not guarantee him a better future. He learned early that he had to educate his mind, and impose on himself the discipline of gaining the advanced degrees required for success in teaching, the field to which he aspired. Home itself, therefore, provided a complex influence as he embarked on preparations for a career in academia. On one hand, it was an unswerving source of support for him, both emotionally and, to some degree, financially. On the other hand, it provided a stark reminder of the educational and social limitations that he was struggling so hard to overcome. This tension can be sensed in a number of his letters from abroad.

Reading the marvelously rich record of his Oxford years that Wilson Lyon has left us, one is struck by the fact that the very richness of the record is a direct result of the fact that there was no other way for him to stay in touch with his family and community except through letters. Nothing but the written word bound them together. In this day and age, when cryptic e-mails have become the most common way for parents and their young adult children to communicate with each other, these letters are a true treasure.

Why, however, at the beginning of the twenty-first century, should we continue to care about letters, written over seventy-five years ago?

Historians may answer this question by pointing out that the letters provide ample illustration of the fact that there are few political or social certitudes in our lives. The world that Lyon knew as he studied abroad between 1925 and 1928 was about to disappear. The hopes engendered by the League of Nations, which he visited in Geneva in the summer of 1926, were already fading with the rise of Fascism in Italy, and would soon be stifled as the Nazis gained power in Germany. In 1935 Mussolini's government flexed its military muscle and invaded Ethiopia; in 1939 they invaded Albania. Wilson Lyon's speculation, after watching a Fascist parade in Naples in the spring of 1926, that Mussolini's vast military buildup would lead to war, proved to be accurate. Republican Spain, where he did research in the spring of 1928, would be convulsed by civil war in less than ten years and become a dictatorship under Francisco Franco.

In the summer of 1926, he and his Rhodes Scholar friend Frank Gray* spent a month at the home of Michael Halasz*, a young Hungarian who was studying in Oxford. Michael's immediate and extended families had country estates south of Budapest in Gyon. His father was a member of the Hungarian parliament and they were extremely generous and gracious hosts. But in the aftermath of World War II they lost everything when the Russians came into Hungary. Writing to his friend Wilson in August of 1946, Michael described his situation, as he told how "my ancient fields have been taken as well as my whole fortune. I am rather badly off, and ask you to send me anything you could give me. Tea, coffee, fish and meat preserves are just as welcome as any sum. . . . Just twenty years ago in 1926 we have had other days in Gyon! Do you remember?"

In a September 18, 1941 article addressed to Pomona's students that appeared in *Student Life*, the Pomona College newspaper, Lyon himself commented on the uniqueness of the historical period when he studied abroad. "It was my good fortune to spend the years 1925-28 as a student in Europe and to see at first hand the steady improvement of international relations at that time. 'The Age of Locarno'[15] reached its height in 1928, and came to a rapid

15. A series of international agreements in 1925, collectively known as the Locarno Pact, attempted to solve some of the issues left unresolved by the Treaty of Versailles (1919) that ended World War I. Under the Locarno Pact, Germany's borders were established and it was allowed to join the League of Nations.

close with the crash of the New York stock market in 1929. As we now look back upon the past 20 years we realize that they represented not peace, but an armistice." Wilson Lyon's letters capture a moment in history that was never to return.

Interesting as they are as historical documents, however, Lyon's letters are equally important as biographical windows on his intellectual interests and his character. In them, we already see the enthusiasm for history that Lyon would carry into the classroom as a college teacher. His description of his travels throughout Europe and the British Isles helped his family experience these places for the first time with him. His superb memory for historic detail, one of his defining intellectual characteristics throughout his life, is already amply evident in these letters, which offer many brief history lessons. History was a subject that he loved, and his letters offer evidence of that fact.

In their description of his work toward his second Oxford degree, the B. Litt. in modern European history, which he received in the summer of 1928, the letters also reveal qualities that were defining characteristics of his personality throughout his life, qualities that were reflected in the way he approached the presidency of Pomona College. He was both a very intellectually energetic man and an incredibly hard worker. One can have little doubt of this after reading of his determination to learn French during the winter of 1926, when he chose to spend his Christmas vacation in snowy Nancy, living in a student *pension*. Knowledge of French was essential for his B. Litt. thesis research on Napoleon's sale of Louisiana to the United States, a topic requiring extensive reading of primary sources. After discovering that there were additional materials housed in the government archives in Madrid, he taught himself Spanish and traveled to Spain in the spring of 1928 to do further research. One is struck, while reading his description of his efforts to gain access to the archives in Madrid, by his self confidence and determination to succeed.

His letters to his Mississippi family also reveal clearly that beyond self-confidence, he was deeply appreciative of all those who had recognized his ability and helped him along the way since childhood. His gratitude to his parents could never be expressed enough. In letter after letter during his three years at Oxford, he told them how much their support meant to him. He never forgot them, either during his three years in England or as he moved from college teaching into administration. Throughout his life, he wrote weekly letters home, and visited Heidelberg as frequently as possible.

The journey motif is one of the oldest and most necessary patterns shaping human experience. Wilson Lyon's letters to his Mississippi family capture a pivotal experience in his own personal journey as he took a major step toward his goal of an academic career. They reveal the heart of a young man of ambition and hope, who would be determined, throughout his professional life, to create within academic communities the kind of collegiality that he had experienced as central to his own education. They also bring to life the supportive spirit of his parents who loved and believed in him so deeply. For in the final analysis there are no "self-made" men or women. All of us have been helped along the way by others. Lyon's letters to his Mississippi family make clear that he was deeply aware of this truth. As such, they are the fitting autobiographical climax to the story of his preparation for a life in academia.

CHAPTER FOUR
Setting Off
1925-1926

Wilson Lyon's first letter home, written on shipboard as he sailed toward England, captures the wide range of emotions that he experienced as he set out on the greatest adventure of his life: momentary homesickness as the ship pulled away from the pier in New York harbor, enthusiasm for the group of young men in his Rhodes class, deep gratitude to his parents for their encouragement and financial support, and jubilation that the amount in the Rhodes stipend had been increased to £400—approximately $2,000 in 1925. Rhodes Scholars were required to pay all their expenses from their stipend, including college fees, room and board, university tuition, and, in addition, expenses incurred during extended vacation periods. Frugality would be required of him during his three years abroad, but he prided himself on his ability to live within his means and the increase in the Rhodes stipend from £350 to £400 made it necessary for him to ask his family for money only once during his years at Oxford.

His reference to the *New Orleans Times Picayune* indicates that he had contacted newspapers outside of Mississippi, in addition to those within the state, to see if they would be interested in paying him for news reports from abroad.

The shirts he mentions at the end of his letter were all made on a manually operated treadle sewing machine. Heidelberg's lack of electric power in 1925 underscores the importance of his reference to his mother's hard work.

Cunard RMS *Lancastria*
Saturday Afternoon, 6:15 P. M.
September 26, 1925

Dearest mother:
They rushed us around so yesterday that I never had the slightest chance to write, and it was impossible this morning

in the bustle of our departure. We sailed at noon and are now well out to sea. The sea is smooth and no one has showed signs of sickness. From the writing room window I can look out on the blue. Another large outward bound steamer is ahead of us over to the left.

The departure this morning was very impressive. As the whistles sounded and the tug boats pushed us out of the pier, hundreds of friends of the passengers waved us goodbye. Many of the Rhodes boys had their parents and sweethearts down at the pier. I felt a lump come up in my throat when I realized how long it would be before I saw you and home again. There was no one for me to wave goodbye, and I took it all rather quietly.

I have met all the boys, and I like them very much. There are 22 of us from this class aboard. The other ten went other ways. One of them, Hart* of Harvard, is to be in my college. We seem to be the only St. John's men.

Drane and I had a great time in New York. I had to postpone my trip to Yale, as I was too tired of traveling and didn't have the time to spare. I didn't stir over New York so widely, but I had quite a time. We took in several shows on Broadway and roamed the streets considerably.

New York is too much city for me. The place is too big to live in. It's all right for a place to come for a pleasure trip, but it must be awful to live there. It is very easy to find your way around and I had no difficulty at all on that point. In fact, it is much easier than most Southern cities. Of course, we touched only a part of it, a very small part.

The luncheon given us by the Cunard people Friday was excellent. The food was good. You certainly get the service. Your waiter does everything just so. Attired in dress clothes he performs in a most formal manner. His bearing is really marvelous and it almost unnerves you.

Here on shipboard we have our choice of the choicest menus. You can eat the whole ten or twelve courses offered if you are able to stand up to it, but most of us aren't. I'm eating rather healthy, but not nearly that much. It is rather unusual to have another help your plate in such an obliging manner.

I fear I am going to be a long time getting fully accustomed to all the aristocracy of the whole life I'm entering into. Everything is as nice as you could wish or dream of, but I prefer the good old democratic American way of looking at it.

The ship is furnished luxuriously. Drane and I have a stateroom together. It is rather crowded but has running water, a lounge, a bureau, and a wardrobe in addition to our berths. We are located on B deck, the first deck used by passengers.

The *Lancastria* is a nice boat and looks good and safe to me. We have a crew of 320 and only 147 passengers on this trip. There is a servant on every landing. You certainly get what you want and get it quick. The service in the dining room is marvelous.

It is dinner time now, good old American supper, and I must close. In case I don't get back to this tonight, I'll add to it Sunday.

Sunday afternoon

Got to talking with the boys last night and didn't get to write any more. It is now just after tea, which I have taken for my second time. I don't find the custom so bad, and I think I will like it all right. Drane acted as host at our table.

I had saved the best news for the last yesterday and didn't get to tell it. At the dinner Saturday at the Harvard Club it was announced that owing to the increased cost of living at Oxford the annual stipend of a Rhodes scholar had been raised from £350 to £400. The increase begins this October. Won't that be fine? I hadn't dreamed of such luck. You should have heard the cheers that greeted Mr. Kerr's* announcement. He is the permanent secretary of the Rhodes Trust and was our honor guest at the dinner. With this increase we should be able to live and travel in comfort. I certainly hope it will relieve me from the necessity of borrowing.

I was interested in the letter from the *Picayune* and will be sure to send the material the editor desires. With my newspaper work and the increase I should make it very well.

We had a religious service at 10:30 this morning. It was the Church of England form and consisted entirely of songs, prayers, and reading. Quite a number went down to it.

After lunch I roamed the ship and played some of the games up on deck. They have indoor tennis, quoits, a game of tossing rubber disks on numbers, and shuttle cock. All were new to me, but I became fairly adept at the one in which you toss the disks on the numbers.

I like our party and believe we have a fine class. They seem to be rather serious minded boys who mean business. By now I know most of them by name. Last night I talked quite a while with Laurie Leighton* from Maine. We compared notes on New England and the South. He is very much like the English already in his accent and manner. The more I see of the boys the better I like them and I think we will have a great trip over together. We have eight more days on here together as the boat isn't expected to make the trip in less than nine days.

The sea is absolutely tranquil and so far I haven't been affected by any touches of sea sickness. It is rather chilly and an overcoat, although not essential, feels very good. I suppose it is still hot at home. I was surprised to find it so cold coming up.

I am anxious for news from home, and I hope to hear from you soon on the other side. It seems so terribly far away here that every little bit of news is appreciated ever so much.

We are going on to London as it will be cheaper to go from there to Oxford. It is much further from Plymouth to Oxford than from London. We will remain in London until Oct. 7, the date when we join our college. That will be a little more expense I hadn't thought of, but I guess I can make it all right on the $50 I have left. I intend to hold on to it until it hurts if necessary. We will have funds awaiting us at Oxford.

Mother, I can never tell you and papa how I appreciate the sacrifices you have made in giving me the opportunities I have enjoyed. Most especially do I thank you for the education you have given me. It was mighty good of you to deny yourselves in order that I might have money to make this trip.

I am seeing things and looking forward to opportunities I never would have had if it hadn't been for you. But few men have the chance that I am now entering on, and I owe it to you.

My shirts are the best I've seen, and I certainly appreciate what you did in getting my clothes ready. I hated to see you work so hard, but you would do it.

My love to Joe. You have been wonderful parents to me and I love you.

Wilson

JASPER COUNTY NEWS
October 29, 1925

———

Mr. R. Lyon had a letter from his son, Wilson, last week who is attending college at Oxford, England, stating that he entered school and settled down and was liking the surroundings fine.

The letter that Rufus Lyon received from Wilson Lyon is undoubtedly this one, addressed to his mother, which gives a wonderfully detailed description of his living arrangements at St. John's College. It is the first of many typed letters sent home over the next three years, and documents the essential purchase of a typewriter. The "scout" to whom he refers was the man responsible for bringing the meals eaten in his room: always breakfast and tea as well as meals ordered for special occasions. The long trip to the bathroom from his room seemed daunting even to a country boy whose Mississippi home did not have an indoor toilet. He had been spoiled by years of convenience at Ole Miss and the Jones County Agricultural High School.

Although Lyon had been educated away from his country home since the end of the eighth grade, both the Jones County Agricultural High School in Ellisville, and the University of Mississippi in Oxford were located in small towns with unpaved streets. Oxford, England with its population of 60,000 (a number cited by Lyon in a newspaper column written in the fall of 1925) was a bustling city, twice the size of Mississippi's capital Jackson, as he notes in this letter to his parents.

It is clear from reading this letter that he had not yet mastered the exchange between dollars and pounds. The pound was valued at approximately $4.85 during Lyon's Oxford years. In saying he would only have $100 left for all other expenses after paying college fees and equipping his room, he underestimated the amount by almost half.

The Green Hat, which inaugurated Lyon's London theater-going, was a romantic drama based on a popular novel by Michael Arlen. It was also running in New York in the fall of 1925, where Katherine Cornell and Leslie Howard were cast in leading roles. In London, Katherine Cornell's part was played by an "Alabama girl", twenty-three-year-old Tallulah Bankhead.

> Oxford, England
> October 9, 1925

Dearest mother:

Oxford at last. Arrived yesterday afternoon at 3:04 on a fast express from London, making the distance in an hour and nineteen minutes. It was the quickest sixty-three miles I had ever covered on the railroad, and the smoothest too. I can certainly say that English railroads are good. They are rather odd though with separate compartments for the groups of passengers and smaller cars and much smaller engines.

I am very enthusiastic over the prospect here at St. John's. The college is very picturesque and the grounds very beautiful. The St. John's Gardens are the most beautiful in Oxford so everyone tells me. I roamed around in there this afternoon and I was amazed with their beauty. Flowers are blooming everywhere here, and the grass is as green as it ever gets in spring at home. I am told that the grass never dies here during the winter. The excessive moisture keeps it green and luxuriant.

St. John's is one of the oldest colleges, founded in 1555. The buildings look almost that old too, but they are beautiful and interesting. The interiors of course are newly finished and the rooms are very nice.

Almost everyone has single rooms, but I have a room-mate. Hart of Colorado, another new Rhodes Scholar, has been placed with me. I like the idea of a room-mate fine, for I like company. It would be rather lonesome at first with no one to talk to when you weren't busy. Also, it makes it less expensive for us as we half the coal, light, and furniture bills.

You will no doubt be interested in our room, its furnishings, etc. We have a suite between us. There is a small ante-room to begin with, then an extra large living room, and two small bed rooms. The ante-room has racks for our overcoats, hats, etc, and also a place for the boy to arrange dishes, and other things relative to our meals. In the living room we have two sofa chairs, two other padded bottom chairs, five straight chairs, a large desk with nine drawers, a tea table, a small dining table, a large table for meals and study, a cupboard for tea dishes, a sideboard without the mirror, an extra large four-shelved book case with two compartments, a large mirror over the mantel, a big carpet on the floor, and a small rug, and a rather nice sofa. Then we have a desk lamp for study and a two-globe light over our other table. In my bedroom, I have a chifforobe large enough for all my clothes, a wash-stand, a towel rack, and a cot-like bed. I hang my suits at the foot of my bed on a set of racks placed there for the purpose. Of course, we have a grate fire, which the scout keeps burning when we are out. The fire is very cheery, and I think I will rather like it. We have to heat our hot water on the gas, and a cold face wash awaits in the morning when we arise. All toilets and baths are down three flights and then around about a hundred yards. All in all rather antiquated, but I suppose I will get used to it in time.

I went around to see Mr. Wylie* this morning and received a check for fifty pounds. We were supposed to get a hundred but he gave fifty of it to the college for caution money. It is a deposit that will be returned to us at the end of our three years in Oxford and is a proviso to take care of our expenses in case we should leave college in bad standing, etc. Of course we will get it back eventually, but I wish he had waited a while before depriving us of it. However, we won't have to pay our *battels*, that is board and college expenses until our next installment of money is due, and I suppose we can make it somehow. If I just have to have more money, I will cash one of the checks which father gave me signed. I understand it will go through all right. I owe the college nine pounds for fees, and that will be all I have to pay them this term. That leaves me forty-one pounds, or approximately one hundred dollars. I think I have made most of the necessary purchases at present. I have purchased my tea set and table cloths, all told my part of the expense was a pound and four shillings. My greatest need now is some clothes, and I will have to order a suit and my dress clothes right away. Drane says he can show me a tailor shop where I can get a tweed suit, like they wear here, with two pairs of trousers for about twenty-five dollars. There is then the dress suit to be considered. I think it will cost about fifty complete with shirt, collar, and studs. Speaking of expenses there is this typewriter, which I have out on trial and expect to buy. The cost of it is fourteen pounds, which I can buy for part down and the rest on the installment plan. It is a real good machine, a portable Corona, and I believe it will give me good service. I am to try it out until Monday and then decide whether I want it or not. I must have a typewriter, of course, and that is a necessary expense. I neglected to say that I can get the clothes on credit too, so I ought to be able to manipulate things fine.

Oxford is a quiet picturesque town. Although the population is twice as much as Jackson, it gives you the impression of being a small town. The traffic is rather leisurely, except when the multitude of bicycles almost run over you, and everything is quiet. You feel free and easy and as if life were great. I am certainly glad to get to a quiet place after the days in New York and London. Speaking of London, I suppose you would like to hear something of my two days there.

We landed in a fog at London, and my first impression of the city is rather poor, yet I liked it better the other days. It is quaint, yet much like New York in a number of ways. In the character of people on the streets you don't notice very much difference. The buildings are not very high in London and all old. The streets run every way, and it is much harder to keep your direction. A pedestrian literally takes his life in his hands when he crosses the street. The traffic, if ever stopped, is done in such a way that it doesn't profit you. In New York crossing is safe, for all traffic is stopped periodically.

I spent part of one day in the National Gallery in London. There they have a collection of art treasures second only to the Louvre in Paris. The pictures were simply wonderful, and I am going back for a longer stay when I pass through for my Xmas vacation. One day was spent out at Wembley at the British Empire exposition. You have probably heard of this collection of exhibits from every British colony on the globe. The whole exposition is very interesting and educational in its value. Over seventy-five thousand people visited the exposition the day we were there. I saw a good play in London, "The Green Hat." An Alabama girl was playing the leading part and was excellent too.

I also saw the parliament buildings, Westminster Abbey, and the government district in London. Hope to look at these more carefully in the future.

I have an invitation to call on the Presbyterian Church pastor at 8:15 Sunday evening. Mr. M. B. Swearingen, the Millsaps scholar, has invited me around to tea Sunday afternoon. I haven't seen him yet, but I received his note this afternoon.

Drane and I went to the show tonight at the Palace Theater. It was very good, and the orchestra furnished excellent music. When we come in after nine o'clock we have to pay a small fine, so I had to pay mine tonight. It was charged on my expenses, so I don't know exactly what it was, about a dime, I suppose.

So far I have received no mail from you. I had four letters from Hattie May but nothing from Heidelberg. Certainly hope I will hear soon. I am very anxious to get some news from home. Hope you are all doing well and that everything is coming as nicely as it was when I left.

Won't you send in my subscription to the *Jackson Daily News* and ask them to start the paper immediately. Subscribe for only six months now, as that will last to the summer vacation when I will probably come home. Even if I didn't the paper would never reach me on my travels. Ask them for a chap rate, stating that I was their correspondent.

It is after eleven o'clock and I must close. I'll try and get some pictures of Oxford for you tomorrow so you can form an idea of the place. I like it very much and think I will enjoy the three years here very much.

My love to all of you,
Wilson

No letters exist from October 14 to December 13, 1925. What does remain, however, is a series of newspaper articles written during that period and continuing through the spring of 1926. Building on the contacts he had made while reporting Ole Miss news, before he left Mississippi Wilson Lyon approached the *Laurel Leader Call, Meridian Star, Jackson Clarion Ledger,* and the *Hattiesburg American,* with the proposal that they pay him for reports on Oxford life and his European travels. He hoped that these reports would give him funds to supplement his scholarship stipend.

The Mississippi newspapers were very interested in his proposal, based on their acquaintance with Lyon's reporting. They liked the idea that these reports would bring their readers personal impressions of life abroad by a native of their home state. As the editor reminded Mississippi readers with many of his headlines, this would be England or Italy or France as seen "by a Mississippian".

The reports are interesting biographically because his choice of subjects reveals those facets of British and European life that struck him most forcefully during his early months abroad. In the two columns that follow, written shortly after his arrival, he draws a picture of the life he discovered when he arrived in England and then gives us a vignette of the life he lived as a Rhodes Scholar inside Oxford's walls.

David Lloyd George (1863-1945), who is mentioned in the first column, had been Liberal prime minister of Britain from December 1916 to October 1922, and was head of the Liberal Party when Wilson Lyon arrived in Oxford.

THE MERIDIAN STAR
November 15, 1925

—

English Life Through Eyes and Ears of Eastern Mississippi Boy
by E. W. LYON
*Rhodes Scholar from the University of Mississippi at
St. John's College, Oxford*

Indications of an economic crisis are seen on every hand in England. The country, now facing its sixth winter of unemployment, seems almost as baffled with its economic problem as it was at the end of war. The industries of the nation are not supporting the population, and this winter a million men will be without work on the British Isles. Schemes have been advanced and others are being advanced for an attempted settlement of the unemployment situation, but no statesman has yet found a workable solution.

Oxford Has Share

Unemployment is not as prevalent in Oxford as it is in many other cities, of course. But even here in the historic university town, the seat of aristocracy and the home of lost causes, beggars stand supplicating under the walls of Oxford's colleges. One meets them on the street at every turn, some selling matches or vending trinkets, others standing by signs telling of their destitute condition and holding out their caps with a hungry look in their eyes. I recall one in particular, an old man, who keeps his daily station by a church, just across the street from St. John's. Each day he stands there by a group of water color drawings and begs for bread. Another, a whistler, often appears in the same neighborhood, and many times I have heard him whistling some jazz tune popular in America a year or so ago. These are but two from England's million men who beg and roam the streets looking for work and the bread it will bring. In Northern England the situation is many times worse. A student from Sheffield told me that twenty-four thousand were unemployed there when he came down to Oxford.

Docks Are Crowded

A Canadian friend, who landed at Liverpool, informs me that the docks there were crowded with hundreds of idle men. During the few days I was in London before coming down to Oxford, I noticed the hundreds of beggars and peddlers which roamed the street. A band was marching up the street and a man was begging on the side claiming it to be an ex-service band. It is significant how many of the unemployed are of that class which saved England on the fields of France. The great contrast between New York and London in the number of beggars and poor vendors serves as a correct measure of that want and need prevalent in these two great cities. In New York few beggars were seen, and little was heard of unemployment. Here it is quite different.

Blame on War

It has been the style with us in America to blame everything on the war, but I think the present economic position of England may be correctly attributed to that great conflict. Loss of trade has brought unemployment and a certain stagnation of British industry. England fought a war to protect her commercial interests, and now she seems to be in worse commercial circumstances than ever. England is no longer the possessor of commercial supremacy; the war weakened her position during the inactive years and other nations got a start. I refer particularly to the United States which at the present time is flooding these islands and the world with its goods in enormous quantities. We hear a lot about protection for our infant industries, but I am sure the British manufacturer does not think they need any aid. Here in conservative Oxford one sees half of the traffic handled by American motor cars, writes his letters on an American typewriter, buys his trinkets at Woolworth's, selects his choice from the latest American novels at the book shops, sees his favorite film star at the cinema, drinks Horlick's malted milk, and shaves with Colgate's cream using Palmolive talc afterward. Almost any well known American article can be obtained here without trouble and most of the lesser known manufactures can be obtained in London.

U. S. Movies Dominate

In the matter of motion pictures the American producers have an almost complete monopoly. An English audience sits through three hours of glorification of American life, and then stands while the king's picture comes on and sings "God Save the King," the only real British part of the program. Last week hundreds stood in line for a chance to see the popular Broadway production, "No No, Nanette." Only the heavy tax, just put on, is keeping American automobiles from dominating the highways in the same way that the films control the screen.

With such a quantity of goods coming in, with many of the colonies trading with America or some other country, and with German manufactures beginning to pour free goods into the country, British industry is having a difficult time, and the British people are suffering.

Battle Foreign Goods

The whole nation and the empire is making a terrific battle against foreign goods. Signs greet one everywhere and newspapers tell you to buy British-made goods. There has been a superhuman effort to awaken the colonies and the mother country. This was largely the actuating motive of the great Empire Exposition which has been running for almost two years at Wembley. It was hoped by this exposition to encourage emigration to the colonies thereby relieving the problem back in the home country.

The government is doing all in its power to relieve the situation and at the same time is seeking some measure of permanent relief. The unemployed are kept from starving by a government dole of some few dollars a week, about enough to maintain them in the rudest comfort. The hope is a revival of trade by the awakening of an empire consciousness and if necessary the emigration of laborers from the overpopulated districts. But at present these do not seem to be working as might be hoped.

Tries New Policy

Mr. Lloyd George, who happens to be considerably in disfavor just now, has just enunciated a new land policy which the Liberal party, also politically out of power, is supporting. His aim is the disestablishment of the landlord and further protection of the tenant, the reclamation of wet lands, and the improvement of farm labor conditions. This proposal, other than attracting considerable publicity, has not been taken seriously and has little chance of becoming law. Mr. Lloyd George's land policy was debated last evening at the Oxford Union, the world's most famous debating society, and I gathered that the bulk of the audience thought little relief could be obtained through it. Nevertheless, it is true that much of the countryside is uncultivated, and it seems practical that this could be farmed to produce food for a nation which now imports the bulk of its food.

See Signs of Reds

England is also disturbed with political unrest. Communists are agitating revolutionary measures in the streets, twelve have been arrested and are being tried at London. Red propaganda arises here and there among the working people. Yet the communists have made little progress. The Labor party repudiated them at its recent conference, and there is little danger that they will gain any ground here. But the fact remains that the poorer classes are suffering.

THE MERIDIAN STAR
November 8, 1925

English Life Through Eyes and Ears of Eastern Mississippi Boy
by E. W. LYON
*Rhodes Scholar from the University of Mississippi at
St. John's College, Oxford*

Certain elements of American people have always been interested—more or less—in Oxford University, but Oxford has taken a new place in American education since the famous bequest of Lord Rhodes nearly a generation ago. Now that American boys to the number of over a hundred are always in attendance at the English University, Oxford has become a place about which many of our people manifest the keenest interest and curiosity. Everyone knows that Oxford has many beautiful towers and wonderful buildings of stone, but few know the life that the Rhodes scholar lives after coming into residence at his college. It is with the idea of showing the real Oxford in its human relationships that I am setting out in my articles this week to give an account of the life there.

Scout is Servant

At 7:30 in the morning the student is suddenly conscious of another's presence in his bedroom and on opening his bewildered eyes sees his scout standing in the door and is greeted by these words, "Good morning, sir, what will you have for breakfast?" Before passing on it might be noted that this scout, as he is called, is the student's personal servant. He is in fact the greatest of Oxford institutions, and without him the University would have to close its doors. He knows everything to be known about the place and can give you the most unerring advice. As has been said, he does everything for you except thinking and a part of that, too. But to return to the student, the scholar, accustomed to steam-heated rooms, dresses and shivers in a cold room and rushes rapidly into the living room where the scout has kindled a fire in the grate. By this time it is time for chapel, at which attendance is required four times each week. The service consists of a prayer service according to the Church of English form with the new Anglo-Catholic tendency predominating. The college chapels are wonderful old buildings and are among the leading show places of Oxford.

Eats in Living Room

Breakfast is waiting in the room by the conclusion of the morning prayer service, and the student eats his meal alone in his own living room. The table when cleared is used for study or any other purpose desirable. The dishes are kept in a cupboard also in the living room.

Very little work is done at Oxford before ten, the hour at which most of the lectures begin. Students usually go to only one or two lectures a day, and attendance at these is optional. Your tutor simply recommends certain lectures, and you attend them if you like. There are no roll calls and the lecturer rarely knows any of the students who face him. My lecture list is counted rather heavy, and it requires only eight hours a week, less than half the time one would spend in classes at any American college. There is very little similarity between these lectures and our American classes where a check of attendance is made and the professor very surely inquires what you know about the assignment. The tutor, whom you see once a week, is the only one at Oxford authorized to ascertain if you know anything of your subject. The student prepares an essay for each tutorial, reads it to his tutor, and is criticized on his findings. The tutor recommends the books to be read and the work to be done during the week. However, it is not to be understood that students do not work at Oxford, for fully as much study is done here as at home. The work is mostly outside the classroom and is in the form of reading. A student is spoken of as "reading" a subject instead of "taking" it, as we say in the South. The Oxford system also anticipates and really requires considerable study in vacation, "vac time", as the students say here.

Serve Cold Luncheon

Cold luncheons are served in the rooms, and a hot meal at noon is had only on occasions and at an exorbitant cost. My room mate, for instance, entertained four people at a hot luncheon, where food was none too plentiful, at a cost of eight dollars. Can you imagine such a charge being allowed in a Southern College, particularly at state university where the student's inalienable right to cry "graft" is always considered in proper form?

After the solitary lunch the student turns out for athletics, almost everyone playing some game. Soccer and rugby football, rowing, hockey and lacrosse are the leading sports for this season, though a number of track and tennis devotees keep up their activities in those sports. Athletics at Oxford are not subsidized by the college or the University, and personal equipment is paid for by the student himself. A general fund assessed each member of the college pays for the upkeep of grounds and the necessary general equipment. With such a result there is a better system of sportsmanship and play only for the sake of the game. The American plays to win; the Englishman plays for the game.

Finish Athletics By Tea

Athletics are generally over by tea time, which is anywhere between four and five o'clock. Tea is not improperly called the most English of all English institutions. No matter where you find him, the Englishman must have his tea. It is a very delightful custom, and it is altogether to be regretted that the taking of tea in America has come to have an effeminate atmosphere and therefore is avoided by those who would be real "He-Men". One of the greatest joys of Oxford is the friendship which one enjoys late in the afternoon sitting around the fire and drinking tea with intimate friends. Here the inter-change of ideas and the fellowship lift life away from the drab weather and give friendship a full welcome. The tea hour is the great social time of the day when friends are invited in to share your hospitality. Of course, a breakfast invitation indicates the most extreme intimacy, but on account of mankind's overpowering love for sleep, these are rare.

Only One in Dining Hall

Dinner is the only meal of the day served in the common dining hall at most of the colleges. Cap and gown must be worn, and attendance is required at least four times each week. One feels rather important with oil paintings of famous Englishmen looking down upon him, but he can't help wishing that the chef would occasionally substitute something for the ever-recurring cabbage and cauliflower. But for those who think Mr. Volstead misguided, there is abundant solace in the spirited contents of the huge silver cups which polite servants bring at your command. All the beers, wines and other light alcoholic drinks can be ordered from the college buttery, but whiskey must be sent in from the outside. In direct contrast to this great liberty students are positively forbidden to enter public saloons and will be expelled immediately if found drunk outside the college walls. Within the walls you may drink to your soul's content.

Go To Cinemas

The theatres and music houses, known as cinemas here, claim great crowds in the evening. Contrary to our American custom, they begin the performances very early, and the theatre crowd is usually off the street about ten-thirty. This is very probably done in order to reduce the gate contributors to all kinds of shows. All the college gates are locked at nine o'clock, and a fine is charged those coming in after that hour. The porter, when letting you in, says "good night" very obediently and then very independently writes a fine of two, four, six, or twelve cents against your name, according to the hour. Admission after twelve is serious, and in addition to the two shilling six pence fine, questions are asked rather cruelly by various officials of the student's college. Of course, everyone at Oxford does not go to the theatre. Many study, read, attend some organization to which they belong, or engage in some other college activity. Somewhere near midnight all the wanderers come in, no matter where they have been, and an Oxford day is over.

During his first Christmas vacation break, Wilson Lyon and several friends traveled to the south of France, visiting Marseilles and Cannes. A letter to his sister Josephine details some of his experiences. Its reference to her recent "operation" for an unspecified problem is a reminder of the ongoing health problems that marked her childhood and adolescence.

Comparing the population of Cannes to Meridian, which was about 23,400 at the time of the 1920 census, Lyon gives his sister a sense of the size of the city but no sense of the dramatic differences in the two places, differences which, combined with his very limited knowledge of French, probably contributed to his homesickness during the holidays. *Ciboulette* the operetta he saw, but did not understand, was a fantasy love story, written in 1923 by Reynaldo Hahn. Its great popularity rested on its music; however, Lyon could not carry a tune, so even its musical appeal was probably lost on him.

> Castelflor Hotel
> Cannes (A. M.) Alpes Mmes
> Sunday, December 13, 1925

Dearest Joe:

I've been intending to write you for several days, but as I've moved six times in the last seven days you must not be too hard on me. We left Oxford last Saturday, London last Sunday, Paris Tuesday, Marseilles Thursday, and we changed our hotel here yesterday. We stopped first at the St. Nicolas here but the food was very poor, and we moved here. We certainly made a good exchange. This is a much higher class place and the food is wonderful. You can bet we are enjoying it too.

There are three of us now and there will be four of us in a day or so. All of us are Rhodes scholars from St. John's, three Americans and a Canadian. We have two double rooms joining each other with running hot and cold water, etc.

We came here from Marseilles Thursday. I mailed papa and mama two small presents from there. Hope they come in all right. For a part of the way we came along the Mediterranean coast. Olive trees and vineyards were everywhere along the railroad. Mountains rose back from the sea and we passed through a number of tunnels. The houses are all either red or yellow and palm trees and orange trees fill the gardens in front. The country here has quite a tropical appearance.

Cannes is a city about the size of Meridian. Most of the people come here for the climate and the sea, for it is one of the most famous resorts along the coast. They call this section of Southern France on in to Italy the Riviera.

You ought to be in France to see the displays in the store

windows. They are the most inviting I've ever seen. What makes it nice is that things are so much cheaper than at home. The most tempting things are the arrays of candied fruits in the windows. They certainly know how to arrange things to look good.

We are getting our board very cheap here. Our room and meals cost us only a dollar and forty cents a day. At this rate I think I will be able to make my scholarship carry me through. It is very much cheaper here than in college at Oxford. They are the best in the world for taking your money for nothing.

Last night we put on our dress clothes and went to the Opera house. The production for the evening was "Ciboulette", an operetta. As it was in French and as my seat was poor, I didn't enjoy it very much. Between acts we watched the dancing and the gamblers at the table betting on the numbers.

Hope you are feeling fine after your operation and that you are back in school again. Guess you are looking forward now to the Xmas holidays. It won't seem much like Xmas to me here so far away from home. The French don't celebrate Xmas like we do, but most of their celebration is at New Year. You will notice the card I sent papa and mama and see that it is quite different from anything you ever saw for Xmas.

Drane and I have joined the Cannes tennis club and have been playing every day. The courts are excellent, and they are kept in good shape. At the clubhouse you can get refreshments, supplies, etc.

A Merry Xmas to you all. You should get this about Xmas day. Write me again at Oxford, won't you?

Love, Wilson

Returning from the sunny Riviera to snowy Oxford, Wilson Lyon complained about the cold in a letter to his mother written on January 19, 1926, and she subsequently sent him a union suit, a reflection of the extent to which he remained a central part of her life, even though he was thousands of miles away from home. The January letter also reflected the difficulties he had had adjusting to the Oxford tutorial system. "I didn't study any too much here last term," he wrote, "and I am resolved to do better this term. Now that I am acclimated I will find it much more enjoyable, I am sure."

The letter he wrote home on February 16 comments primarily on the rhythms of life in Heidelberg and the activities of Mississippi family and friends: the death of a family friend who was a contemporary of his parents, letters from a college friend now studying at Princeton, and from a local friend now attending Mississippi College, a private Baptist college in Clinton, just west of Jackson.

Spring planting had not yet begun, and Rufus Lyon was busy as town tax collector, an elected position that he had held since at least Wilson Lyon's junior year at Ole Miss, based on a report in the *Jasper County News* for January 21, 1924. It is noteworthy that Willia Lyon was writing some newspaper stories that covered more than social events. The Morgan case, as reported in the Chancery Court listings in the January 28, 1926 *Jasper County News*, was a trial of W. M. Morgan, administrator of the estate of W. B. Morris. Morgan, who was being sued for his handling of the estate by family members, was probably a descendant of the pioneering Morgan family that settled in Mississippi with the Lyon family in the early nineteenth century.

A visit from his recently widowed maternal grandmother, Josephine Yongue Wilson*, is also noted. After the death of her husband, Confederate veteran Thomas Wilson, in the fall of 1925, she often spent several months visiting each of her adult children, some of whom were raising young children. With no young children in the Lyon household, her Heidelberg visit would be particularly restful.

Despite feeling more acclimated to Oxford life, by February Wilson Lyon's thoughts had begun to turn to spring travel. Listing the names of his traveling companions on his upcoming trip to Italy, this letter introduces three young Rhodes Scholars who would be close friends throughout his life: Frank Gray, Reuben Borsch*, and Owen "Dusty" Rhoads*.

The letter is most interesting, however, because of reminders, at its conclusion, of the connection between race and politics in Mississippi in the 1920s. Wilson Lyon had turned twenty-one on

June 6, 1925, and for the first time was eligible to vote. Apparently, however, he did not register before he left Mississippi to study abroad. He comments in this letter: "Hope (father) doesn't forget to pay my poll tax. I suppose the circuit clerk registered me." His assumption that the circuit clerk would be able to register him *in absentia* is a dramatic example of the discretionary power that Mississippi's election laws gave local registrars, allowing them to bend the rules for whites, as well as to exclude blacks from voting. Wilson Lyon was a white male, a scholar, and a local hero. For him the registrar was happy to make an exception, not requiring his personal appearance for registration. The tone of Lyon's comments vividly illustrates his casual acceptance of the privileges of race afforded by Mississippi's laws and customs.

Oxford, England
Feb. 16, 1926

Dearest mother:

I was beginning to wonder what had happened at home when I received your two letters yesterday. It had been a month since I had a letter from you, and I suppose you have been waiting some to hear from me as I have been very slow about writing myself. I am trying to write at least once a week now, though, and hope to keep it up.

I was very sorry to hear of Mr. Herrington's death. Your letter came before the paper which carried a notice of it. I see you did well in getting a good headline on the Morgan case at Bay Springs. In regard to the *Daily News*, tell them that as a special concession Mr. Johnson, the business manager, agreed to give me the paper free in addition to paying for my correspondence. This you see was a breach of their usual custom, for they do charge even correspondents as a rule—a rule which seems unfair to me. If the *Clarion* has stopped using my work I think I will see if I can't work in with the *News*. It is a pity that I got in with the *Clarion* to start with, but Mr. Gadmer seemed so enthusiastic that I thought things would go nicely. Wish the *Star, Leader,* and *Hattiesburg American* would send me some money. Except for ten dollars from the *Clarion* I have received nothing from any of the papers.

I suppose grandmother is with you by now and that you are enjoying her visit. I hope she gets rest with you; there will be freedom from children at any rate.

I got a long letter from Ellis the other day telling me about things at Clinton and Heidelberg. It was a good letter, and I was pleased to hear from him once more. I also heard from Harold Barber* after such a long interval. He seems to be delighted with life at Princeton. For the past two days we have enjoyed sunshine, which is quite unusual here, as you probably saw from my diffusion on the weather in the papers. It is a long way to spring, but just the same it does feel a little like the better season is on its way, though it be a long way off. It will certainly be spring when we come back for the summer term here, May and June. There are three more weeks of this term left after the present one. I will be glad when it is over and we are able to leave Oxford for sunnier climes. I have become a confirmed Southerner since coming here, and in the future I plan to devote myself to a land of sunshine and warmth. Did I tell you that I was going to Italy for the Easter vacation. Three other first-year men, Gray of Minnesota, Rhoads of Pennsylvania, and Borsch of Illinois, will be in the party. This is of course the most wonderful season of the year to visit Italy. It is warm but not hot, just right in fact.

I have been running lately, but I plan to play tennis this afternoon. There is a track meet on the running ground which keeps me off, and then the weather is excellent for tennis today. See where a girl I know in McComb has married. Hattie May is still out of the lists a while, anyway. She wrote me yesterday that she had decided to take an M. A. and was planning to go to school this summer. She has ambitions of teaching in a Junior College for girls. She thinks girls are much easier to work with than boys; what do you say after your long experience?

We are having quite a quiet time after our stir of last week when the Oxford Union censured the Vice-chancellor* for his action in restraining two Communist students from expressing their opinions on political questions, that is, on

Communism. After Shakespeare at the theater last week the present bill is a decided come-down.

I suppose father is busy collecting taxes and making farming plans for another year, if the rains have stopped at last. Hope he doesn't forget to pay my poll tax. I suppose the circuit clerk registered me. Perhaps you heard something of it.

My love to all of you.

Wilson

In the spring of 1926, Wilson Lyon and his three friends, Frank Gray, Reuben Borsch, and "Dusty" Rhoads, made the trip to Italy that they had anticipated all winter long. Writing to his mother from Rome, exhausted after extensive traveling, his letter of March 31 provides numerous reminders of what an inexperienced and naive traveler he still was: discovering for the first time the differences in cleanliness and affluence existing between southern and northern Italy; forced by his own economic circumstances to venture into the Mediterranean in a rowboat on a blustery day; learning, firsthand, about the importance of safeguarding valuables after his friend Frank Gray was the victim of a pickpocket in Naples. The letter also reveals that he is an astute political commentator as he observes a Fascist parade in Naples and speculates on the possibility of war.

Pensione Albion, Roma
Via Sicilia 166, Rome, Italy
March 31, 1926

Dearest mother:

Here we are at Rome again after having gone two thirds of the way around Sicily and a good way up and down the boot during the past ten days. It has been a very tiresome trip but all in all very worthwhile. However, it has somewhat cured me of my desire to go so far away from Oxford in the future. Especially, do I intend to avoid the more Southern countries. Their sanitary conditions and living conditions are none too pleasant to one of Nordic blood and breeding.

After leaving Syracuse we had a nineteen-hour ride, from

11 in the morning until 6 the next morning, to Naples. Of course we took no sleeper, we never do here for the money means too much to us. After finding a hotel in Naples we took a train out to Pompeii and spent a good part of the day at the ruins of the city. I enjoyed that more than anything we have done so far. It is marvelous to see the civilization that the people had in those days 79 A. D. The houses appear to be much better than the Italian houses of today. In some of them the paintings on the walls have a color as bright as if they had been painted only a year or so ago. The decorations in the houses are extraordinary and show the artistic sense of the Latins. The temples and other ruins of public buildings were very beautiful. Pompeii was a very large city, and it has been uncovered in its old form, with regular streets and its general plan intact. The ashes came down first and covered the houses, and they were preserved from the lava flow. In the museum were cakes of bread, nuts, and other articles of food which were covered in the flow of lava and thus turned into rock. The original shape is perfect. Bodies were also turned to rock.

Sunday we saw the Fascist demonstration in Naples. It was the seventh anniversary of the founding of Fascism, and the party celebrated throughout the kingdom. In Naples the soldiers and civilians marched by for at least two and a half hours. There must have been thirty bands in the ranks. All ages filled the civilian lineup. Everybody in Italy is Fascist now, and Mussolini is worshiped as a God. Signs of "Viva Mussolini" are posted everywhere, and everyone you talk to thinks he is the leader of all that is to the benefit of Italy. There are more soldiers here than I have ever seen any- where, more even than in France. Out of it all there is bound to be a war. How Mussolini can maintain his position with- out a victorious war I cannot see. As for the internal admin- istration of the country he has helped things tremendously, and the *Fascisti* must be praised for what they have done. Italy is much better off since they came in many respects, but what will it all lead to? One wonders what will happen when Mussolini dies. As a side issue to the *Fascisti* celebration Gray

had his pocket picked and lost some seventy dollars, fifty of
which was in travellers' checks and which he will eventually
recover for the bank will repay him his money in a year.
Luckily he had enough money to complete the trip, but I
don't know what I would have done had the bad luck fallen
to me.

Sunday afternoon we took a boat across the Bay of Naples
to the island of Capri, a very beautiful little island famous as
a health resort in both ancient and modern days. Tiberius,
one of the Roman Emperors, had a villa over there. We took a
row boat and were rowed around the island. I have never been
so near sea sickness before. In fact, we all thought we would
go several times. The wind was rather high, and our little
boat was standing on end. A row boat in the Mediterranean!

We took a boat from Capri to Sorrento the next day and
from there had a three-hour street car ride back into Naples.
It turned out to be a rather poor day after the tossing of the
boat in the morning; I had a headache for the remainder of
the day.

We came here yesterday and are settled comfortably in the
pensione, boarding house, whose name appears on the enve-
lope. It is a very good place, one of the highest priced in
Rome, a dollar and eighty cents a day. But after our cheap
places in Sicily we were ready for a good place. You feel much
better and enjoy things more when you are in a good place.
The food was very good here last night, a rather strange
thing for Italy. The comforts here cannot compare with
France, which is really a very pleasant place in which to
travel. France is also cheaper than Italy, and you get much
better accommodation.

We hope to study some here. We are leaving here after a
week for Florence where we will stay two weeks, and then we
will return to Oxford. I am enclosing some pictures of places
we have visited. Joe should be interested in the Roman and
Greek scenes. Hope you are all well and feeling fine.

Love to all of you,
Wilson

In Florence, Wilson Lyon took time in the midst of his sightseeing to purchase a high school graduation present for his sister, Josephine. Although the Heidelberg high school had been recently accredited, a great step forward since Lyon's own high school days, it still did not offer enough preparation to qualify her for college admission, and she would take an additional year at the Jones County Agricultural High School, her brother's alma mater, in 1926-27.

Heidelberg's pride in its four high school graduates, notably all young women, is reflected in the program of events leading up to graduation exercises—all detailed in the *Jasper County News*. Thomas Bailey, a Meridian lawyer who was the commencement speaker, was a member of the Mississippi House of Representatives and would later become a popular governor of Mississippi (1944-1946).

Written at the end of his Italian trip, Lyon's letter also charmingly reflects his increasing self-confidence as a traveler, proud of both his growing ability to speak Italian, which he had never studied, and his ability to travel economically. With a turn of phrase that reveals he is a Southerner, he notes that he "carried" his Italian landlady and her niece to the movies one evening. It is almost the only local idiom in his letters that marks him as a resident of the South. Even as a child, he never spoke with a Southern accent, and thus left those who met him for the first time unaware that they were talking with a native of the American South. It is appropriate to note here that his lack of accent extended into his speaking of French, Italian, and later Spanish, probably often to the amusement of those with whom he spoke during his travels abroad.

JASPER COUNTY NEWS
April 15, 1926

Heidelberg, Miss., April 13: Professor C. A. Williams, principal of the Heidelberg High School, has announced the following program which will embrace the closing exercises of the school here.

Friday night, April 23rd, the Senior play, "Honor Wins," will be given. *Sunday, April 25th,* the commencement sermon will be delivered by Rev. B. H. Wiggins, pastor of the Presbyterian Church, in the school auditorium at 11 o'clock. *Monday evening* the grammar school department will entertain with a miscellaneous program. *Tuesday evening, April 27th,* Hon. T. L. Bailey of Meridian will deliver the baccalaureate address at which time the following pupils will receive diplomas: Bessie May James, Hazel Bethea, Margaret Clayton, and Josephine Lyon.

Florence, Italy
April 18, 1926

Dearest mother:
I went shopping yesterday afternoon, and am mailing the result to sister tomorrow for a graduation present. I know it will be late for commencement, but you can't expect to get things from here on time. I bought a silver bracelet set with amethyst stones and an amethyst ring to match. I am trusting that they will fit. To the best of my judgment I think they will be all right or can easily be made so. The bracelet is sterling silver and the stones are pure amethysts, the ring is the same. Silver is very cheap here, and the Florentine workmen are among the best in the world. The outfit cost about four dollars, and I fear you will have to pay duty.

Last night I carried our landlady, her daughter, and niece out to the movies. It was very interesting to witness the crowd and attempt to read the words on the screen. Let me say to my credit that I was able to read practically everything that came on. Since coming to Florence I have learned to speak Italian very well in a halting fashion, and I carried on a conversation very well. I sit by the landlady at meals and we talk Italian entirely, as she knows no other language. If I stayed in Italy much longer and would study a little more, I think I could soon speak the language fluently. It is really easier than French.

The museums, galleries, and other such things are free on

Sunday, and we put in the whole morning sight seeing. We finished up the Uffizi Gallery, the Old Palace, and the Medici Chapel. The latter is the most ornate and richly decorated chapel I have ever seen. We calculated that we saved thirteen lire this morning, which isn't bad.

We have been having quite a time here in Florence, about the best I've had since leaving America. Some girls from Minneapolis, friends of Gray's, have been here, and we have all been having a gay time taking in the city together. We had several tea dances, they entertained us at dinner once, and things were very pleasant. I was sorry when they left for Venice Thursday.

We will be here until Wednesday morning when we go back to Paris. I suppose the trip will require about three days, and we will be in Oxford Friday night. I think Friday is our last day of grace at Oxford. I am not very anxious to get back; at present I am very well satisfied with Florence. The city is very interesting, our *pension* is delightful, the food is wonderful, and the price is very reasonable, so why shouldn't we be contented?

The vacation has been very cheap. With all my travelling and even with some purchases it has been cheaper than last vacation. My whole trip won't cost me more than thirty-two pounds, which is cheaper than nine out of ten would have made it. We have really economized at every opportunity. It is surprising how cheap you can travel and how comfortably you can go when you know the ropes, and I may be pardoned for saying that I think we know them rather well. I challenge almost anyone to do better than we have on the same money.

It is cold and rainy here today and was the same yesterday. The city is said to be the most unfavored climatically of any in Italy, and I quite agree. It might be truthfully called the Oxford of Italy.

As this vacation is nearly over, Gray and I are beginning to think of going to Hungary and France for the summer. Think we will both stay in England a while first.

Hope you are all well and that the bracelet and ring fit.

Love, Wilson

Returning to Oxford, and settling in for his first English spring, Wilson Lyon and three friends rented a punt for the term in anticipation of many happy hours on the Cherwell. Surveying the state of his finances, he was relatively optimistic that he could stretch out his £400 Rhodes stipend until its renewal in the fall. He was also recognizing that the demands of Oxford study and student life would make it impossible to read the daily Mississippi paper that he was receiving by mail. Nevertheless, as he skimmed the papers, he was pleased to find published articles on Jasper County social events submitted by his mother.

His mention of Holly Springs, which would not accept his sister Josephine when she graduated from Heidelberg High School, is a reference to the Mississippi Synodical College for Women, a two year college located in Holly Springs, Mississippi. Annie Ford, a 1926 graduate of Ole Miss who was to teach at Holly Springs, married Harold Barber, Lyon's Ole Miss classmate in 1927.

The letter clearly shows that the limitations of life in Heideberg were also felt by Wilson Lyon's contemporaries: his friend Ellis Travis had decided to remain in Clinton for summer school at Mississippi College, rather than return home. Another young member of the Travis family, Carl, was recently married. Such means of escape, however, paled beside life in Oxford, as Wilson Lyon contemplated traveling to Stratford to see a Shakespeare play.

However, his thoughts did turn toward home, and spring planting. He concludes this letter to his mother by remarking that he hopes "father succeeds in getting the patch planted for you. I am heartily ashamed of myself for not having carried out my many pledges to repair the fence." The fence surrounded his mother's large kitchen garden. How clearly his statement reflects his embarrassment over being such a reluctant farmer, as well as his own disinterest and ineptitude in dealing with any sort of mechanical matter, a disinclination that would stay with him throughout his life. Equally important, the statement is an assurance to his family, especially his father, that the privileges of his Rhodes Scholarship would never separate him from remembering his responsibilities to them.

Oxford, England
April 28, 1926

Dearest mother:

I have been here since Friday now, but have been so busy try-ing to straighten things out that I have had no time to write. My tutor began by giving me an essay for Tuesday, and that forced me to study immediately. Then everything was out of order and had to be set straight again, which is always a labo-rious process. As usual the weather got bad for our especial benefit. We have been here five days now, and the sun has hardly shone at all during that time. It rained yesterday, the day before, and is raining again today. The vegetation is well along, flowers are blooming in profusion, and all the world is green, but it is very cold just the same. I wouldn't think of trying to go without a fire like a lot of the English are doing. We are on daylight-saving time, and on normal days it does-n't get dark until after nine, or nearer ten later in the sum-mer. That makes the evening very delightful, but makes studying very hard.

I am writing essays for two tutors this term. I have one in political science and the other in history. This means almost twice the work I have been doing before and will keep me very busy. It will be better for me in the end, though, for it is difficult to work anyhow unless you are forced to it.

My papers accumulated on me, of course, and so far I haven't been able to do much with them. I hope to get through them the latter part of the week. It seems that I can't really afford the time to read them. I enjoyed the clip-ping that you sent me about Mary Hassell's wedding and the baseball notes. I see in the later papers that you are getting quite a lot of material in the *Jackson Daily*. Summer is always a better time for news than winter.

In company with three English boys I have hired a punt for the term and hope to have some fun on the river. A punt is a flat bottom boat with room for five and is moved along in the water by means of a pole which is stuck in the river bed. There is an art to using the pole, and I will have to acquire it. There is danger of being jerked in unless you are careful.

Punting is the great sport here in the summer, and great
crowds of people crowd the river in the afternoons. The
Cherwell is no wider than an ordinary creek at home, but the
water is of a more uniform depth.

My college *battels* for the past term were six-pence (twelve
cents) less than fifty-one pounds, about the cheapest I know
of. This included my tuition, board, room rent, coal bill, laundry, light bill, service, and other college dues. I think if I can
live for less than fifty-five at the college that I will be able to
make my four hundred go. The Italian trip is considered
expensive, and I did that, including ten dollars for a visa, for
only thirty-five pounds. At present I have paid all my bills,
have a seventy dollar typewriter paid for, have bought a suit,
and a tuxedo suit, some books, shoes, sweater, and other
things, and have about fifteen dollars left. I will get another
hundred pounds for the summer, and I hope to get something
from my American newspapers by then. I am hoping to save a
little during the summer in order to have a reserve fund to
fall back on. It is tiresome to be always from hand to mouth;
however, it shouldn't bother me for I am used to it. I am
much more fortunate than Jug* who writes me that he is several hundred dollars in debt.

My congratulations to Joe on finishing High School. In
the future she won't have to take mathematics and school
should be more pleasant. It is a pity that her work didn't fit
in at Holly Springs, as Annie Ford, a girl whom I knew well
at Ole Miss and who is in love with Harold Barber, is to teach
there another year, and I feel that she might be of some assistance to sister as we were very good friends at Ole Miss.

I see by an advertisement in the bus that a Shakespeare
festival is being held at Stratford now and will continue until
May 15. The round trip can be made from here in a day, and I
am thinking of going up for one of the plays. The bus fare is
seven shillings, and I think it would be well worth it if the
day is pleasant. The theater there burned down not long ago,
but I think these plays are given in the open air. A campaign
is on now to erect a Memorial Theater there to the poet.

Had a long letter from Ellis not long ago. He plans to

spend the summer in school, as he can't face the prospect of a summer at Heidelberg. He says that Carl urged him to marry, saying that he would never know real life until he did, but it seems that he neglected to name the girl.

Hope father succeeds in getting the patch planted for you. I am heartily ashamed of myself for not having carried out my many pledges to repair the fence. Hope you are all well and that the bad weather has let up at home.

Lots of love,
Wilson

One of the major political events of Wilson Lyon's three years in Oxford, the British General Strike, occurred in early May, 1926, shortly after his return from Italy. For a week, almost all essential services ground to a halt in Britain, as workers showed their support for the wages and benefits sought by striking miners. According to a May 4, 1926 news report of the strike published in the *Laurel Daily Leader*, between 2,500,000 and 4,000,000 workers walked off the job, approximately 1,000,000 of whom were miners. Writing home to his mother on May 8, while the strike was in progress, Lyon stated that "I sympathize with the strikers, the miners in particular, and believe their cause is a just one and that the government by its bungling and pig-headiness is largely responsible for the present situation. There is too great a difference between the upper and lower classes here, and it is time the workingman got a better chance. England, as I see it, is by far the most aristocratic of the civilized countries of the world. In no country will you find greater wealth and luxury at the top and greater poverty and suffering at the bottom."

Lyon's own news report of the event, which follows, contains a description of how people got news, when the papers themselves were on strike. It was a topic of particular interest to him as a reporter. Stanley Baldwin (1867-1947) was the Conservative Prime Minister who led Britain during its troubled economic times. As Lyon reports, Baldwin's son, a student at Oxford, took a far different view of the strike from that held by his father. Winston Churchill, (1874-1965), chancellor of the exchequer in Baldwin's

Conservative government, was very critical of the miners, and edited the government's paper, *The British Gazette*, during the strike. Although the coal miners would continue to be on strike into the fall of 1926, the General Strike itself lasted only a week.

THE MERIDIAN STAR
Sunday, May 30, 1926

English Life Through Eyes and Ears of Eastern Mississippi Boy
by E. W. LYON
*Rhodes Scholar from the University of Mississippi at
St. John's College, Oxford*

It is sometimes said that Oxford never changes, yet the atmosphere during the strike was far different from that of a week ago. Academic questions for the time were forgotten, and the Oxford of the general strike was far different from any I have ever known. This is a statement which applied to all England.

In answer to the call of the government for volunteers to act as special constables and dock hands, half of our college have left for Oxford. [*Editor's note*: London is obviously meant here.] The diminished crowd in the dining hall reminded one of the first meal after the Christmas holidays at home. All weary of the strike and the real question, some spoke of leaving for government duty Monday, others wondered if the college would be dismissed. Americans and other foreigners faced the prospect of having no place to go if the college should require them to leave.

Finds Queer England
It was a queer England that we awoke to that Tuesday. *The Times*, that companion of the national public, was not delivered in the houses and rooms as usual. In fact, no newspapers at all were printed, and for the moment a wave of darkness seemed to pass over the world. No one knew what had happened, but all knew that the united British workingmen were on strike. Before noon the broadcasting agencies began to come through with the news. The government took over all

broadcasting, and announced the regular distribution of news. Since the first morning the radio items have been posted as received on the college bulletin board, around which an eager crowd could be seen at almost all hours. Then came the announcement that the government would print its own newspaper, and the first issue of *The British Gazette* appeared on the second day of the strike. The workers, on the other hand, began the issuance of *The British Worker*. The government paper, which came from the office of *The Morning Post*, a very Conservative journal was dubbed "The Morning Ghost" by the Labor people.

The Oxford strikers began the publication of a single mimeographed sheet which stated their point of view. One issue concluded with the exhortation: "Remember! If the Miners' wages come down, all other workers will follow. Stand firm, Workers: Do not believe lying rumors."

Indicate Their Stand

The above quotation is illustrative of the workers' stand. The strike was a moral crusade with them for the betterment of all classes of British labor. They felt that industry in England should be reorganized on modern lines and that if the miners lost their fight it would be the beginning of other reductions and a weakening of the powers of the trade unions. In support of this crusade labor leaders were speaking throughout the country urging the workers to stand firm and win their battle. The general meeting ground in Oxford was in the Broad street just in front of our college. There I have "listened in" on two labor rallies. I never heard stump speakers exhort their audiences with more eloquence or apparent earnestness of purpose. University men, women, labor leaders, and others have mounted the platform on the back of the Ford truck to represent the miners' case.

Has Unique Experience

I was treated to a unique experience at a rally. Politics often make strange things, but I never witnessed any political trick like this. Oliver Baldwin, son of the Conservative Prime

Minister, bitterly denounced the present government and upheld the cause of the trade unions. While the son was denouncing the Conservative government in Oxford, the father was devoting all his energy against the strike from his office in Downing Street, and the mother was organizing a transport service for women workers in London. Well, who ever attempted to explain the tricks of politics anyway!

Not Opposed to Strike

I was a guest of a friend at the University Labor Club. Americans are apt to think that all Oxford undergraduates are opposed to the strike but anyone present at this meeting would find reason to alter his opinion. There must have been five hundred students there, all rabidly in favor of the strike, cheering the speakers at every turn, and contributing money for the support of the strikers during the time they are not at work. G. D. H. Cole*, the famous guild Socialist and an expert on one of the early coal commissions appointed by the government, defended the miners. He was the second University instructor who upheld the cause of the miners during the meeting.

It is a great tribute to the English people that not one person had been killed. The meetings in the street had been attended with perfect order. Interruption had been very slight, especially for England where it is thought that anyone had a right to ask questions of the speaker at any time during his address. Of course, Oxford is about the last city of the kingdom where rioting would be expected. The city is only slightly industrial, and the proportion of nonunion men is rather high. The busses, for instance, had never stopped, and other local services except printing were uninterrupted.

Speculation as to who would win the struggle and what the end would be was running rife. The Conservatives termed this a blow at the Constitution, and Labor emphasizes that it was only an economic move.

Oxford terms were short, with the expectation that students would also spend some time studying during extended vacation periods.

As they prepared for the long summer break, Wilson Lyon and his friend Frank Gray were planning a trip to Hungary to visit in the home of their Oxford friend Michael Halasz, as well as planning visits to Vienna, Venice, Milan, and Geneva. They were also looking forward to time in France at the end of the summer, where they would be studying before returning to Oxford in October, 1926.

As Lyon sorted books to take with him on the trip, he also purchased and mailed a book for his father's fifty-ninth birthday on July 16—*The Life and Letters of Walter Hines Page*. Its choice as a gift reveals much about the way he saw himself in the spring of 1926. Never one to talk a great deal about personal feelings, he must have identified closely with Page because so many aspects of Page's early life were analogous to his own. Presumably sure that his father would also see the parallels, the book allowed him to speak indirectly to Rufus Lyon about his own hopes for making a contribution to society.

Like Wilson Lyon, Page was a Southerner, a North Carolinian who both loved the South and faced its problems unflinchingly. Page's father was a farmer, like Rufus Lyon. Like Willia Lyon, Page's mother was one of his earliest teachers. Although he was not a Rhodes Scholar, he was a member of the first class selected to attend Johns Hopkins. His extended tenure as a newspaperman, magazine writer, and editor must have helped Wilson Lyon, who loved his own newspaper work, identify further with him.

But it was Page's ideas that Lyon was undoubtedly most eager for his own father to know, because they so closely paralleled the way he saw his own thinking developing. Like Wilson Lyon, Page viewed himself as an American, not a sectionalist. He had great faith in democracy. Because of this, he was highly critical of Southern education, which he did not feel was as good as the education available in other sections of the country, leaving the average person inadequately trained for full participation in a democratic society. Page, even as a young man, was outspoken in defense of the causes he believed in.

Lyon's own concern for improving the quality of Mississippi education would be reflected in letters he wrote during his second and third years at Oxford. Though he knew his career would not follow Page's career path, he hoped it would be marked by equal honor and integrity. The letter that announced the impending arrival of Page's biography is one of the few that he addressed solely to his father. Deeply grateful for Rufus Lyon's constant support, he seemed to be stating through his birthday gift that he would do all he could to ensure that he was worthy of his father's confidence in him.

Oxford, England
June 18, 1926

Dear father:

Today is the day before the university closes the summer term, and the whole week has been a rush. Here we have to plan and think what work we are to do during the vacation, we can't forget our studies for the time being as we always do at home. That has necessitated the purchasing and borrowing of a number of books, and as my room for books in my belongings is limited I have had to choose carefully. Going down after this term is a more complicated matter, for we are away twice as long. Then too I am changing my room for another year, and I have to pack up my things. Hart and I are separating, as each of us realizes we can do much more studying alone. Then too, I was never too fond of him and it will be more agreeable alone.

The annual Rhodes dinner, we would say banquet at home, was given Wednesday night in the town hall. Some two hundred and fifty were present, and the affair was quite nice. Lord Cecil* was the guest of honor and spoke along the line of closer cooperation among nations. The tables were decorated with a profusion of carnations, and plates piled high with strawberries added to the charm.

In anticipation of your birthday, which I believe is July 16, I have ordered a small gift mailed to you. It is *The Life and Letters of Walter Hines Page*. The book has been widely read recently and has received very favorable comment. I think it one of the most interesting works I have seen for quite a while. The two volumes are combined in one in the edition I am sending you. You will no doubt recall Mr. Page as the popular American ambassador here during the war. The work is the story of a Southern man who rose to prominence on two continents. I do not agree with many of his views, particularly his harsh criticism of Mr. Wilson, but that does not detract from the pleasure of the work or the sterling quality of Page as a man. I hope you will like it and that you will enjoy a pleasant birthday.

I am leaving tomorrow for London where I will be until next Thursday morning—today is Friday. Thursday morning Owen Rhoads and myself are going out to a little village in Buckinghamshire to spend a week with an English family. We were invited by Lady Frances Ryder* who is interested in introducing Americans and colonials into English homes. We should have a very nice time, but I imagine it will be very quiet. Perhaps I'll get to do some history during the week. This Sunday I am having dinner in London with an American family that I met on the Riviera. The man is a professor in the University of London, but is returning soon to Colorado.

About July 1 I am crossing to Paris alone, will stay there several days, then go to Munich where I will meet Gray, who will be with me the rest of the summer. Gray is taking a business trip to Hamburg for his father. We go from Munich to Vienna, then to Budapest where Halasz, the Hungarian Count, meets us and will take us out to his country home to spend several weeks. His father is an important man in the present government, and the family seems to be one of the best in the kingdom. Anyhow, I'm looking forward to the visit. As most of his family speaks English it will be quite easy to get along. After leaving there we are returning by way of Vienna, Venice, and Switzerland and will settle down to study in a small village of France.

Drane has been taking examinations for his degree. He finished today I believe. His mother is coming over and he will meet her in London Monday. I suppose I will see her then.

The Emory University Glee Club from Atlanta is singing in London Wednesday, and I hope to hear them. Imagine I will enjoy hearing Southerners sing once more. I am looking forward to going to the theater several times while I'm in

London. There are a number of good plays running now, if
the critics are to be believed.

Love, Wilson

For sixty years Wilson Lyon's Ole Miss friend, Girault Jones, saved
a group of letters that Lyon wrote to him during his three years in
Oxford. In these letters, addressed to Jug, we hear the voice of a
twenty-two year old talking to his closest college friend. "Jug" was
the nickname that Jones acquired in his Mississippi high school. In
1997, he provided the following explanation:

"In our small Woodville High School, we had a transfer from
New Orleans my junior year. He was very foreign looking, and I
began calling him Czech for the country which had just been put
together after World War I. He responded by calling me Jugoslav.
He pronounced it 'J' and not 'Y' and it soon was shortened to 'Jug.'
Certain classmates went to Ole Miss the year I did and they trans-
planted it." The nickname, Jones noted, was never used by anyone
except his Ole Miss contemporaries.

Jones was studying for the ministry at the Episcopal theological
school at the University of the South in Sewanee, Tennessee—
hence the reference to the mountains at the end of Wilson Lyon's
letter. Summer pastoral assignments were part of his education
program and in the summer of 1926, he was pastor of Trinity
Church in Hattiesburg, Mississippi. Without a car, he traveled
around the city by laundry truck to call on parishioners.

Lyon's letter to Jones depicts Europe with a youthful exuberance
not present in his letters to his family. It is noteworthy that while
in London his love of tennis led him to Wimbledon. There he saw
the flamboyant French tennis champion, Suzanne Lenglen, defeat
"Miss Brown", probably the American U. S. Open Champion Mary
K. Browne, in an early round. Henri Cochet, the 1926 French Open
Champion, defeated Vincent Richards in the second round of play.
It's clear that after a year abroad, Ole Miss and college friends were
beginning to seem far away as Wilson Lyon was drawn more
and more fully into the life of Oxford and Europe. Doris Lenoir, a
1926 graduate of Ole Miss whose mother's death Lyon notes,
was a native of McComb, Mississippi, and a friend of Hattie May
Benjamin. Jin was Jones' hometown sweetheart, Virginia Wallace.

G. A. Reinwart Hotel Hubert-Hof, Vienna
July 12, 1926

Dear Jug:

I haven't heard from you in so long and not knowing your
address I'll send this to the old hometown from whence I
suppose all things reach the reverend in due season.

I am here with Frank Gray, Rhodes from Minnesota, and
we are walking our legs off and spending all our money trying to see the sights in about the second finest city of
Europe. For Vienna in my estimation is right up with Paris,
even better in some ways. But with the present rate of
French exchange no Rhodes scholar could ever think high-
priced Vienna superior to Gay Paris where one can have
three meals and a good room with running water for less
than $1.50 per day. Then too, French food has all Southern
home cooking beat for me. I could never tire of hors d'oeuvres and a few other of the specialties of the Paris cuisine.
But I started out to tell you about Vienna, and I'm digress-
ing. We came here several days ago from Munich where we
were for several days. Munich was wonderful, most mam-
moth beer gardens you've ever dreamed of with thousands
drinking, beautiful buildings, quaint atmospheric restaurants,
great parks, open air cafes, operas, art galleries, etc.

But I can't go back to Germany now that I'm in Austria.
Gray and I have been doing the sights here. Sunday morning
was spent in the gallery, this morning we were in the other
good picture gallery. This afternoon we went through the former imperial palace, rather boring after all is said and done.
Of course I saw the rooms where the Czar staid during the
famous Congress of Vienna, but that didn't mean much to my
aching legs. I felt like the American girl I overheard in the
gallery yesterday. "This may be art but lunch would look better to me." We plan going out to the Hapsburg country palace
tomorrow. I think it is about an hour by train from here.

As I wrote you before we are going to Hungary to visit
our Oxford friend. So day after tomorrow we set out for Hungary. Halasz is meeting us in Budapest, will show us the
sights for a day or so and then take us out to his country

home for a while. I suppose we'll remain about two weeks. From there we return here, then we go to Venice, Milan, and back to Paris by way of the Italian lakes and Switzerland. We will stop in Geneva for a while and perhaps somewhere else in Switzerland.

To go back—I left Oxford on June 19, spent a week in London going to the theaters and other attractions about town. Saw Suzanne beat Miss Brown at Wimbledon and Vincent Richards lose to Cochet, the new French champion. Have struck a real good boarding house in London at a reasonable figure, so am all set for the city now. Hitherto the expense of staying there has been prohibitive. From London I went up to Buckinghamshire with Rhoads of Pennsylvania for ten days in an English country home. We were treated in real style while there. It was a great experience to have a valet at one's beck and call. At eight he knocked and came in bringing your tea, which he placed nicely on a chair by the head of the bed. He took your evening clothes down and brushed and pressed them. At the same time he laid out your clothes for the day, straightening things and turning the sox so you could get in them quickly. In the evening you found your tuxedo all laid out for dinner, your shoes shined and all in readiness. In the afternoon it was the same with your tennis costume. Our hostess drove us all over the surrounding countryside, we went to the rowing regatta at Henley, a horse show at Aldershot, a polo match, spent a day on the river, played tennis, etc. Despite the English frigidity of the place it turned out to be quite an experience. I calmly handed the valet a $2.50 tip as I left and the next day was riding third class on my way to France. I doubt if he knew such would happen when he so carefully packed my bag for my departure.

I was in Paris for a good part of a week, more or less alone. One of the boys from Idaho was staying at the same hotel and I saw some of him. There were a couple of girls there I knew and I spent quite a while with them and some money too. I came on down here alone, that is, the twenty hours from Paris to Munich. Despite an all-night ride the trip was very good, as I was going second class which is really very good. Compared with third it is very, very good.

How have you found Hattiesburg? I am sure you have enjoyed the change after the strenuous work in the mountains. . . . Hattie May writes of Harold, but I haven't heard from him in ages. Maybe I will hear from all of you again when I get to Gyon, Hungary, in the next day or so.

I'm supposed to be studying, but so far I haven't hit a lick. I have a bag full of books in Paris and several with me here, but they aren't being put in use. They seem to be a lot of dead wood on my hands.

I am rapidly losing touch with the old gang, and I suppose you are too. But if you have any news let me have it. Hattie May just wrote me of the death of Doris' mother. I know it is a blow and I feel for her very much. I would write a note, but I fear it would do more harm than good. It seems that disasters come in rapid succession when one is away.

Hattie May is as sweet as ever, so far as I can tell from letters. I hope things are the same with you and Jin. Guess you knew Hattie May was at Tulane.

My regards to any of the Ole Miss crowd you may see in Hattiesburg.

E. W. Lyon

Wilson Lyon and Frank Gray spent almost a month in Hungary at the insistence of the Halasz family, not the two weeks that they had originally envisioned. In Budapest, they had an "insider's view" of the city, made possible by the fact that Michael Halasz' father was a member of parliament. The family's hospitality at their country home in Gyon, south of Budapest, was remembered fondly by Lyon throughout his life. The estate, including land owned by aunts, uncles, cousins, and grandparents, was very extensive. In addition to the crops mentioned by Lyon in his letters home, the family had fifty acres of wine grapes, and made their own wine. Tennis on the grass court, at the home of Michael Halasz' aunt, was one of the happy memories that stayed with Lyon. Describing the experience to his family years later, he recalled that a young boy retrieved the balls they hit out and then threw in a new ball to them whenever they called out *labda*, the Hungarian word for "ball".

Budapest, Hungary
July 16, 1926

Dearest mother:

I've forgotten whether I wrote you from Vienna. We were so rushed trying to see the city that I fear I didn't write you about it. We found it very delightful and remained there for four days. We are planning to stay a day or so on our return.

We have been here in the city some three days now and tomorrow we go out to the country, to Gyon—Michael's home. Michael met us at the train here and brought us to his aunt's home—from which I am writing. I have never seen such hospitality before. We aren't allowed to raise a hand or spend a penny. Everything is paid for us, taxis, street car fares, museum fees, everything. The food is wonderful, and there is such an abundance of it that I fear I shall be sick. The aunt speaks excellent English, so we've had no trouble at all. She speaks excellent French too, so we are doubly insured.

They have been amusing us and showing us all the places of the city. Yesterday we took a bath in one of the famous city baths, with sweating box, steam room, etc. This morning we had a real Turkish bath in a bath built by the Turks when they were masters of Budapest 400 years ago.

We were shown through the royal palace by a private guide. It was not open to the public, but our hostess, because of her family, was able to secure an entrance. We have been through the coronation church, the houses of parliament, on the island, in the parks, and to a circus last evening. The last was very funny—with all the usual clown, horse, acrobatic, and wild west stunts.

Michael's father is a member of parliament, and it was only through his influence that we were allowed to go in. Because of our friends we have seen Budapest in a way that we could never have touched otherwise. They are being so nice to us that we will be obligated to them forever.

In the country we will have a different kind of life. There we will play tennis, swim, read, dance, etc. Michael is anxious to get us out there, for he thinks we will enjoy it much more than here.

The ride from Vienna reminded me very much of the middle west at home. On every side the plain extended as far as you could see—fields of wheat, corn, potatoes, and alfalfa. The harvest was on and the fields were filled with hands cutting the wheat. We saw binders in only one field.

Michael says I have a lot of mail at Gyon, so I am sure I will hear from you then. Guess we will be there for some time.

Love, Wilson

Time spent in Gyon gave Wilson Lyon an opportunity to compare the crops and farming practices he observed there with those he knew in Mississippi. The letter that follows provides a number of reminders of the differences between the country life he experienced at Gyon in 1926 and his family's country life in Mississippi. His statement that his home was presently unable to receive his friends as overnight guests reflects his embarrassment at the somewhat primitive rural conditions in which his family was living, without a bath or indoor toilet. His reference to "the springs" refers to Stafford Springs, Mississippi, near Heidelberg, popular for its pure water. The *Jasper County News* reported on March 4, 1926 that a small hotel complex was planned for the site.

His thoughts are primarily on Mississippi as he writes, commenting on his news of Ole Miss friends to keep his mother up to date on their activities. Marjorie Jackson, whose marriage he mentions, was his classmate at Ole Miss. Her sister Harriet*, who graduated from the university in 1924, maintained an ongoing correspondence with Lyon during his years abroad.

His mother was apparently still trying to decide whether Josephine should enroll at Jones County Agricultural High School in September, 1926, to gather enough credits for college. It is clear that Lyon hoped that his faculty friends at Ellisville would help her fit in.

Gyon, Pest vm, Hungary
July 20, 1926

Dearest mother:

We came out from Budapest several days ago, and we are now

quite well settled here in the country. The family has a beautiful home, a nice white residence set back from the road in a garden of trees and flowers, with a circular driveway leading up to the house. It is peaceful and quiet, far quieter than Heidelberg, for although the village has a population of some six thousand you don't see three automobiles a day. The passing of one is still slightly an event in the village, and some of the horses are still afraid of cars. There is very little motor traffic on the streets in central Europe. I feel much safer on the streets of Budapest, a city of 1,200,000 than I do in Laurel. They have traffic policemen, but to my way of looking there is absolutely no need for them. The family here, as well as all other good families, have a carriage with a coachman dressed in livery that is here to drive us around whenever we want to go anywhere. Yesterday afternoon they drove us out to see one of the family vineyards, and we incidentally gathered a basket of apricots.

It is very much like Mississippi here. However, it is not quite as hot yet. The crops are about the same with the exception of sugar cane, cotton, and sweet potatoes which they do not seem to have. Their watermelons do not ripen until about the middle of August. The wheat harvest is over now, and the threshing will begin immediately. The corn fields here remind one very much of home, for this is the only place in Europe that I've seen it.

I suppose we will be here for about a month, as we won't be able to leave sooner. They seem to expect us to stay all the summer. Hungarian politeness is really overwhelming. However, we will have to leave after a month, for we must get back to France where we can study. We will be able to do some here, but it is always difficult to work when you are visiting. I have some books with me, though, and I hope to use them.

Did I tell you that Marjorie Jackson was married? I have never been so surprised at the news. Hattie May is in Tulane University at New Orleans in summer school. She will teach at McComb again next year. She has just been on a short visit to the Barbers at Gulfport. Harold has had his girl down from Lexington and they had Hattie May over. Hattie May had been at Gulfport previously this summer with a girls' camp. . . .

Ellisville will probably be all right for sister after all. There are a number of very good friends of ours there who would be able to help her, and that would be worth a lot. I am sure the Smiths and Gantts would be nice to her on our account. Then as you say the expense is a great consideration.

I am very much interested in the house repairing, also in the water and light project. I would like to have some friends over home when I return next year or the year after, and as you know the place is in poor condition to receive them at present. The development of the springs furnished a place for entertainment, and with the house improved we might be able to have a nice time.

The duty on the bracelet was outrageous. I shall take care about what I send in the future. To think that it cost only three dollars and a half here and that the duty was four-fifty. The tariff laws at home are disgusting. I shall quit sending things that will require a tariff duty and will bring them with me when I return. Then I can bring in the value of a hundred dollars free of duty.

Hope the new cotton pest does not get in our fields. How is the crop this year and how is business at home? I have been wondering about these things for some time.

It is time for lunch.

Love, Wilson

In letters to Girault Jones, Wilson Lyon often continued the personal confidences and banter that marked their friendship at Ole Miss. Writing of those college days, over seventy years later, Bishop Jones recalled many late-night discussions in the dormitory. "We were assigned to the first floor on West Gordon. Gordon Hall was E-shaped, with the central arm the college dining room. We had an inside room which looked directly into the dining hall. Many a night we propped in bed and watched the dances, for neither of us attended them. I did not go for lack of interest and a slim budget; Wilson had never learned to dance."

Instead of dancing, they talked. Characterizing those talks, Jones remembered that "many of our night sessions had to do with the state of each's love life. I had little to contribute, for while I did date on campus, my destiny was already tied to a home-town girl whom I knew some day I would marry. But Wilson did considerable casting about, first one and then another, and he needed an Ann Landers on whom to place some of the load. . . . By the time we were seniors, his interest had settled on one person and he was genuinely interested in knowing how I could be so certain I had found mine. I wish I had tape recordings of those late night sessions."

A year after sailing for England, Wilson Lyon was still love-struck over his college sweetheart Hattie May Benjamin, the "one person" he had settled on. Their relationship, and its eventual breakup, was to be the subject of much of his correspondence with Jones who, as a close college friend, knew them both well and was in a position to understand and comment on Lyon's feelings.

His mention of R. Malcolm is a reference to Malcolm Guess, the director of the YMCA at Ole Miss. Wilson Lyon was president of the YMCA during his senior year, and Jones was Guess's office secretary for two years. In his mention of "the Dean", Lyon refers to their mutual Ole Miss friend, A. B. Lewis.

Mrs. S. C. Heidelberg was the sister of Callie Findlayson, who was married to Allen Lyon, Rufus Lyon's first cousin. Her husband, who had a furniture business in Hattiesburg, was a son of Washington Irving Heidelberg, who founded Heidelberg in 1882.

One political allusion is made by Lyon when he speaks of hell breaking loose in Paris, an apparent reference to the fact that between June 15 and July 23, 1926 the French formed four governments. This was part of a larger pattern of governmental instability between 1924 and 1926 caused by inflation, the falling value of the franc in relation to the American dollar and the French government's inability to decide on the type of spending and taxation policies that should be put into place to help control the situation.

Gyon, Pest vm, Hungary
July 21, 1926

Dear Jug:
Jones, you are about the best letter writer that ever warbled

on an Underwood. By the way, how is the old machine? I always feel an interest in the old girl. I found your two recent letters of June waiting for me here, both of them over several weeks of age, and my how I enjoyed them! If I had another correspondent or so like the reverend I would like to spend the rest of my life reading and writing.

I've just finished a long letter to Hattie May, one in which I poured out all the passion I possess—the kind of a letter that says everything possible. I really flatter myself that I can write love letters now, for I'm genuine, and this and one I wrote yesterday are among the best I have ever done. I'm afraid I did backslide a little in my writing. I had hardly noticed it when Hattie May began to check me up and then suddenly began writing me almost every day, the sweetest letters I had ever received from her. I tried to send her a cablegram but it was impossible out here and there is no passing to Budapest. I'm writing almost every day now myself. I'll tell you, Jug, I love her so that without her I don't believe I would be worth shooting. I'm sure I would mope a year or so away if I should lose her. Which by the way, is the very thing I don't intend to do if zealous attention and real love, everything I've got, can keep me from it. American girls are the world's best and for me she is the best and most lovable of them all. I could search ages and never find one I could love so much or one who would suit me so well. This is not written just for you to relay to her, but I wish you would transmit a little of it in your next letter. All this and more is genuine, and I want her to never forget it.

I suppose Hattie May has written you about seeing Harold and Annie at school and also seeing them recently at Gulfport. I say recently, the news will be about five weeks old when you get this. They seem as happy as can be, she says. Gave her a dinner at the Buena Vista, etc. Wonder if they can wait until another year. Hattie May is planning a trip to Europe, and I'm trying to get her to come another year, that is, summer. I take examinations for my degree next summer and will be free from study for a while. If she doesn't come to Europe I am making rapid tracks to America. I would prefer

her coming next summer instead of the year after, because I
would want to come home immediately after the term is over
at Oxford. I get five hundred dollars from the Rhodes trust at
the beginning of that summer, and I want to keep it for a nest
egg to tide me through the summer and support me until I
can draw some salary at the university or college which is
unfortunate enough to receive me for an instructor, or what
not. I can get home fairly cheaply, and I would be very well
set for the time being. 'Twould be a start toward a diamond.

I wrote Margie a letter, rather frivolous in fact. Hope
Hubby doesn't mind. I couldn't help reminding her that I had
prophesied as much last spring when I told her goodbye. Tell
me, wasn't it what we call in rubberneck parlance "a runaway
affair"? In other words, it was rather sudden and not marked
by much ceremony, was it not? I wonder if Harriet was the
sister who accompanied her. I have been hearing from Harriet occasionally every few months, but haven't heard lately. I
suppose it is just as well. Her letters are wonderful, but the
cessation might as well come now as ever. I pledge you there
is not a whit of sentiment about the connection. Merely a literary friendship, very platonic.

Well, Jug, I know you well, I think, and I would bet my
last *sou* that you are a goner this time. The little lady has you
on the way, and by all accounts she is on the same road herself. "I can truthfully say" that I don't think you could have
found a better. Hattie May is wild about Virginia, and I think
her opinion is worth a lot. As for ole E. W. he thinks she is
one of the sweetest and loveliest girls he has ever known.
Just the kind for you, Jug, plenty of pep, nice looking, sensible, loving, and sweet. You know, it has just struck me as
funny that I should attempt to eulogize on the virtues of one
you know many times better than I do. However, I suppose
that like most men you love to hear nice things said about
persons and things you are fond of.

You aren't wasting any flattery on me lately, however.
First you insinuate that I don't know how to fold letters and
then you impeach my character by asserting that I am not fit
to wear the cloth. As to the first imputation I can defend

95

myself, as to the latter I think the untruth is apparent
enough, so will let it slide. At the college envelopes as well as
writing paper are furnished by what we call the Junior Common Room, an organization which handles various student
activities. As I have to pay my subscription to the J. C. R., and
as I don't care to buy special envelopes to fit typewriting
paper, which the English never use, I cram my letters into
the college envelopes in the best way I can. Why reproach
economy, which I claim to be a virtue when rightly used.

Your description of your eating place is what the English
would term "priceless" or better "marvelous". Really it does
credit to Oliver Wendell Holmes. I am delighted that you like
your place so well. I have always considered Hattiesburg a
very nice city for South Mississippi. However, in the matter
of libraries Laurel has it beat by miles. The library there is
rapidly becoming the best in the state. Hattiesburg is such an
Ole Miss town that I'm sure you must feel at home. . . . While
I think of it, Mrs. S. C. Heidelberg on West Pine is a very
good friend of our family, and I'm sure she would be glad to
see you. You might drop by some time, if you ever get up
with your calls. I stopped with her several times last year
when on my way to Woodville, and McComb.

I have just realized about Doris' mother. I remember now
that I heard it before, but I've been on such a rush that I did
not think of it. I am trying to write her a letter today. I am
also writing the Dean. I was under the impression I had
written him, but I will try again. Do you ever hear from R.
Malcolm? Mother sends me clippings about Ole Miss from
the *Daily News*, and they are the extent of my Ole Miss
knowledge.

Now, I'll try to tell you a little something about myself.
After a delightful time in Vienna, I think I wrote you there,
we came on to Budapest, five hours and a half by train—third
class. Our friend, Michael Halasz, met Gray and me there and
carried us to his aunt's home in the city. We remained there
four days while they showed us the city. Boy, I have never
been so overwhelmed with hospitality. I've been here a week
now and the only thing I've spent money for is stamps. They

absolutely refuse to let us pay laundry, street car fares, taxis, train fares, theater admissions, Turkish bath fees—I've had *deux bains Turcs*. The food is splendid and they have about put me under the table by insisting on us eating so much. In fact I did get sick the other night, vomited like a dog. After that I have been all right. Gray did not have such good fortune, and his stomach is still out of order. The father of our friend is a member of parliament so we were shown through, a privilege that is denied to the public. We also had a private guide for the royal palace at a time when it was closed to the public. We did the city up pretty thoroughly and it was very enjoyable.

There have been a number of guests who do not speak English and we speak French with them. I have been surprised with the ease with which we get on. It will really be wonderful practice for us. We are not getting away from here so soon as we had expected, and I imagine our return to France will be delayed until around September 1. We want to go back via Venice, Milan, and Geneva. Just now hell seems to have broken loose in Paris, and I am just as happy that I'm not there. Certainly hope they don't confiscate the books I left there.

We are now out in the country about 24 miles from Budapest. We play tennis, read, walk, and swim, and dance— all of which is very nice. The only trouble is that it's hard to get any studying done. And that is very essential for me.

Continue writing me at the college. My mail will reach me fairly promptly now. Here's to the continuance of our love affairs and the increased pleasure in your work, in which you seem so happy and contented.

> COUNT-ing his money,
> Just a trekking Rhodes Scholar
> who's beginning to weary of the roads
> and hard third class seats.

> E. W. Lyon

Writing to his mother from Hungary, Wilson Lyon offered his reflections on the merits of Jones County Agricultural High School in Ellisville as a place for his sister to study for a year to gain adequate course work for college admission.

As always, he was enthusiastic about the impending changes that his mother reported both for their home and for Heidelberg. He again urged his family to replace their outhouse with a bathroom. He was excited at the prospects for a light plant in town, though in fact it would be the end of 1927 before Heidelberg residents had electric power.

The letter alludes to his having received money from home, the only such reference in all of his Oxford correspondence. As he notes, the hospitality of the Halasz family was of major importance for him in stretching his stipend to cover the long 1926 summer recess.

Gyon, Pest vm, Hungary
August 10, 1926

Dearest mother:

I received two letters from you today, the first I had had for over three weeks. It seems that the college porter lost my address and had to wait for me to write him before he sent my letters. I was furious with him, for his blunder was excuseless, as I wrote him expressly to send my letters here and he had already sent two packets before this.

You ask my advice about sister. I do not know what to say. I am not a great proponent of the cultural value of an AHS, but there are some distinct advantages to be offered for Ellisville. In the first place, it is near home, which might not be bad for the first year that sister is away from home. Then Mrs. Gantt and Mr. and Mrs. Smith, all of whom I esteem very much, are good friends of the family, and they would take some kind of an interest in sister and that personal interest will be what she will need and it will be of great value to her. Then too, it is cheap; and after all, I expect it is fully as good as Holly Springs. As to the diploma, that doesn't make so much difference really. Let sister take the regular work without the extra Home Science, she will be able to enter college and to all intents and purposes she will be through with High School. Knowing her as I do and remembering my own distaste for the more practical things of life, the extra Home Science work, which is really very hard, would probably be the difference between a pleasant and a miserable year. After all, Ellisville is probably as good as we can do. I agree with you that the Laurel project is not commendable. Dormitory life has distinct advantages, and I think it will do sister a lot of good. I think eight years of it gives me the right to speak of its good points. It makes one self-reliant and teaches him to look out for himself. This is exactly what Joe needs. I will try to write to her this winter and will send her little things and some money occasionally; these will all cheer her up a lot. Tell her to be sure and take a course under Mrs. Gantt. . . .

I think you must have been on the coast the same time that Hattie May was there. She was over visiting the Barbers on July 3-5. Annie Ford, Harold's fiancée, was there and they invited Hattie May over from New Orleans. The Barbers are very fond of Hattie May and I think she has been back there again since. Harold writes me that he is going into business in the state, with a firm from Iowa that has some holdings in the state, I think.

I am glad to hear of the light plant. If we can get water works now, the town will be much improved. Be sure to put in a bathroom when you have the house remodeled. I really don't see how we've lived so long without this necessary comfort. I can't afford to invite anyone to visit me until we have one; it would be rather embarrassing.

I hope the family financial condition continues good. I will not be forced to call on you again I am sure. I have gotten myself within my scholarship, and I am sure I can continue there for the future. Also, I may be able to save a little money. I will return home with several hundred I am sure. I plan to spend both of my winter vacations cheaply, and that will also augment my finances. Of course, I'm investing quite a bit in books and other things which I will need, but it is very nice to be able to get the things I will need in my profession. I'm going to buy some French books when I leave here. I read the language well enough to study in it without difficulty. Sounds odd to think of reading the history of England in French, doesn't it?

We will not remain here over ten days longer. We plan to get to Rouen by September 1, which means that we must begin our return about August 20. As I told you we want to stop in Italy and Switzerland. The League of Nations will be meeting in Geneva, and we may get a chance to see a session. It would furnish interesting material for a story to the papers at home. It has been as agreeable as possible here. The Halasz family has done everything possible to make our journey pleasant. I have never been treated with the hospitality that has been accorded us here. Everything has been done for us, and we have been taken into the family circle of the village as old friends. All the many family connections have welcomed us and have shown us every courtesy.

We've had some opportunities to speak French here, and now that I look back on it, I have learned quite a lot. It will be worth a lot when we get to France. The French family with whom we have reserved places at Rouen is highly recommended to us by Paul Havens* and Bob Sams*, two of our best friends at Oxford. Madame Noblet is a Frenchwoman of high class who lost her husband in the war, and now she takes boarders, *pensionnaires* as they say in French, to supplement her income. She has a beautiful chateau with a large garden in front at Grande Couronne, about six miles from Rouen. Rouen is the old capital of Normandy, from where William the Conqueror set out for England in 1066, and is still the most important city of that section. It is only an hour or so from Paris on the train. Normandy is the French apple country, famous the world over for the blossoms in springtime, and I am sure it will be nice to be there when they are ripe in the autumn.

Am glad the book arrived OK. I think father will like it. Tell me, did you have to pay duty? I am under the impression that there is no duty on books, am I right?

Hope you are all well. It makes me rather homesick to hear

you speak of melons and other Southern delicacies. We are supposed to have some here, but the season is so late that they are not ripe yet. You seem to have had unusually good luck at home this year. However, we have fried chicken and corn on the cob, two very famous Southern dishes. I have enjoyed both of them very much.

My love to all,
Wilson

Settled in the French countryside, near Rouen, for a month of studying and learning to speak French, Wilson Lyon had more time for lighthearted self-description when he wrote to Girault Jones and summarized his summer travel experiences. Director D. W. Griffith's film, *The White Rose,* which Lyon saw in Milan, tells the story of a minister who has an affair with a young girl whom he leaves. Eventually he abandons the ministry and returns to her when he learns that she has given birth to a child. The film would have provided him and Frank Gray with a much needed change of pace after their serious sight-seeing.

The letter that follows shows clearly his devotion to the American academic world which he was preparing to make his professional home after completion of his Oxford degrees. The M. A. degree which he mentions was a purchased degree, not a degree earned through study.

In reporting his accidental meeting in Paris with Lloyd Thatcher*, a member of the Ole Miss biology department, he mentions several other faculty members. Eric Allen Dawson had an M. A. from Ole Miss and was assistant professor of French. When thinking back to his college days, Girault Jones remembered having Dawson as his French instructor when he was a sophomore. Elmer V. Levie had an M. A. from the University of Chicago and was a professor of history. Lyon seems to have had little fondness for either man's teaching abilities. Dr. Swan was chairman of the Department of Chemistry. Mr. Moore, also mentioned, was the minister of the Episcopal church in Oxford, reopened due to the efforts of Girault Jones and others.

Chateau de St. Martin, Grand-Couronne
Seine Inferieure, France
Sept. 8, 1926

Dear Jug:

I'm not nearly so formidable as the above sounds. To a less
intimate friend I would keep up the bluff, but honor forces me
to apprise my friends of my situation. I am here with a
French family attempting to learn to speak the dear old language which seems to get further from you the more you
learn about it. The house is a very lovely chateau, the leading
house of this delightful little Norman village of fifteen hundred inhabitants. We have a large *jardin* out in front and the
ensemble is quite nice. I left Gray in the American hospital at
Paris having his stomach examined, and he won't be out to
join me for another day or so yet. As that was about a week
ago, he should be turning up soon. We are less than twenty
minutes from Rouen by train, and the service is frequent, so
we aren't exactly isolated, even if the nearest bath is there!

My French has been slowly but surely improving since I
arrived in Europe, but this is my first serious attempt to
learn to speak it in anything like a scholarly way. I read quite
well and rapidly, if I may be allowed to say it, and I speak the
necessary travel language without difficulty, but the carrying
on of an intelligent conversation on almost any topic is
another thing entirely. I have noticed a great improvement
during the week I've been here, and by the end of my five or
six weeks here, I will understand everything even if I don't
speak any too quickly. To speak without the foreign accent is
well nigh impossible and something I don't hope to accom-
plish. I read the papers every day, am reading a novel *Noblesse
Américaine par* Coulevain, and am reading some of the short
stories of Guy de Maupassant. Yesterday at Rouen I ordered
a three volume history also, *L'histoire du Peuple Anglais au
Dix-neuvième Siècle.* The book is highly recommended by my
tutors and will enable me to kill two birds with one stone.

My day is not the least exciting. I begin to think of rising
at eight and complete the process of shaving, etc., in time for
breakfast at nine or a little after. *Après le petit déjeuner, j'étude*

l'histoire jusqu'au déjeuner. Alors, j'écris ou fais quelque chose comme ça jusqu'au thé, après lequel j'étude encore. The evenings are uneventful also, so all in all I'm having quite a quiet time, not the rip roaring time at all that popular conception attributes to a Rhodes Scholar turned loose in the "iniquities of Europe". I've got about fifteen volumes of histories that I should read before returning to England. I may get through them but the prospect at the present time is rather doubtful. My long travels, if they have enriched my knowledge and afforded much pleasure, have certainly not contributed to my knowledge of English history. I am having my first tests when I return to Oxford, the first I've had since coming to Europe. They don't mean anything except to show your tutor how much you know, but I would like to show some "faint traces of the subject" at any rate.

Just a running account of where I've been since I wrote and what I've seen. I tried to write you from Hungary before I left, and that was some two weeks or more ago, so this letter is sadly behind. It looks like that in spite of myself I'm getting to be a bad correspondent, but you know how it is when you travel with never over two or three days in one place at the time. We spent two more days in Budapest with Michael's aunt, stopped in Vienna for a while, had a delightful ride to Venice through the Austrian Tyrol. Venice lived up to and exceeded all of my fondest expectations. The Piazza San Marco is the most beautiful square I've ever seen, and the city is charming in the evening with the gondolas. I couldn't imagine a better place for a honeymoon, except for the fact that the bride would probably bankrupt the husband right off by buying out the captivating shops which cater almost exclusively to the tourist trade. I think they are the most enticing shops I've seen anywhere. I fell to the extent of buying some beads for Hattie May and an artistic leather purse for sister, but that was the end. Prices were too high for me to get anything for myself (sweet sacrificing soul that I am).

We were two days in Milan, which sounds much nicer if you give it the Italian spelling and pronunciation, *Milano.* I need not rave to you about the beauties of the world famous cathedral, the arcade, the Scala theater, the Camp Santo. There, I say in disgrace, I descended low enough to see D. W. Griffith's "La Rosa Bianca", The White Rose. We then hopped off to Geneva, enjoyed the breezes off Lake Leman, visited the church and cathedral of Calvin, the Reformation Monument on the University grounds, saw the League building with the famous Salle de Glace, the International Labor Office, met and conversed with some of the professors of the Carnegie delegation who were there studying international relations, roamed the Quai Woodrow Wilson in the evenings, and made mild attempts to flirt with a very captivating little French waitress at our favorite ice cream emporium. In Paris I remained for a day, picked up my bag of books, which had slept peacefully there since the first days of July, and trotted out here where I've hid myself from the world, so to speak, for the next four or five weeks.

Perhaps many questions about me come up in your mind, perhaps old prophecies of my doom, comparable to Wigglesworth's famous version, have disquieted your clerical brain with visions of your former roommate locked in the grips of sin. Well, don't lose your sleep. I'm going to enter the confessional and open up on a few things which as you would say "are close to my curls". To my mind I've not descended into the vale, but of course you must allow that my point of view has undergone certain quasifundamental changes. My love for Hattie May sets your mind at ease on one point, so I need not delay there. Although I have in no way left the path of strict sobriety and gentlemanly conduct, I find wines, especially the French and Italian, very delightful, and I drink them regularly with my meals when I'm on the continent, as the cost is practically nothing. In England I drink lemonade, lemon squash, or ginger beer, a harmless non-alcoholic beverage, and these cost more at the college than the best table wines do here. The old gag about the French never drinking water is not true. They drink it often especially mixed with their wine, but at the present price and with my taste as it is I shall continue to drink wines, have more pleasure and safeguard my health from the many

WILSON LYON
Heidelberg, Mississippi, 1904

THE LYON HOME
Heidelberg, Mississippi, ca. 1912

———

Left to right: Willia Lyon, Josephine Lyon,
Elijah Washington Lyon

DEDICATION OF THE CONFEDERATE MONUMENT
Heidelberg, Mississippi, September, 1911

—

Front row, second from right: Wilson Lyon

Special Collections, Honnold/Mudd Library,
Claremont University Consortium. Reprinted with permission.

MISSISSIPPI STOCK JUDGING TEAM, 1921

Clockwise from left: Wilson Lyon, Aubrey McLemore,
Armos Beaman, Myres McDougal

OLE MISS SENIORS
Girault Jones & Wilson Lyon

Special Collections, Honnold/Mudd Library,
Claremont University Consortium. Reprinted with permission.

RHODES SCHOLARS
on RMS *Lancastria*

———

September, 1925
Back row, far left: Wilson Lyon
Front row, center, in light suit: Frank Gray

ITALIAN TRAVELERS
Spring, 1926

———

Left to right: Frank Gray, Wilson Lyon,
Reuben Borsch, "Dusty" Rhoads

THE HALASZ FAMILY
Gyon, Hungary, 1926

———

Back row, center: Wilson Lyon; *far right:* Michael Halasz.
Front row, center: Frank Gray

WILSON LYON
Venice, August, 1926

MARJORIE DANCE &
WILSON LYON
Oxford, 1927

RHODES SCHOLARS IN SPAIN
March, 1928

———

Left to right: Wilson Lyon,
Reuben Borsch, Frank Gray

TWO MEN ON A DONKEY
Spain, April, 1928

Reuben Borsch & Frank Gray

RHODES SCHOLAR TOURISTS
Madrid, March, 1928

—

Third from left: Wilson Lyon

RUFUS LYON
Heidelberg, Mississippi, ca. 1925

WILLIA &
WILSON LYON
Heidelberg, Mississippi, ca. 1928

JOSEPHINE LYON
Senior picture, 1929

———

Holly Leaves,
Yearbook of Mississippi Synodical College.

PASS CHRISTIAN, MISSISSIPPI
August 29, 1935

———

Left to right: Girault & Kathleen Jones,
Wilson & Carolyn Lyon

RHODES SCHOLAR FRIENDS
who directed Lyon's career path
toward Colgate University & Pomona College

———

Thomas Hoben Robinson & Paul Swain Havens

E. WILSON LYON'S INAUGURATION
as sixth president of Pomona College
October, 1941

———

Left to right: Frank Aydelotte; Robert G. Sproul, President, University
of California; Bernadotte Schmitt; Lyon; Charles K. Edmunds

Left to right: Lyon, John Kemble, Bernadotte Schmitt

PRESIDENT LYON
in his Sumner Hall office

WILSON & CAROLYN LYON
Pomona College's young presidential team
Claremont, September, 1941

———

THE LYON FAMILY AT HOME
Claremont, November, 1941

Left to right: Wilson, Elizabeth, John, Carolyn

possible impurities of their *l'eau naturelle*. That I can still
advocate prohibition, I assure you, but a lot of the arguments
about drinking at home are positive bosh—as are a lot of the
other provincial trends of thought in the States. Even with
that, I prefer our small town knowledge to the listlessness
and ignorance of the European peasant, even if he does live
more sanely at times. But to compare anything other than
negroes in American life to the peasants is obviously unfair
to both parties, for we don't have a class as low as that.

I think I have found my place in the affairs of the world at
last, as a professor of history. I have fallen more in love with
the academic and cultural spheres of life and have lost still
more taste for the business side. All of which means, I will
never be rich and will never be in want. I find the history
work very interesting, think I'm developing the historical
mind, and believe I can rise to a fair degree of prominence in
the field. I don't see why I shouldn't perhaps be able to do
some writing in the field. The only thing that jars me now is
the lack of a Ph. D., which we foolishly require in America.
The fact that I've spent the time necessary to get one in perhaps the leading university of the English speaking people,
certainly as far as English and European history is concerned, won't have much weight with the trustees of some
two by four university where they turn out rah rah college
boys with a faint idea of who Napoleon was and the firm con-
viction that Queen Victoria was a prude and Henry the
Eighth a reprobate. As I see the situation now I will have to
spend two years at some American University to get the necessary credentials to mount on high in the American University world. If things go well I should get the B. A. next
spring, then the B. Litt. the next spring, and two years later
I will be entitled to my M. A. provided I pay a nice little sum.
If I were all alone in the world with no settled plans of trying to induce another to agree to spend her life with me that
would not be so terrible. But being in love as I am, with one
of the most charming young ladies of the country, and not
having enough money to support two during the process of
giving myself my eighth and ninth years of college life, I'm

somewhat up the tree as just what to do. The lack of a Ph. D. won't reduce my salary for the first two or three years, and if I should enter one of the larger universities, I could put in the summer and other time working for my degree which I might eventually take without too much loss of time or expense. That seems to be the best course at the present time. Of course, if Hattie May should change her mind about thinking me "the one and only", and mind you she's not bound to me by any fast ties of engagement or any promise to wait until my return, I would have plenty of time to think and might find two years of work for a Ph. D. not too inconvenient or unpleasant.

I had a most pleasant surprise the other day in Paris when I ran into Professor Lloyd E. Thatcher in the American Express. After I had changed my money we went out to the Café de la Paix, where he had some beer and I an orangeade, and discussed the affairs of Ole Miss. He's the first Mississippian I've seen here whom I knew at home. He was leaving that afternoon at four on the boat train from Boulogne and sailing for America that evening. Apparently, being one of those few gentlemen who do things ahead, he had completed his tour of Paris and only waited for the train to leave. I invited him out to lunch with me and over a bottle of Vouvray we spoke of Ole Miss. I saw him off on the train after some six hours of most pleasant conversation. Most of the things he told me must be old to you, but they were all news to me even if I did have some inkling of them. Thatcher was very amiable, said he had inquired about me at Oxford, and had seen one of my friends on the Rhine. He seemed to think the University was prospering, thought there were better things in store, and seemed to think I would find it an agreeable place to begin my work after leaving here. He seemed to have some news of you, through Mr. Moore, and paid you a number of well-deserved compliments. He didn't hesitate to give his opinion of Dawson, Levie, and one or two others. Silence, of course. I sent my best especially to Guess, the chancellor, Dr. Swan, Dr. Bondurant, Dr. Milden.

Your ravings, pardon the word, remind me familiarly of

myself and seem so like me in olden times that I feel like the shoe has jumped in some measures to the other foot. I wish I could write like that now, but I've lost some of the spark during the year's absence. Don't misunderstand, my love is just as strong as ever, but you know it's much harder to relate your sweetheart's sweetness a month after than the day after. It's that kind of inspiration you miss most over here at a time when you need it the most. The charm of the American girl, especially one you love, is something unique in all the world. Nothing else can make up for it. If anything can it will be the desire for that which will draw me home next summer. Hattie May talks of coming abroad, and in that case, I certainly shall not come home. Otherwise I probably shall, but I can't make definite promises so far ahead. Where do you think you will be another summer? I shouldn't count a return half complete unless I should be able to see you.

I shan't read over this, that pain is reserved for you. Suppose you are at Sewanee so I'll send it there.

Cheerio, Wilson

Wilson Lyon's ongoing concern for his younger sister is reflected in this letter, written to his mother just after Josephine left for Ellisville. Apparently Aunt Vera* had driven her to the Jones County Agricultural High School in her new car, so Josephine would not have to make the trip by train alone, as her brother had always done. His deep desire to retain a sense of family with his parents and sister, despite his own growing independence, is reflected in his request for a family picture. It is interesting to realize that he apparently took no family picture with him to England in the fall of 1925.

References to Mrs. Heidelberg and Miss Hemeter, both of whom lived in Hattiesburg, suggest that Josephine had visited them there earlier in the summer. Both were friends of the extended Lyon family. Emily Hemeter had taught in the Heidelberg elementary schools before moving to Hattiesburg, where she taught middle school English

The letter also illustrates what were, for Lyon, the sometimes unreasonable requests of local friends who hoped for a letter from him, or advice on how they might peddle an invention.

The description of the circumstances surrounding his move to a new *pension* in Rouen is marvelously vivid and youthfully cocksure. It's clear that his desire for ample meals at a reasonable price won out over his desire to immerse himself in French.

Pension Lemercier, 107 Rue Beauvoisine
Rouen, Seine Inferieure, France
Sept. 30, 1926

Dearest mother:

I was delighted to receive your letter this morning telling of sister's beginning at Ellisville. I certainly hope she will be pleased. If she is satisfied, the year should mean much to her. Write me and tell me, how is her health, does she hear better, has her side trouble improved, etc? These were difficult questions to ask when she was at home, but now that she is away I can write you more plainly. I have thought of her many times since I've been over here and hoped so ardently that something could be done to fit her in more with the life around her. I want to send her little gifts from time to time, but I'd like to send things that she'd appreciate most. You might help me by sending me a few suggestions, or do you think a little money would please her more? I think books constitute one of the best gifts for her because she seems to like to read, but I really don't know what things she likes. If she'd write to me more I could tell. I'm going to write her today and maybe she will answer. You might tell her that I'm still waiting for an answer to my letter from Hungary.

Aunt Vera's car should prove of great joy to the family. 'Tis nice that she should come by to pick up sister, as it was nice of Miss Hemeter and Mrs. Heidelberg to see her. With people being so nice, I don't see why she should be lonely in the first few days. I will try and write to Mrs. Heidelberg. I have some faint recollection of promising to write Mr. Avery, but I thought he only suggested it to be polite; and then I never had the address either. My correspondence is heavy

enough without taking any chances on wasting letters by
sending them to the wrong address. Everyone seems to think
I should write him from Europe, but it doesn't seem to occur
to them that it is just as obligating on them to write me
occasionally. However, all this is not directed at Mr. Avery,
and I shall be delighted to write him if papa will get the
address. I remember now that I never did answer something
you said about Mr. McClellan and his invention. You realize
no doubt that it would be very difficult for me to do anything
with it over here. I have no connection in the business or
manufacturing world. Does father seriously think there is
anything to it? At any rate he doesn't seem to be doing much
with it, considering the length of time the thing has been in
the air.

I'll drop a card of congratulations to Carl. Is he returning
to Louisville? It seems odd to think that he, two months
younger than I, is married, a father, and hitting out trying to
beat the world out of a living. It may be the thing to do, as he
advises all his friends so generally, but I'm still from Missouri. At any rate, I'm financially independent and able to live
in a style better than I've ever known. It is not always advis-
able to rush into marriage tumultuously and blindfolded to
the problems arising out of it.

You probably wonder why the change in address. It proved
very disagreeable at Grand Couronne, the food was horrible,
the service poor, and the price out of reason for France. As
things failed to improve we determined to leave. We found
this *pension* (boarding house in English) to be far superior to
Madame Noblet's, and the price is only thirty francs whereas
we were paying fifty out there. Naturally, we had a little
difficulty in getting away. We decided to tell her frankly we
weren't satisfied and that her place was not worth the money.
She insisted so that I told her frankly but politely that her
meals were entirely too poor for anything like the price. We
parted pleasantly and outwardly peaceful, but, of course, she
was not pleased though what I told her was for her own
good, as I knew the others who had been there this summer
were dissatisfied also. She was honestly one of the stingiest

women I have ever seen, and no one can charge me a big price, half starve me, and expect me to stay. We speak very little French here and it was too late to find a family, so I won't learn as much as I had hoped. I think now I'll come back to Paris alone at Christmas and find a family to live with there. If I came alone I would learn a tremendous lot in the six weeks. After all, you don't learn much if you are with someone who speaks English, for the mixture of the two languages retards the French.

You speak as if the cotton crop had been good. I certainly hope so. The price is certainly none too good. Tell me, how are business conditions at home, and how is the family treasury? I hope you are getting along all right.

We are spending most of our time studying, with strolls about the street and an occasional theater for diversion. We will leave here for England in about two weeks. Then the expenses begin. Whereas, I live here for ninety-three cents a day, tips and all included, there I'll pay about five dollars, just a slight difference. What's more, the food here is much superior to that in college.

Did you give Joe a Kodak at commencement, and if so, why haven't you sent me some pictures? Why don't you and father have a real photographer make some first class pictures of you? It seems odd that I have no pictures of anyone in the family. It looks rather cold blooded and unfamily-like. I wish you would do this. It wouldn't be much trouble to drop down to Laurel some day and have your pictures "took".

Love, Wilson

CHAPTER FIVE
Settling In
1926-1927

On his return to England in October, 1926, the unfinished business facing Wilson Lyon was making arrangements to be paid for the articles he had written for Mississippi newspapers in 1925-26. After having no success on his own, he turned to his father for help. The letter that follows, and its enclosure (not included here), detail a history of his agreement with the newspapers. Although his father's assistance did lead to his receiving payment for his articles, the demands of his academic work prevented Lyon from continuing his newspaper writing during his second and third years at Oxford.

The insurance referred to in this letter was apparently a life insurance policy. Setting aside adequate money for payment of the premium on the policy proved to be next to impossible for Lyon during his Oxford years.

William Inge (1860-1954), whom Lyon heard preach, was a popular writer on religious and social issues, as well as being dean of St. Paul's Cathedral, a post he held from 1911 to 1934. *Lay Thoughts of a Dean*, published in 1926, is probably the book to which Lyon refers.

The letter provides a glimpse of "Wilson Lyon at home" as he decorates his room and invites new American Rhodes Scholars to tea. He had purchased the "flashing Hungarian table cover" in Budapest to match an embroidered pillow cover given him as a farewell gift by one of Michael Halasz' cousins.

Beulah (Lyon), whose marriage is noted in the letter, was the child of Rufus Lyon's first cousin, Eugene. Her grandfather was Jonathan Lyon, a younger brother of Wilson Lyon's grandfather, Elijah Washington Lyon. Uncle Rufe (Rufus Uranius Lyon) was the youngest brother of Elijah Washington Lyon. A resident of Fort Smith, Arkansas, and a widower since 1912, he frequently paid extended visits to family members, including his nephew and namesake.

The letter's mention of the continuing coal strike provides a reminder that the grievances that had precipitated the General Strike in the spring of 1926 had not been resolved. Britain's economy, in the fall of 1926, was still deeply troubled.

Oxford, England
October 17, 1926

Dearest father:

The enclosed letter to you is self-explanatory. I have been unable to secure a reply to my letters asking the *Star* to pay me for my work, and consequently I have ceased work until I can get some understanding with them. As they seem to be inclined to ignore me, I want you to take the matter in hand and push it to a decision as quickly as you can. I have written the enclosed letter with two points of view, one to present the situation to you, and secondly, to give you something to show the *Star* so the matter will be simplified for you. I suppose Mr. Skewes* is the man to see. It may not be necessary for you to go to Meridian in person, and if you think you can settle the matter by letter, well and good. Do whatever you think best, but please do something immediately as the matter has dragged out a long time. I have hoped against hope that I would hear from them but I have given up since they failed to reply to my letter written from Vienna early in the summer. If you go in person I would strongly advise making an appointment before hand.

Unfortunately I am unable to send you all of the money for my insurance. Fifty dollars will be all that I can afford to part with now. But if you get the money out of the *Star* be sure to keep back twenty-five for the remainder of the insurance and deduct all the expenses of collection. I am going down to town in the morning and send you a money order or check for the fifty and will enclose it in this letter.

The Salvation Army is holding its regular Sunday evening street service just below my window, and I have the benefit, or the disadvantage, of their brass band. My new room looks out over St. Giles Street, the widest and one of the nicest streets in Oxford.

This morning after the church service at the Presbyterian Church I went down to hear Dean Inge preach. He is the Dean of St. Paul's cathedral and the outstanding religious leader in England. His new book on England of the present day is being widely read. The sermon was a very scholarly and able presentation this morning. Saw my Hungarian friend at the Presbyterian church for the first time since our return. He reported that his father had been very ill since we left but that he had recovered now.

I've been down here since Wednesday. I came a day early in order to be here to take my autumn examinations. I have taken five in the last three days, finishing yesterday morning. They were fairly difficult, and I have little idea what kind of a class I will get on them. They were the first I've taken since I came over. However they gave me an idea of the kind of questions they ask and an idea of how much I know and what I need to study most. Speaking of study, I will have to work very hard this year to get ready for the "schools" which are coming in the spring.

Before coming down from London we went to the theater three times, seeing among other things a very good troop of American negroes which I enjoyed. Coming over on the channel I had my first attack of sea sickness and I hope the last. The sea was the roughest I've ever seen, and the water was washing up on the decks. Gray went down also along with about half the people on board.

The new Rhodes scholar from Tennessee* lives at Okalona, Miss., and I've just had him in to tea along with a new man from South Dakota*. Both seem very nice and pleasant. The Mississippian was at Sewanee and knew Jug.

I was very glad to get back to Oxford. It is beginning to seem a bit like home now, and I find the English boys very friendly and congenial. My rooms are quite nice, and I feel like the possessor of a castle now that I'm alone and have two rooms to myself, to use as I see fit. I've carried five etchings down to the shop to be framed, and they will help my walls very much. The etchings, all colored ones, are of Venice, the Alps, The Tyrol, a French valley, and Beethoven's house. I also have out my flashing Hungarian table cover that I wrote you about.

I wrote sister some time ago, and hope she will answer. Am glad she seems satisfied. She will enjoy it if she once gets into the swing of things.

Beulah's wedding was a surprise, though I had wondered if it might not come off some day. If he has a good position it should be quite nice for both of them.

As I'm not getting any Mississippi papers this year, will you send me the Sunday *Jackson Daily* when you've finished with it, especially the sports section. Of course, mother must take her write-ups out first. The Sunday paper will carry all the football returns and enough of the local news to keep me in touch. I have no time to read more. The paper every day was very nice last year, but a bit too much for this year now that I have to study so much.

The coal strike still continues and our coal is rationed to a ridiculously small amount. I fear we shall be cold if it continues much longer. However, I'm rather well acclimated now, and I find I can stand it all right. The temperature never gets any lower here than it does at home, but the dampness is bad.

Adeline Aldrich, an American girl whom I knew here last year, has presented me her portable victrola. She left it with her landlady and wrote me to call for it. It is a very nice instrument and I shall enjoy it very much once I get some money to put in records. Adeline is teaching English in Hollins College, Virginia, this year and says she likes the South fine. Her home is Albany, N. Y.

Hope you have gotten rid of Uncle Rufe, for mother must certainly be in need of rest.

I am distressed at the low price of cotton and other farm produce in America. Looks like the good times are on the wane. How is the progress on the house? Mother has never told me what you were doing on it, although I've asked the pointed question.

Certainly hope you will be able to settle the *Star* debt for me. In case it turns out that the *Leader* did not use all the material as the *Star* did, the debt would be about a third less, or two dollars a week for the seven months.

Love, Wilson

P. S. On the advice of my banker I am sending you a personal check. You will deposit it like any other. The bank at home will have to convert it into dollars. You should receive just a few cents over fifty dollars. Certainly wish I could send more, but it is impossible.

Wilson Lyon had never ridden a bicycle in Mississippi and therefore the following description of his late afternoon bicycle ride with Thomas Robinson* may have evoked for his family a picture of him wobbling down country roads toward Abingdon for tea.

His reference to his test results at the end of this letter indicates he already had a more than respectable knowledge of modern European history, and foreshadows the class he would earn when he received his Oxford B. A. in 1927. More significantly, he makes reference to his tutor, William Costin*, though he does not name him in this letter. Costin, a young man in his mid-'30s when he tutored Wilson Lyon, is mentioned by name only twice in the surviving correspondence from Lyon's Rhodes Scholar years. However, their weekly tutorials were of increasing importance as Lyon prepared for his B. A. examinations at the end of his second year at Oxford. By the time Lyon left Oxford in 1928, their tutorial relationship had evolved into a deep friendship that would survive until Costin's death on October 6, 1970. Grateful for his guidance and support, Wilson Lyon returned to Oxford many times to visit him throughout his life. The depth of his friendship and respect is reflected in the obituary for Costin that Lyon wrote for the April, 1971 issue of *The American Oxonian*, which is included in the Directory of Names.

St. John's College, Oxford
Saturday, Oct. 30, 1926

Dearest mother: '
I've just come in from a bicycle ride with Robinson, the Canadian who was with us at Cannes. We went out to Abingdon,

a small town about nine miles west. It is a rather famous place in history, and the ruins of the old abbey are beautiful remains of early English architecture. We had tea out there and then came back, arriving after dark. We pushed our cycles through town in order to avoid being stopped by the police for riding without a lamp. I learned to ride a little in France this summer, and I'm completing the process here. As everyone here rides a bicycle it seems odd when you can't. But every year there are several Americans and Canadians who have never ridden. Now that I can navigate one I'm going to buy one as they prove rather useful here.

The debating society, of which I'm secretary, held its first meeting night before last. As the officers wear dress clothes I felt somewhat distinguished. It was the first time I had worn my tuxedo since July.

The coal ration has been doubled so I hope to be able to stay in my room more. Lately I've been studying in other men's rooms, following the fire, so to speak. Each man has his day to provide the heat. Luckily it's been rather warm lately, so it hasn't been so very inconvenient.

The letter you forwarded me was an announcement of Lawrence Corban's wedding. You will recall that he was my predecessor as president of the YMCA at Ole Miss. His wife is a daughter of the chemistry professor at Millsaps.

The timber will prove a valuable resource in this time of low cotton prices. Whether father sells now or not is immaterial, for he has the resource whenever it is necessary to call on it. Now that father seems so well fixed I hope nothing will happen to set us back again. It is a great feeling to be independent and not in debt. I'm enjoying it very much over here, as I make my £400 see me through. I think it will do it quite comfortably in the future.

Hope you are all well. My tutor seemed to be pleased with my tests and thinks I will get a second class which is quite good.

Love to all,
Wilson

Writing to Girault Jones as the term began, Wilson Lyon was already beginning to reflect on life after Oxford. With the perspective gained by a year away from home, this letter also contains his first comments on areas needing strengthening at Ole Miss. Dr. Snydor, a history faculty member, must have been one of Girault Jones' Ole Miss professors. Because he had a Ph. D. (from Johns Hopkins), Lyon probably viewed him as a competent teacher and scholar.

Hattie May's travels in the states, alluded to here and mentioned in a letter Lyon wrote to his mother on September 19, 1926 from Grand-Couronne, France, included a two-week trip to New York, Washington, Philadelphia, and Atlantic City. In New York she missed the first act of a play because her cab was caught for an hour in a traffic jam caused by mourners of Rudolf Valentino, the great matinee idol of the silent screen, who had just died at age thirty-one of a ruptured ulcer.

Jones had visited Wilson Lyon's parents in Heidelberg late in the summer while he was doing his summer internship ministry in Hattiesburg. The reference in this letter to Willia Lyon's food is an allusion to that visit. In recalling his day in Heidelberg over half a century later, Jones commented on the enormous gas stations. His memory is confirmed by reports in the *Jasper County News* which, on April 8, 1926, reported the completion of the Pan-American Oil Company station, the second station in town. Despite poor roads, many Heidelberg residents had cars.

St. John's College
Oxford, England
November 4, 1926

Dear Jug:
I fear I've become a very poor correspondent recently, but I'll try to drop you another letter soon after this when enough has happened to me to make it worth while. It has been rather difficult to get settled here, due principally to the coal strike. When it's real cold, and you aren't able to have a fire in your room for stretches as long as a week at a time, it is not the easiest thing in the world to write. As a typewriter is

a novelty here, you can't think of using it in another's rooms for fear of causing a nervous breakdown. You know the English are terribly averse to noise. They have the idea we are all about to go crazy with the rushing and clang of our cities. America signifies noise to them, and overdriven men on the verge of collapse. They regard us as a recreationless folk.

We've been back here some three weeks to the day. I found myself quite pleased to return, and I'm developing a great attachment for Oxford and the college. It seems entirely different now that I have that feeling of being sure of myself. In plain American slang: "I know the ropes." And you know that is about three thirds of the fight.

I'm rooming alone this year, in true Oxford custom. As I thought, it is much pleasanter for Oxford. Where you entertain at teas, breakfasts, luncheons, etc., it is much more convenient to be alone, unless your roommate seems to be friendly with the same bunch you are, which was exactly the opposite last year. I have the usual two rooms, a "sitter" and a "bedder", as we call them in Oxford slang. I have two lounge chairs, a couch, three tables, a cupboard, bookcases, and more straight chairs than I can count. And above all, I'm the possessor of a Victrola! Fortunately I didn't have to buy mine, for an American girl who was here last year willed it to me on her departure. They are quite the common thing here and serve to while away and dissipate an enormous lot of time. Their best justification is for the river in the summer term when you take them out in a punt and drift down the stream to the tune of a dreamy waltz. The scout on this staircase is exceptionally good and I get service par excellence.

I went through a set of tests when I came back, five in all, and came out fairly well. They seem to think I will probably get a second class, which is very good, though of course a first is better—that I have little chance of getting. At the present moment I've left English history behind and am dealing with the French Revolution and nineteenth century Europe. All my reading has been in French, and I've gotten to where I can read the French direct without having to mentally translate it into English. That I think is my greatest

accomplishment in the language so far. I shall never forget
Dr. Brown's* words on the first day we started French at Ole
Miss. "You must think in terms of French. *Cheval* must mean
cheval and not horse to you."

I am accumulating a rapidly growing little library myself.
So far I've acquired about fifty new volumes since I arrived. I
am buying continually, and I am going to buy a number of
French books when I go to Paris at Christmas. I'll never have
a better chance than the present to get together the begin-
nings of a real historical library. Money, of course, is the
main drawback, but I manage to get along, and the path looks
much smoother for the future.

I'm beginning to give a little thought to getting a position
after I finish here. My ideas are very vague at the present. I
think it would be to my advantage to go where I can get a
Ph. D., as I could shorten the process by putting in my spare
time on the thesis. What a nuisance the process and expense
of getting it is going to be. However, I may prefer to teach at
a smaller University where I would get more money and put
in my summers somewhere else. There would be the proba-
bility of going back to Ole Miss, but I hardly think that
would be desirable at the present. One thing certain, I could
never stand to take a subordinate position with such a man as
Levie above me. As a historian and professor he's about the
worst I know. What did you think of Dr. Snydor?

Hattie May has been blaming herself in her letters for her
lack of consideration toward you in not notifying you when
she would be away, so you need feel no regret for your own
inability to go over to McComb. She said she was afraid you
would think she hadn't been in earnest about the invitation
since she had left no time open for you to come. I'm afraid her
travels in the States dampened her ardour for coming over
here. I certainly wish she could come another year. Know you
and Jin are getting along famously. You know, Jug, in all seri-
ousness, I don't know but what the girls are right. It is a
rather long time to promise definitely to bind yourself when
there are so many possibilities of change, and when we aren't
about to offer them anything besides our love. But each day

brings us that much closer to some kind of an end of the trail, so we may hope for better in the future.

Ole Miss seems to have the football team that may take A&M down this time. Perhaps at last the great year is coming. If so, I shall get a thrill as great as if I were once again a follower of the Red and Blue.

Hattie May writes me that McDougal and Satterfield are the Ole Miss nominees for the scholarship this year. Mac has been owing me a letter for months, can't understand why he hasn't written. What do you think of their chances, rather of Mac's? I would certainly like to see the old boy over here, but it will be some change for him! *Comprenez-vous?*

By all means you must spend the week with me, longer if you can, just as soon as I get back to the good ole USA. I regret that I've never been able to have you before. If I come home next year I hope to try and have a gathering of a few friends. You, Jinnie, and Hattie May, certainly, if I can get things fixed up a bit. You understand, of course, what I mean. Glad you liked the food. Mother has always been famous for good food, that has certainly been something that I could not have wished changed.

I hope you found no widespread opinion on the campus to the effect that I had gone to the devil. Hope we can go back together sometime (campus, of course). What do you think of a class reunion, say about 1930. I think we might get quite a nice crowd. L. E. seemed to think the old place was coming, and I hope he's right. But Dr. Bondurant's right. We don't need increases in students half so much as we need strengthened faculties, higher standards, and a stronger cultural atmosphere. Above all, Oxford and Ole Miss need a real bookstore. It is appalling to think of a University trying to carry on with the poor facilities for buying books that exist at Ole Miss.

But I'm getting didactic, the one thing I want to avoid. Sit down "subito" and write me all about yourself and the fatherland.

E. W.

Lyon's search for vacation lodgings in Paris was unsuccessful, and on the advice of a Rhodes Scholar friend, Ed Ham*, he found a boarding house in Nancy. There he celebrated the season with French families, in their homes. As he grew more competent in French, he was no longer an outsider, as illustrated by his being invited to spend a few hours in a nearby café on Christmas night with a new French acquaintance.

Near the end of his stay in Nancy, he received the news from his mother that his Mississippi friend Myres McDougal had won a Rhodes Scholarship and, in a letter written January 9, 1927, told his mother that he had written to St. John's College asking that McDougal be accepted there.

Hotel Deux Hemispheres, Nancy
18 Dec., 1926

Dearest mother:

I'm afraid it has been rather long since I wrote you but you can appreciate my difficulties, I'm sure. I left Oxford a week ago today hoping to spend the vacation with a French family at Paris. The man with whom I had been in communication could not take me so I was reduced to searching for another place. I obtained several addresses in Oxford and then in Paris I got some more at the American University Union. But I was without success in Paris as the prices were more than I could pay. The one or two places where I could have paid the price were full. I was in Paris Sunday, Monday, Tuesday, and Wednesday until noon. It was a vacation; I learned some more of the city, had some good food, and danced one evening. Ed Ham, of Maine, knew two American girls in Paris and the four of us had dinner and remained for the dancing at Romano's, a very good but modest-priced restaurant just off the Boulevard des Italiens.

Ed knew a family here with whom I could live, so I came here with him. The place is really a boarding house for French students in the University here. I am the only person in the house who can speak English, so my opportunities for learning French are excellent. For the first week I am only taking my meals at the place, for there is no room in the house, but after Thursday I will have the room of one of the students, who will be home for the Xmas vacation. Frenchmen are easy to know and the people seem cordial, so I should have no trouble getting along well. I understand without difficulty, so I've slipped into the conversation without too much trouble. The meals are nothing to brag about, very simple in fact, but the food is well cooked and there is plenty of it. All in all I'm quite well satisfied and I think the vacation will be very profitable. The price is very cheap (27 francs or $1.08 per day). The prices they asked me in Paris ranged from 40 to 60 francs a day. While I'm in the hotel I pay five francs (20 cents) for dinner and the same for supper. At the Paris prices my money would not have lasted through the vacation, while here I should make it quite well.

Ed is staying in another place, though at present we are sharing a hotel room until rooms are available for us. He was here last summer in a family, and we have been invited to take Xmas dinner with them. Tonight we are escorting the two girls to the Grand Ball of the School of Mines, said to be the biggest social event of the season. I hope we shall enjoy it, as I guess we shall.

I haven't received any mail yet, so I haven't had home news for a long time.

If you should have any curiosity as to where and what Nancy is I might say that it is a city of 125,000, two hours from the German border. It is in that part of Lorraine which was French before the war and it was heavily bombarded, though never captured by the Germans. There remains no sign whatsoever of the damage. One passes through Chateau Thierry coming from Paris to Nancy.

This should reach you just after the new year, which I hope will find you all well and happy. About a month from today I shall be returning to England.

Lots of Love,
Wilson

Nancy, France
Dec. 24, 1926

Dearest mother:

This is about the coldest day I can remember for a long time.
The temperature has never been this low in England any
time that I can recall, and I've experienced cold weather no
where else over here. There is ice several inches thick in all
the ponds and puddles. Seems quite appropriate for Xmas
Eve, or *Reveillon de Noël*, as the French call it. I've just come
in from a French lesson, my first. I've gotten in touch with a
lady who gives lessons to foreigners at forty cents an hour. I
learned quite a lot this afternoon, and I think she will prove
very valuable.

Yesterday I moved out here, where I will have a room for
the next ten days. I got rather tired of coming every day
from my hotel for meals. I lost too much time from my work
by that system. Certainly wish I could stay in this room until
I go back to England, for it is comfortable and I am in the
family all the time.

Christmas Day

I didn't get to finish this yesterday, as I had to go to a French
lesson, and then down town to buy a Christmas gift for the
Madame. Last night, Christmas Eve, Ed and I were invited to
spend the time with the French family he stopped with last
year, Madame Hodez. We had been invited there for Xmas
lunch, so I've been there most of today since noon. After the
lunch, which was quite good, the two girls, their brother, Ed,
and I took a long walk to the heights above the town from
where we had a good view of the surrounding country and the
valley of the Meurthe. I got mighty cold before we returned.
Yesterday was one of the coldest days I've seen in Europe. The
temperature was seven degrees below zero, Centigrade. I don't
know the relation between the two systems so I can't reduce it
to Fahrenheit. All I know is that the French papers consider it
very cold, and consider the weather worth two columns on the
front page. There was some sunshine though and the day was
not disagreeable, though the temperature might give that

impression. I'm sending you a picture of the situation at Paris.

We came back from the walk and took tea at the Hodez's, and I got home just in time for dinner, 7:15. I had intended to work in the evening, but one of the French students here asked me to go out and have some coffee with him and listen to the music in a café; and as it was Christmas and as I regarded this as a good opportunity to learn some French and make an acquaintance, I consented. I came in about ten and here I am writing letters.

Naturally the day has been very different from Xmas at home. In fact there has been practically nothing to remind one of it. I've had no mail for two weeks, so I haven't received any cards or news from home to remind me of it. I hope you have all had a pleasant gathering at home. I need not say that I would have liked very much to have been with you. Christmas never seems like Xmas unless you can be at home, see the loved ones, and smell the fragrant odor of the turkey cooking in the kitchen (or as Neil Crone*, an American from Iowa says, stick the turkey to see how it's coming along).

My experiment here is proving very satisfactory from the standpoint of learning French. I find that I'm progressing rapidly. I understand nearly everything one says to me and can follow most conversations without great difficulty. Also, I can converse fairly well on any topic that I could talk on in English.

I've begun to take some lessons from a lady who seems to be very good, and those should begin to help me. I shall feel very gratified if I make as much progress per day for the next three weeks as I have made in the past two.

Nancy has the saving grace of being cheap, as Ed Ham promised when he induced me to come here. Had I not struck such a cheap place I would not have been able to make my money last. I pay two hundred francs a week for my room and board, which on the present rate of exchange is exactly eight dollars. The only other regular expense I have is tea, which costs between three and four francs, or about fifteen cents. I'm having some books bound and I'm buying a few books, but those will not come too high either.

I shall be here for a little over three weeks longer, as the University reopens on January 20. Our vacation is a few days less than six weeks this time, just a bit shorter than usual.

I will close and do some studying.

Love, Wilson

The tone of this letter to Girault Jones, written shortly after Wilson Lyon's return from France, reminds us again of his youthfulness. His reflections on art and religion provide a wonderful window into his mind and heart: he brings his visit to the Louvre alive; he defines his feelings about religious practice. He and Jones had often contrasted the Presbyterian and Episcopal churches during their time at Ole Miss. In this letter Lyon acknowledges the beauty of the language of *The Book of Common Prayer*, compiled in 1549 by Thomas Cranmer, the archbishop of Canterbury appointed by Henry VIII.

"The present business" refers to Jones' request that his friend Wilson purchase and send to him a graduation present that Jones could give his sweetheart, Virginia Wallace, in the spring. Lyon's own Christmas gift to Girault Jones seems to have been *The Caravan Stories* by John Galsworthy, a collection of fifty-six short stories written between 1900 and 1923.

Jones had gone to McComb, Mississippi, to visit Hattie May Benjamin, Lyon's Ole Miss sweetheart. His report of the visit apparently suggested that Girault thought that after almost two years, Hattie May's ardor for her friend Wilson might be fading a bit. In fact, their breakup would soon take place. However, Lyon's enthusiasm in this letter about the prospect of a European visit from Hattie May in the summer of 1927 makes clear that in January, 1927 the possibility of a such a breakup was far from his mind.

St. John's, Oxford
Jan. 21, 1927

Dear Jug:

I left Nancy a week ago tomorrow and spent until Wednesday in Paris. Spent all Sunday in the Louvre, pictures alone.

Tuesday I spent the afternoon in the Greek and Roman sculpture, which I knew a little better than the pictures. These two days made me familiar enough with the gallery so I can see only the things I want to in the future. You know the "Mona Lisa" does smile—what an exquisite picture. And the "Winged Victory" and the "Venus de Milo" are Greek sculpture *en sa façon la plus merveilleuse*. I would give anything to go and see them with Dr. Milden. Placed as it is there at the head of the long staircase and visible from below for nearly a quarter of a mile it grips you and refuses to let you go. You can just see the prow of the ship moving in the Mediterranean or the Aegean with the victory in wings guiding it through the blue water to triumph. I don't know any Greek, but I'm certainly impregnated with a love and admiration for Ancient Greece.

We pulled out of Paris at 6:25 Wednesday morning and arrived here at 6 in the evening, changing and coming immediately from London. I had been foolish enough to enter a scholarship examination here for which there are several prizes in books and a couple of scholarships of considerably more value. I didn't get a chance to look at the subjects on which we are doing them, so I don't expect to get anything. However the four I've done so far haven't been too bad, and I am better prepared on the one which comes tomorrow. The Englishmen don't think anything of the £5 book prizes which are being offered, but I should certainly be happy if I could get one. My financial situation is not as bad as yours seems to be, but the task of making the four hundred do the year is awfully difficult especially if you buy books, pictures, and other things you want. Of course, having to deposit fifty pounds with the college last autumn didn't get me off with a fair start. That fifty pounds comes back at the end of the three years, and I should be well set for the last summer, but it makes it hard now. Like you I can't afford to call on father, and if you reckon what I've sent home in the way of gifts I haven't had a pound from them since I've been here. Whether you believe it or not I'm a good economist. I know how to cut the corners and I shave them as close as comfort and reasonable pleasure will allow. All Rhodes scholars ought to enter Wall Street; as financial training the sojourn here is what Ole Miss is for politics, the finest in the world! I'm always drawing ahead on my scholarship. It's the only way I can make ends meet.

This term and another and I face the "schools", examinations for my degree. It means work, work, work. However, I've learned more than I gave myself credit for if the exams of the past two days are any indication. I have no fear of getting the degree, but I want to get a second class. Otherwise I won't be able to go on with a B. Litt. and research next year. If I miss that it will be rather serious for a future professor, for the road looks long enough as it is. How on earth I'm going to get a Ph. D., found the happy home I have in mind, and live like I want to are questions which my poor brain finds exceedingly difficult. You are finishing your schooling at any rate next year and are going to start to be of some use to the world, while I will still be far from the goal.

You know, Jug, I'm happy to see you in the ministry of the Episcopal Church. It is a church which stands for enlightened thought, for real Christianity as opposed to the narrow mindedness of the circuit, or the Baptist pulpit. Unfortunately the latter two organizations have by their preponderance sadly contaminated the Presbyterian influence in Mississippi. The more enlightenment I receive the more I admire and love the Episcopal Church. I said some silly and foolish things to you about ritual, etc., during our Ole Miss days. Forget them and know that I have seen the light. Cranmer's prayer book has come to mean to me what it is—the climax of beautiful English.

Now to come to the present business. I wish to goodness you had written me while I was in Hungary because I could have gotten something in Northern Italy when I passed through Venice and Milan the last week in August. Beyond doubt the most distinctive gifts to be had here are in Italy, Florence or Venice especially. A thing I've been intending to get for Hattie May before I come home is an Italian shawl. They are really exquisite in Florence or Venice. The prices vary but I'm afraid it would take at least fifteen dollars to get one of the class you would want to give. As I suppose the duty on silk is very high so that is probably out of the question. Another beautiful and perhaps even more appropriate thing would be an Italian leather desk set. You have a huge blotting pad, a stand for letters and paper, a pad for engagements, a paper knife, one or two ink stands, and another piece or so. The designs vary—you can have Dante and Beatrice, children of the classic times, etc. The colors vary also. One of these complete should cost between ten and fifteen dollars. I have no idea about duty. As to ring and bracelet, like sister's, that cost me about $3.50. The exchange is a little more against us now and it might cost four. Etchings can be had in abundance on almost any variety of topic. Did you see the one I sent Mrs. Benjamin, a Venetian scene, or the one of Magdalen College that I sent Hattie May for Xmas? The Venetian one cost about three dollars and a half, while the Oxford one cost almost eight. But the trouble about all these Italian things is that I cannot possibly go to Italy before the time you will want them. However some of my friends are going, and I might entrust the matter to one of them, if you can give me explicit directions. Also, I might write a firm in Florence about a desk set, for I think Frank Gray can give me an address or I could write to the Italian lady with whom we stayed there. *Le dernier cri de Paris en ce moment* is jewelled heels for evening shoes. You take off the ordinary heels and replace them with the jewelled ones. They are awfully lovely things, just a fad of course but very beautiful. I saw the displays on the Rue de Rivoli and thought of sending a pair to Hattie May, but I'd already sent the etching and I couldn't afford another seven or eight dollars, which is the price. If you should be interested in them and would tell me the color you prefer, I could get them without difficulty. I have no idea where I'll be next vacation, so I can't promise much definitely. I've promised to spend the time with another would-be historian, a Rhodes scholar from Connecticut*. We are going off somewhere to study, the quieter the place the better.

What you asked for is difficult to obtain here, for any

English article does not appear foreign or out of the ordinary to an American. Think the matter over and if none of the above suit you give me some more suggestions. If you want to give me plenipotentiary powers I will consider it a favor to be allowed to do all I can to get something that makes Jones stock at 100% "and still going strong". I appreciate your dilemma. I hesitated so long this year that Hattie May's gift didn't arrive until after Christmas day.

Now as to the dollar seventy-five, please forget it. You may consider it a Christmas gift for last year or as an expression of my good will for countless favors in the past. Even pay for reading my English papers while I filled a date if you wish. Any old thing, but by all means don't send it. I refuse to accept it. Glad you hadn't read most of the "Caravan" stories. I hesitated a long time before sending it. I always have a half conscious fear that any book I send will be one that the receiver has read. Harriet unfortunately slipped into that path in sending me a book this Xmas.

I was indeed delighted to know you had been to McComb. Hattie May too lamented the fact that she had little time to talk to you alone. Your report sounds good. It isn't wildly exciting with tales of rapturous devotion, but I value it all the more for I realize it is the conservative opinion of one who reflected and thought before he spoke. At the present moment I'm all beside myself with excitement. Doris, bless her soul, has convinced Hattie May that they should come to Europe this summer. Moreover, she has already assumed control of Hattie May's finances, has made her transfer part of her money to a separate bank where she has started a savings account for the trip. I'm going to send Doris a note of encouragement and thanks just as *toutely* and *suitely* as possible. Boy, won't I be glad to see that ole liner come into Southampton. I'll probably blow out completely on my exams due to the excitement. You can imagine all the thousand and one reasons that impel me to want to see her. Two years is an awful long time, let alone three. I'm going to do all I can to promote this scheme. I'm convinced that otherwise Hattie May would waste her money, while this way she can have the trip of a lifetime. I know all the short cuts and we can do all the cutting of corners possible. Doris fits ideally—Mrs. Benjamin won't hesitate for a minute to let them come together. I'll have plenty of cash to stand the gaff, at least five hundred and things should be rosy. I will get to go back to all the places I love most of all, Italy, France, Switzerland, and will also travel in England with them. Venice with your sweetheart—heaven on earth! A girl who was here last year has just written me that one should be lonesome to really enjoy Venice, but I've had the lonesome experience. Now I'm ready for company.

[End of letter missing]

This letter's picture of Wilson Lyon completely "at home" in Oxford, after his Christmas break in Nancy, provides ample proof that by his second year of study he had really settled in. His rigorous weeks of study during the Christmas break had led to his winning £5, for the purchase of books, in a history essay competition.

The detailed discussion of his wardrobe, prompted by his purchase of a new suit, makes clear that he was the same Beau Brummell recalled by his friend, Jug Jones, from their undergraduate days together at Ole Miss. It's noteworthy that he comments on the perilous condition of his finances, and in the very next paragraph announces he has ordered a suit—his wardrobe was not an area where he was willing to scrimp! Throughout his life, Lyon loved nice clothes, and was always impeccably dressed, usually in jacket and tie. He was six feet tall but in his Ole Miss and Oxford days was very thin. The twenty-pound weight gain he reported to his mother at the end of this letter must have reassured her. Even so, he probably weighed no more than 140 pounds.

In commenting on his letter from his Heidelberg friend, Ellis Travis, Lyon's remarks reflect his disdain for education shaped by religious fundamentalism. Longino (Ellis), who had family in Heidelberg, had apparently come back to town to live, as had Curtis, whose identity is unknown. Mrs. Morrison was a close friend of Wilson Lyon's mother, active in the UDC and so interested in

Wilson Lyon's life abroad that she sent him a laundry bag during his first year away from home.

Jan. 28, 1927

Dearest mother:

I realize that this letter is nearly a week overdue, but somehow in the rush of early term activities I haven't had time to get around to it. After the examinations were over there was my weekly essay to get onto and other duties. I am now completely settled again and feel somewhat relieved to have the homelike feeling once more. After all, whatever we may say at times about the food, this is more home than any other place in Europe. It is our one recourse when all others fail, the base of supplies and the retreat when all other helps fail. One learns to love it very much and to feel quite at home in the Oxford atmosphere.

I might begin by telling you of my little piece of good fortune. Several prizes were offered for excellence in our examinations, and I won five pounds to be applied in buying books. When you translate the sum into its equivalent of twenty-five dollars it seems like a whole lot more. This will enable me to get a lot of things which I need and which otherwise I could not have afforded. I have the privilege of choosing what books I want. The books are stamped with the College Coat of Arms to show they were won as a prize, and that gives them a slight mark of distinction. My papers seem to have been rather good, and my tutor seems very well pleased. He told me last night that I had done better than any of the history people in the college who entered the examination, which means he thinks I will get the highest class when we take our examinations in June. I am speaking of the college, of course, and not of the University.

Also another piece of good fortune. The lost letters came home finally. By some unaccountable blunder they had been sent to Grande-Couronne where I was last summer. They finally came back after a long wandering and were all a month late. Worst of all one of them was an invitation to see an American girl and her mother in Paris, I had met the girl here last spring. I received it here after I had returned! However, your letter with the advice on coming home was in the batch. It looks like I ought to stay as there is so much one can do, and there is so little to do at Heidelberg. I hate awfully to stay away from home so long, and I would give anything to see you, father, and sister, but it seems to me wiser to stay. The third-year men I know best here applaud the idea very strongly. I think Hattie May is coming. She has practically said as much.

I may go to Brussels for the next vacation, and I will call on Aunt Vera's friend. Belgium is very much cheaper than France, and as I've never been this would be a very good opportunity. You get 175 Belgian francs to the pound while you get only 120 French, and the prices are about the same in the number of francs—which means a lot saved. There is no danger of things going up in Belgium, for the franc is stabilized at the rate of 175 to the pound. As my finances are about as low as possible I must look to saving every penny.

I ordered a new suit yesterday, the first I've had this year. I did without it until my clothes were beginning to get a little too worn for real polite society. The fact that we always wear evening clothes at all dinners, dances, and such affairs is of course a great help and makes it possible to do with ordinary street clothes. The suit I ordered is a very nice bluish gray mixture, cost eight pounds and eight shillings, almost exactly forty dollars. I am going back for the first fitting tomorrow. Needless to say it is much superior to the twenty dollar suit I bought last year. However the latter is still serving me well, and I've worn it all over Europe. It has been my travelling suit on every vacation. The clothes I brought from America have lasted wonderfully well. The blue suit with the two pairs of trousers, though three years old, is still plenty good enough for ordinary Oxford wear and continental use. The spring suit I had the last year at Ole Miss is also good, but too light in weight for use now. Then I have my knickers and a pair of flannel trousers, the most usual thing here. Finally there is another old American suit which can be made to do in an emergency. These with my dinner suit usually suffice, but I didn't have anything presentable for nice teas and select afternoon occasions.

The prospect of your orchard sounds very good. I shall be delighted at the thought of delicious fruit in the home orchard, free for the asking. I can play the part with perfection of the long departed son, long from home and now returned to enjoy all its good things. I will send Mrs. Morrison the card as you suggest. Hope Joe's temporary improvement of spirit will last.

You asked me some time ago about my throat. It bothers me but little. My general health is excellent and I weigh nearly twenty pounds more than I did when I left home. So you need have no worries about me. Oxford and Europe are treating me fine.

I finally had a letter from Ellis. Like a true Mississippi College product, he can't write a friendly letter to a friend without dragging in a lot of narrow-minded prejudice and incriminating charges against Ole Miss. He could have told me lots of things about Mississippi and affairs in general which would have been far more interesting. I hope I'm above all such petty disputes, for my time here has given me the perspective to show me how ridiculous they are. But if my time here has given me a truer view of things it has decreased enormously my already minute enough opinion of Mississippi College. That place is the American denominational college at its worst, narrow minded, egotistical, depreciating of everyone else, intent on prying into everyone else's affairs, and at the same time doing everything itself that it accuses others of doing. Mississippi College is in short everything a college ought not to be. I pity the state of mind of one who really lets their philosophy take hold of him. Ellis is too sensible to embrace it all, but he can't help from doing things that show the Clinton influence. He seems to be doing rather well in chemistry and talks of a fellowship in one of the larger eastern universities next year. His disgust of Heidelberg seems to mount with every visit. He talks at times of never going back to the place.

Your mention of Longino and Curtis puts me in mind of

the old saying the "birds will come home to roost". Seems funny to think of Longino being back with a wife.

I was at a very nice little dance in North Oxford last night. An American girl here celebrated her twenty-first birthday by inviting a number of us for dancing. We had souvenirs from Boston, her home—mine being a rubber doughnut! After the dance Hope French, whom I had escorted, asked me by her home and I had my first turkey of the year. I'll say it did taste good! I think this was by far the nicest dance I've ever attended in Oxford. It was the night after my essay so I was ready for entertainment.

Hope the nice sunshine continues for you. We've even had some in Oxford this term. At the present we are having a regular March day, and the wind is whipping about my window with terrific speed. Hope you are all well and happy.

Love, Wilson

Images of hatred, violence, and racial inequality defined much of Mississippi's public image during the years when Wilson Lyon studied in England. Coming in after a tutorial session when his tutor had joked "about the way we treat the negroes at home", he was bothered about it enough to mention it in this letter to his parents. His comments, almost impossible to decipher because we don't know the lessons of history he and his tutor were discussing, seem to reflect conflicting loyalties between his sense of justice and his love of home.

The letter also shows that women students at Oxford were not always looked upon as equals by their male counterparts, a point suggested by the frivolous topics scheduled for debate with two women's colleges.

One important piece of good news is noted here. Rufus Lyon's trip to Meridian to collect the money due his son for his newspaper columns had been a success. The check itself had arrived from home. In the same mail there were apparently some Mississippi newspapers whose headlines were a source of great perplexity and/or amusement to Lyon's English friends.

Discussing the illness of his "scout" at the end of the letter, Lyon talks of having to get his own coal for the fireplace in his room. Although the miners' strike had continued into the fall of 1926, by the beginning of 1927 most of the miners had drifted back to work, many of their goals for improved hours, wages and working conditions still not achieved.

Feb. 10, 1927

Dearest father and mother:

I'm afraid I've been awfully bad about writing this term. I will try to do better in the future. I've been so busy with my studies this term that I've neglected you far more than I should. I shan't let this long go again without a letter.

I want to thank papa with all my heart for the check. I had almost despaired of getting my money when I thought of the brilliant scheme of writing father to go and see about it. I don't know why I didn't think of it before. I wish I could have let you keep the money, but unfortunately I just had to have it. I had been cutting things close, and without it I would have been very short for the vacation. As it is, I'm a little overdrawn on my scholarship, that is, I will be when the spring vacation is over. I drew a check for forty dollars; that leaves five to pay father's expenses at Meridian. I had just ordered my new suit, so I had the money to put into it.

All my mail is straight at last. I thank you so much for the handkerchiefs. I was needing some, especially nice ones like these. The L gives them distinction, fit for any company. You asked about the papers. I have been getting them regularly and thank you for them. They give me considerable news of what is happening and don't take too much of my time as they did last year when I got them every day. I showed some of them to some English chaps the other day and they thought them very funny especially the headlines. The following struck them as very humorous as well as puzzling "Normal Girls Will Meet Ole Miss Co-eds In Cage Battle." If you remember that they don't know that "Cage" refers to basketball and that "Normal" has any other than its usual significance you can easily see why they were puzzled.

Another they thought funny was "Health Causes Man to Cut Throat." English headlines are generally something like the following: "Portuguese Revolt", "Church Assembly", "Negotiations at Hankow", "German-Polish Relations", "Spanish Claim to Tangier", and "Irish Free State and Imperial Defence." I have been quoting from today's "Times." Quite a difference, are they not?

Spring is beginning to show signs of approaching. The snowdrops and croci are beginning to bloom in our garden, which as you know is about the most beautiful in Oxford. Other bulbs begin to show some signs also. Of course, the hyacinths are a way off yet. I would give anything to be at home for the Mississippi spring. I don't think they are any lovelier anywhere, not even in Italy or England.

I was grieved to hear of father's illness. I certainly hope this letter will find him better. This is the first time his back has hurt him recently, isn't it?

I'm having more trouble trying to make up my mind what books I want than I had in winning them. We have to get them all at once, so I must take off some time and make up the list. I've just finished my weekly tutorial, so I may work on them tonight.

My tutor has just been joking me about the way we treat the negroes at home, calling them slaves and me a Ku Kluxer. Of course, there is much to be said on both sides, as Abe Lincoln once remarked when he was pushed into a tight place; but I gently reminded him that he knew nothing of the situation and that his argument was in violation of all the lessons of history we had just been discussing.

I wish you'd get Joe to write me. I wrote her months ago and yet no reply. I never received the copy of the Ellisville paper. I will try to send them something some time as you suggest.

I'm going to speak Monday night in a debate on which I take the affirmative of the question: "That this House deplores the modern taste in dress." We are debating against one of the girls' colleges, St. Hilda's. Yesterday afternoon I went to tea with the President and Secretary of the St.

Hugh's Society to arrange a debate with them. The question is frivolous again, as are all the debates with the girls' colleges: "That this is the Best of all Possible Worlds."

My scout has the "flu" and as the college staff is limited now, we are having very poor service on this staircase. I am taking my meals with Callaghan*, an Australian Rhodes scholar, until my scout returns. It puts things out considerable not to have the good attention and service I had grown accustomed to. I'm afraid we get awfully pampered here. For instance, I resent having to get my coal. However, it isn't so much that I mind the work but because someone else is supposed to be doing it and is neglecting the job.

I hope you are all well and enjoying nice spring weather.

Love, Wilson

Concern for his sister and the desire that his mother, father, and sister be able to enjoy a closer sense of family were deep worries for Wilson Lyon throughout his life, and he addresses these issues seriously in this letter, written approximately half way through his Rhodes experience at Oxford. In the letter we see him planning for his own future and urging his mother to send his sister to college after her graduation from the Jones County Agricultural High School so that she can look toward a more promising future also.

Pecans and watermelon seeds sent from Mississippi had just arrived from home, providing wonderfully tangible reminders of the love and support he had received throughout his life from his parents. Lyon had requested the seeds for the Halasz family in a letter written from Hungary on August 18, 1926. They came from melons grown by Sam Hales, a black resident of Jones County, who, according to a letter from Willia Lyon as well as a report in the August 12, 1926 *Jasper County News*, had brought a sixty-two pound watermelon into Heidelberg. Allen Lyon (1868-1940), who sent the pecans, was owner of the Heidelberg gin, and Rufus Lyon's favorite first cousin. He was the son of Jonathan Lyon, a younger brother of Wilson Lyon's grandfather, Elijah Washington Lyon. It is not surprising that this letter, reflecting Wilson Lyon's own loving concern for family, was written in response to these family gifts.

Feb. 24, 1927

Dearest mother:

I've just received the pecans and I thank you very much for
them. Don't know when I've enjoyed anything so much. I've
had a lot of fun giving them to my English friends—who
have never heard of or seen any before. I learn on consulting
the dictionary that the word "pecan" is thought to be of
American Indian origin. So you see how when far away we
sometimes learn a lot about things we had never questioned
before. It was very nice of Allen to send them, and I am writing to thank him.

This is the time when the college is in its biggest athletic
stir. All the teams are playing in the tournaments for the
intercollegiate cups, and the boat races have commenced. Our
luck in the games has been rather bad, as we are now out of
all the tournaments, hockey, rugby, and soccer. However, our
first boat made a bump and went up one place today, which
somewhat compensates. I was not down on the river as Bob
Sams and I were trying to look at some rooms for another
year. We haven't settled on anything yet. You see one looks
quite a long way ahead over here.

I hope you will let me wait until my next letter to talk
about sister's school for next year. I'm afraid I haven't had
time to think, that is, seriously. But I may say I do think she
should continue her school work by all means. So long as she
seems to make progress, nothing will be better for her. If she
can learn to appreciate literature, music, etc., she will be able
to entertain herself all the better, and find something in life
without the necessity of too many friends. As fate seems to
have decreed that she should live lonely, we should spare
nothing to help her enjoy the kind of a life she will have to
follow. Don't you think sister might become an instructress
of some kind, school or music? I have always thought and
still think she is really very bright. If we can teach her to
love the quiet retirement of the scholar and cultivated person, she will come nearest to getting the most possible out
of life under the circumstances. Heidelberg as you know is
no place to develop such tendencies. I can think of no worse

place to dampen and kill any spark of culture and real education. From that standpoint the place is hopeless.

I quite agree with you about the car. I do wish we could get it for sister. It, above all things, would go a long way toward making her content. She and you and father could get away from home for little picnics, trips over the country, etc. It has seemed to me more and more a tragedy the older I've grown that we have never had much society in the family between us all. Every year has tended to draw us apart rather than throw us into a common society. My friends have all been found in a different order of life from our own, and forces have tended to separate our interests. I do not refer to our love and affections, which are as strong as could be, but to the fact that we have never had a real family society like so many other people have. I, unfortunately, can never spend much more time at home, but the car would help tremendously for the rest.

You asked about my weight and hair. I only wish the latter were as well as the former. I weigh close to 140. But my hair keeps coming out, in spite of all my attempts to save it by cutting it short and treating it. The fact remains that it is going and I don't think there is any way to stop it. At present I have quite a lot, but the signs of the times are unmistakable. A few more years and most of it will be scattered over the sands of Europe. I hate it, of course, but there seems to be no help for it. Anyhow, tradition demands that a professor be bald.

I will send the watermelon seed to Mrs. Halasz real soon. They were so nice to me that I am delighted to have some real opportunity to return their courtesy. I thank you and father ever so much for getting them. May they thrive in Hungary.

Three weeks of our term remain; then I go to Brussels. Meanwhile I am working hard, about as hard as I ever studied in my life, I think. My one thought now is the hope of the freedom that will come after June 22, the day when all the examinations will be over. You asked what time I could come home next summer. I don't know definitely, but I suppose I would be able to get off fairly early after the term was over, about July 15 or a bit earlier.

As soon as I get through with my examinations, I want to begin prospecting for a position in the States. It won't hurt to be a year ahead if I want something good. I have no idea where I will go, but I don't suppose there is much chance of me coming back to Mississippi for the present. I hope you don't mind. You see I will want to continue my studies for the Doctorate and there is no university in Mississippi of sufficient standing for such work. In many ways I would like to teach at the University (Ole Miss) but I fear I would run into a rut there. However, I must go where I can to begin with.

My letter will no doubt find you enjoying spring weather. We have had some slight touches of it here. Perhaps I shall see Holland in tulip-time this spring.

Love, Wilson

There was little vacation during Wilson Lyon's spring break in Brussels in 1927, since he studied almost constantly in preparation for the upcoming June Oxford B. A. exams. The letter that follows provides a picture of the pattern of his days. He was accompanied to Brussels by his Rhodes Scholar friend John Whiteley.

This letter also makes his growing cultural sophistication clear, as he reports on Lady Astor's* ball for Rhodes Scholars and attends the opera twice a week in Brussels.

Commenting on the improvements his family had just recently made to the house, he was particularly pleased that at last they had installed an indoor toilet, "a source of embarrassment" now removed.

Tallahatta, mentioned in the same letter, was the largest of the Lyon family farms. His remark about "being the planter's son that I pass for here" arises from the fact that any farm of more than 100 acres was referred to by Mississippians as a plantation. In the Rhodes directory, Wilson Lyon was listed as the son of a plantation owner. One can imagine his quiet pleasure in the inaccuracy of the image of his home that this title suggested.

His questions about the elections refer to state elections. Former Governor Theodore Bilbo* initially had to face a number of Democratic candidates in a summer gubernatorial primary.

Brussels, Belgium
March 29, 1927

My dearest mother:

We are now all settled for the vacation and I don't suppose we'll move again until we return to England. We stopped in a hotel on the outskirts of the city for the first two or three days until we could locate a good *pension.* At the moment we are the only boarders (*pensionnaires*) here—which means that conditions are ideal for study. We have two large connecting bedrooms and a sitting room and the dining room all to ourselves. The food is marvelous and well served. We are only one block off the Avenue Louise, a broad street wider than Canal in New Orleans with two great avenues of three rows of chestnut trees each on each side. There one can walk with never a fear of passing traffic. At the end of the avenue (at least half a mile away) is the *Bois* (wood). With all these attributes of nature around us we can enjoy and follow the spring which is beginning to approach. The budding of the trees on the avenue is already well advanced.

I am charmed with Brussels and our situation. For comfort and study we could hardly have done better. The city itself is extremely beautiful and elegant—though of course not up to Paris. As nearly everyone except the uneducated speak French one thinks he is in France. I have realized again this vacation how much progress I made at Nancy, for I am beginning to speak and understand French with an ease that is indeed gratifying as well as useful. In conversation I rarely ever fail to follow everything. I'm inquiring to see if I can find a professor who lives near and in case I find such a one, I'm going to take further lessons while I'm here. My history is pressing but I can spare an hour a day for French I think.

The opera here is one of the finest companies in Europe. We went for the first time last night—they played "The

Tales of Hoffmann". You probably know the best known of the pieces in it. We are going tomorrow night to see "La Bohême". We hope to spare twice a week for the opera.

I'm going to call on Aunt Vera's friend this week. So far I haven't had time.

Lady Astor's dance was a great success, much better as a dance than last year. The Prince was there but I didn't meet him. The Prime Minister was also mixing with the boys. I had met him last year, you will remember. I saved you a copy of the report in *The Times*, which I enclose. The list of names will explain how good our social standing is at the moment. Would that we Rhodes Scholars could keep up the bluff that carries us on now!

Whiteley and I came on to Brussels the day after the dance, so have been here now about a week. The channel crossing (Dover-Ostend) was a new one for me. Fortunately all was well.

You have certainly changed things up at home and I am all curiosity to see it. What you wrote sounds awfully good and will make lots of difference. The old home will be looking like a mansion when I finally manage to set my feet once more on Jasper's soil. The new big room will be fine for entertaining and for a library. And as you remark—the bath will be invaluable. What a source of embarrassment it removes! Its convenience will soon make us all wonder how we ever did without it. You have certainly been energetic and you deserve congratulations. Wish I could be home this summer to help you enjoy the changes.

By the way, I finally sent the pictures, just before I left Oxford. I had kept them intending to send some etchings of Oxford along with them. But the etchings are a bit expensive and my money was too low to get them this term. I will be able to get them when I return next term. They are beautiful things and will fit well at home. The reproductions that I sent were after all rather cheap, and I was a little disappointed in them when I got them back to Oxford. The etching is a street scene in winter near the Church of St. Ouen at Rouen. I bought it during the summer, and had thought a bit of putting it up in the room but I thought maybe you could find a better use for it. I shall probably have an opportunity to get some things here, and I will send you something if I am favorably impressed.

Things must be moving out on Tallahatta from what you say. I am indeed the planter's son that I pass for over here. What is father planting mostly and how is the farming outlook? I even yet sometimes get that "farming" spirit in my bones.

I heard from grandmother and I'm going to answer her letter right away. I know I should have written her before but I always seem so rushed.

As to Murray and the Naval Academy—all I know is that one gets an appointment through your Congressman or a Senator. The appointment allows one to take the examinations (which are stiff) and the passing of these admits one to entrance. I don't think the appointments are too hard to get but some political "pull" is necessary—I suppose.

I hope for letters tomorrow. They will be the first I've received since leaving Oxford. Hope Joe is improving as she thinks.

Love to you all,
Wilson

P. S. It would do your heart good to see how hard I'm studying. W.

By the time Wilson Lyon returned to Oxford in the spring of 1927, the great Mississippi Valley floods, which destroyed the Delta cotton crop, were the subject of major articles in the British press. The floods, which in totality covered more than 26,000 square miles, took 214 lives and required the evacuation of 637,000 people, according to Hodding Carter in his 1970 history of the river, *Man and the River.* The April 28, 1927 *Jasper County News* reported that in the Delta, 159,238 people were homeless. Thousands of farm animals drowned. The catastrophe put Mississippi at the center of the national stage, and would lead to the federal Flood Control Act of 1928, as the national government assumed responsibility for controlling the river's waters.

The letter that follows reflects Lyon's hope that federal help could lead to permanent control of the river. Heidelberg's farmers, never threatened by the flood, benefited from the complete loss of the Delta cotton crop in 1927. The price of cotton rose to over twenty cents a pound, an almost eight cent increase from the 1926 price.

Home improvements are the initial subject for this letter. The tank referred to would have been set in a tank house in the yard where it was used to collect water that could then be piped into the house. In the spring of 1927, an open well with a bucket was still providing water for the family.

Mansel Hill, mentioned here, was a close friend from Jones County Agricultural High School and was a member of the school stock judging team with Lyon.

Gaston Doumergue (1863-1937), whose visit to Oxford was occasioned by the spring degree granting ceremony, served as the twelfth president of France (1924-1931) and was the first Protestant to hold the post.

St. John's

May 9, 1927

Dearest mother:

I'm afraid I'm at my old trick of letting the days slip by without writing, and I did enjoy your four letters that I found here more than I can tell you. Everything has now reached me OK. It seems that they merely neglected to forward anything for the last three weeks! I also had a letter from sister, who seemed quite cheery.

It must be very pretty at the house now that all is painted. I am indeed anxious to see the old home once more. After what you say, I don't imagine things will look very much like they used to. Everything seems to have been changed. You are right about the tank. We ought to have it, and I hope you will succeed; or better still that the water works man will really do something. Really, the town of Heidelberg ought to be right royally ashamed of itself. I think we must live in one of the most backward sections of the United States. Papa is to be congratulated on all the new work, and I am sure it cost him quite a bit. I'm glad you and father decided to fix things up and remain at Heidelberg, for I'm afraid our income would not carry us far if we divorced ourselves from the old homestead. From my conversations with other Rhodes scholars, I find that Mississippi is about the cheapest place in the country; and while our income may not be so large in dollars and cents, it is as much as several times the amount would be almost anywhere else. Can you believe that my board and room alone cost me over $100.00 a month here; and I live economically too. If we can just manage to get a car now, Heidelberg wouldn't be so bad. It isn't that things are so dull there, but the trouble is you can never get away. One would tire of any place; even Florence perhaps gets boresome to the Florentines.

Father is no doubt very busy now, especially if you are having the fine weather we are experiencing. Is he planting mostly cotton? I see the price is quite a bit better, on account of the floods no doubt. From all you write me I am looking forward to hearing of a lucky deal almost any day.

I didn't get sister anything in Brussels, but I must send something from here. Is she getting a diploma? I've been under the impression that she wouldn't, all this time. I sent Jug a Venetian bag for his girl. The one I got was very beautiful, and I think she will like it.

The weather is the finest I have ever seen in England. We are having one of those marvelous summer terms that you read about in the books on Oxford life. It is warm, even what would be considered warm for Mississippi in May. I play tennis or go on the river in a punt in the afternoons. The temptation is so great that I'm getting very little studying done in the afternoons. But I'm getting in excellent physical condition. I have a nice rosy complexion and weigh 143! You'll hardly know me when I return.

The comedown to this horrible English cooking after Belgium is a bit tough. Robinson, my Canadian friend, and I look at the menu every day and grumble in despair. Cooking is certainly not one of the accomplishments of the English.

Just a little over five weeks now and our examinations

begin. We finish on June 22, and about a month later we have
to come back for our oral examination, the "viva". That
means I'll be tied up until about August. Between those dates
Frank Gray and I are going to take a trip in Northern England and Scotland. Lady Frances Ryder is inviting us to
spend some of our time with some of her hostesses, the same
thing you will remember me doing early last summer.

May 20, I have been invited to tea to meet the American
Ambassador*, who is paying a visit to Oxford. The French
president, M. Doumergue, is receiving a royal reception here
on May 17.

I have certainly been perturbed over the flood situation.
The papers here have followed it with great care, and the
explanatory articles have been very good. The great question
of the day was "Will they save New Orleans". I judge from
recent news that the city will be saved. It would have been an
inestimable historic and artistic loss. After all, New Orleans
is probably the most interesting city in the U. S.—even if we
people at home haven't yet realized it. But more important
still is the appalling loss of life and property. Of course, I
don't suppose there is any possible danger at Heidelberg. But
I imagine many of my Ole Miss friends in the Delta have lost
everything. I received the papers you sent telling me all
about it. Perhaps good will come out of seeming disaster in
the shape of a national project to control the water. The
question in my mind is if anything permanent can be done
to adequately cope with such a crisis as this.

. . . It is very seldom that I hear from old Mississippi
friends now. Mansel keeps me in touch with AHS things a
bit; but he is out of the run too now.

Sister will perhaps be home when this arrives. Wish I were
free for the year.

Love, Wilson

With references to the state United Daughters of the Confederacy
convention in Jackson and his description of the spring degree
granting ceremony in Oxford, Wilson Lyon anchored this letter in

both his Mississippi and Oxford "homes". Willia Lyon was president of the Heidelberg chapter of the UDC during her son's Rhodes Scholar years. Because UDC members were influential leaders in their communities, and despite the complexities of dealing with the Mississippi River floods while facing Theodore Bilbo in a Democratic primary, Governor Dennis Murphree* took time to address the convention.

The dignitaries who participated in the Oxford degree granting ceremony were some of the most important statesmen in post World War I Britain and France. Two had worked tirelessly together to guarantee peace in Europe in the wake of unresolved issues following WWI and were Nobel Peace Prize recipients: in 1926 Aristide Briand (1862-1932), French minister of foreign affairs, shared the prize with Gustav Stresemann, foreign minister of Germany. They were honored for their roles in negotiating the Locarno Agreements, which attempted to address European security problems that had not been resolved by the Treaty of Versailles. Sir Austen Chamberlain (1863-1937), British foreign secretary from 1924 to 1929, had shared the Nobel Peace Prize in 1925 with Charles Dawes of the United States for their initiatives in providing a factual basis for the British/French/German dialogues that led to the Locarno Agreements. Haig (1861-1928), was the commander of British Expeditionary Forces during World War I.

In its conclusion, this letter describes the end of Wilson Lyon's love affair with Hattie May Benjamin, which he seems to have accepted as inevitable. Though disappointed, he is far from despair as he enjoys a wonderful spring social life at Oxford.

May 21, 1927

Dearest mother:
I was quite surprised to get your letter from Jackson and delighted to know you had had a delightful time. Evidently the Convention was quite a success. What did you think of the Governor? No doubt he has had a trying time with the floods on hand.

Speaking of the floods: it looks as if everything will be swept away in Louisiana, judging from what the English papers say. Everyone here is following them with closest interest, and the leading morning papers have a column on the situation every morning. If such a catastrophe had occurred in England, there wouldn't be much of the island left.

The weather on the whole is good, but we've had a bit of rain lately. At the moment, Saturday afternoon at 2 P. M., all is a state of uncertainty. I've invited two girls to come punting on the river, and I'm trying to decide whether to 'phone them and ask them to come for tea. We play tennis or go on the river in the afternoon, and Oxford is quite pleasant. My tennis game has improved several hundred per cent over here, and I'm beginning to play rather well. I ought to try and get good in it as it is the only game I've ever been able to play with any degree of success.

I suppose you got the paper with the articles and pictures about the visit of the French president to Oxford. I was at the awarding of the degrees, and it was indeed an imposing spectacle. It was the first time I had ever seen this ancient university in all of its splendor. The chancellor*, President Doumergue, the vice-chancellor and M. Briand, and numerous other dignitaries including Field Marshal Haig and Sir Austen Chamberlain came in in a procession followed by the proctors and led by an official bearing the mace. All the university people were in their gowns, and the mass of doctors wearing red might have induced a Communist to think he had reached the promised land. Most of the ceremony was in Latin. For minutes at a time not a thing but Latin would be spoken. The chancellor spoke a few words of welcome in English and then addressed the visitors in French. M. Doumergue read a short speech in French, which I was happy to be able to follow. After the ceremony a lot of undergraduates including myself assembled out by All Souls College to give them the final send off.

Yesterday afternoon most of the Americans in Oxford were invited to meet the American Ambassador who was down for the day. The weather was nice fortunately, and the garden party was quite successful.

My examinations are less than a month away. I paid my

entrance fee of £5 this morning. I have also been admitted to standing for the B. Litt. degree which I hope to do next year, and I had to pay £10 for that, so at the moment my finances are not very strong. By getting admission this year I should be assured of time enough to complete it next year before I return.

Frank Gray and I have completed our plans for a trip through Northern England and Scotland after our examinations. We will go from here to Cambridge and then work up the East coast through the cathedral towns. From Aberdeen we will cross to Inverness and come back down the West coast. Lady Frances Ryder is inviting us to spend a week with one of her hostesses—the same sort of thing I did last year immediately after the term was over.

I have been intending to write you some time about Hattie May. She is not coming over, and our affair is over. I have known this over two weeks, but I just haven't taken the time to explain it all to you. Just after I returned from the vacation I received a letter from her telling me that during my long absence I had become a dream and that she had fallen in love with another. I was naturally surprised but not completely as I had often thought of the possibility of such during the past months. Everything had been perfect until about April, but when she found out definitely that she didn't have the money to come over she gave in and accepted the other man—who he is I do not know.

Of course, I am not happy over the whole affair, but it never interfered with my work after the first three days. I had often thought of such an end to our affair, as I began to see the many practical difficulties that stood in the way. I would have given almost anything to have retained her love, for I loved her far more than any other girl I have ever known. We were admirably suited to each other (at least when last we saw each other), and I know she loved me with all her heart when I left. To have expected her to wait three years without seeing me was demanding too much. Then I would have had little for several years after I return. She was a few months older than me and age means more to a girl than to a man.

As much as I hated to say "good-bye" it will be the best for us both no doubt. She can marry, and I can go on with my studies and establish myself in a way that would have been impossible otherwise. Knowing the difficulties ahead far better now than I did in 1925 I shall take good care not to fall too much in love again until I am in a position to offer something to the girl rather than imposing sacrifices on her as I have done with Hattie May. Then there is the possibility that we might not have found too much in common after my return. I am sure that I have changed a lot, and she probably has too.

I shall continue to seek girls' company and enjoy their society as I've always done, but a serious entanglement is the last thing I would think of now. I'm having quite a good time at Oxford with the girls I know, and at present I'm rather fond of a very cute little brunette English girl, so you need have no worry of me becoming ascetic or hanging myself in desperation! I am too philosophical and have inherited too much of father's optimism to nurse a broken heart or worry very much over something that reason tells me was almost the inevitable.

I'm going down to London tomorrow with the American baseball team to watch them play an American team composed of Americans resident in London. Borsch, the captain of the team, is one of my best friends here and the chap I went to Italy with. We are getting a saloon bus and will make the day of the trip, stopping en route for lunch and dinner. It will be the first baseball game I've seen since I left the states, and I think I'll enjoy it.

Hope the weather has been better for farming than one would judge from the numerous newspaper accounts of rain and storms in the U. S.

Love to all,
Wilson

After the completion of their written B. A. exams, Wilson Lyon and his friend Frank Gray set off to explore northern England and Scotland. The two letters that follow describe their experiences.

One of the most important events was their visit in the home of the Biblical scholar, Dr. James Moffatt*. The two Disraeli novels that Dr. Moffatt gave Wilson Lyon from his library both dealt with aspects of class in British society, a situation that troubled Lyon when he arrived in England, and which is mentioned from time to time in his correspondence throughout his three years abroad. *Sybil, or the Two Nations* (1845), was set during the period of the Chartist revolts (1837-1844) when workers were trying to get equal social and political rights for all classes. *Lothair* (1870) was popular in both the United States and Britain because its portrait of the upper classes was created by a former British prime minister who had personal acquaintance with the aristocratic world which he described.

In Scotland, Wilson Lyon also noted, in a July 12, 1927 letter to his mother, that he had discovered that the Lyon family was part of the Farquharson clan. Confirming that his own family roots lay in Scotland must have given him pleasure, since his Oxford education was making Great Britain a second home for him.

His letters describing the trip provide vignettes of many aspects of Scottish and English life. The picture of drunks reeling in the streets of Aberdeen outside his hotel contrasts dramatically with pictures of life in a country home in Perthshire, also described in his letter of July 12. Mr. Fyfe-Jamieson, who, with his wife, hosted Wilson Lyon and Frank Gray at Ruthven, their home in Meigle, was owner of a coal mine.

As a Presbyterian, it is understandable that Lyon would have wanted to include a visit to the home of John Knox, who led the fight that resulted in Presbyterianism becoming Scotland's state religion in 1560.

> Hotel Central
> High Bridge, Lincoln
> Sunday, June 26, 1927

Dearest mother:

Frank Gray (Minnesota) and I began our Scottish trip yesterday and came this far. We have just returned from a service in the Cathedral. The Cathedral, as you know, was what brought us here. The building is beautiful Early English architecture and lived up to all our expectations. The great nave, with its Gothic arches, and the three towers are very fine.

This is the longest trip I have ever taken in England to date. We are now some 120 miles north of Oxford. This evening we are going on to York. I'll give you the rest of our itinerary when I write again. Just now I should tell you something of what has been happening at Oxford.

We finished the history examinations Wednesday noon. Some of the papers were difficult but on the whole the questions were fair enough. I didn't particularly distinguish myself but I could have done worse. The greatest strain of all was the physical ordeal. Eleven three-hour papers stretched over five days is an enormous strain. I doubt if I could have got through much more—even though I was in perfect condition. My oral examination is set for August 8—a rather inconvenient date for it ties me close to Oxford for a good part of the summer. The results will come out August 13.

After the *schools* the St. John's tutors gave a dinner for the history students who had been in for the examinations. They came off their reserve a lot and the evening was quite pleasant.

The next day I invited the English girl I mentioned before to lunch on the river. We had quite a time rejoicing and celebrating the end of *schools*. The next night, Friday and my last in Oxford, we dined together and went to the theater. This particular girl is exceedingly charming and her company has made the past term indeed pleasant. So you see, mother dear, there is little chance of me pining away or being sad over what has passed. When Hattie May wrote me I made up my mind to forget at once. In two months I've forgotten so well that I wonder if I ever remembered. You are quite right. I am too young to let disappointments sit heavy with me.

I think you were too hard on Hattie May. I don't think you made allowances enough for the difficulty of remaining faithful without having seen one for three years. There was also the uncertainty of how each of us would feel when we met again. She did all I could expect. She told me when she fell in love with another and did not lead me to believe what was

168

not true. I do not blame her. Her position was difficult, and I think she acted wisely. It will no doubt be better for us both.

I have just received an announcement of Harold Barber's wedding on June 9. I must try and get up a present for him and Annie. Perhaps I can get a nice etching of one of the cathedrals up here.

An old Mississippi Rhodes scholar* was back at Oxford the past week. He was an Ole Miss man of the class of 1916. He is now in the Department of Commerce at Washington, and he came over as a secretary to one of the American delegates at the recent economic conference at Geneva.

Your news about the farm sounded very hopeful. I am so glad that father's great effort has brought such splendid prospects. I know he feels elated over it.

I enjoyed sister's letter and I am going to write her soon. Have you decided anything yet about her school for another year?

You might be interested to know that an overcoat is necessary to comfort today. What a country!

I will write more promptly now that the vacation has begun.

Love, Wilson

The Balmoral Hotel
52 Market Street, Aberdeen
Sunday, July 3, 1927

Dearest mother:

We have covered quite a lot of territory since I finished writing you at York. After York we spent a day at Durham. The cathedral there is the finest specimen of Norman architecture in the world and one of the most impressive sights I've seen in Europe. The cathedral and the old castle are placed in impregnable positions up on the rocks hundreds of feet above the Wear River. This immense bank with its circular paths is covered with trees and has been converted into a park. The view of the Cathedral and Castle from the opposite side of the river is majestic and sublime. Both the cathedral and castle were begun by William the Conqueror and they served as fortresses against the Scots.

We went from Durham to Glasgow where we were the guests of a Scotch girl whom Frank knew at Oxford. Her father, Dr. James Moffatt, is the celebrated Presbyterian minister who translated the Bible into modern speech and has written a number of books on religious questions. He goes to New York in September to assume a chair at Union Theological Seminary. They made me feel more at home there than any place I've been the past two years. Margaret, Mrs. Moffatt, and Dr. Moffatt accepted us as old friends and gave us the liberty of the house at once. When we left Dr. Moffatt presented each of us with two books from his library. Mine were two novels by Disraeli—*Sybil* and *Lothair*.

The weather cleared up one day while we were at Glasgow and we were able to drive out to Loch Lomond, a lake some 20 miles away. It is in the edge of the highlands and the scenery was quite lovely. Another day Margaret went over to Edinburgh with us and a girl friend of hers there showed us over the Castle, St. Giles' Cathedral, and the home of John Knox. We will stop there again on our way back.

Aberdeen is some 150 miles from Glasgow. Frank wanted to come here to try and locate his father's people. He spent yesterday in a little village about two hours further north and succeeded in finding a great uncle and a lot of cousins. I stayed here and wrote letters. By the way, won't you write me all you and father know as to the descent and blood of our family? I've gotten curious about it since I came over. Am I right in thinking myself primarily Scotch—with some English and Irish?

Tomorrow we go South to Meigle, in Perthshire, where we are spending a week in a country home. Our hostess has invited us through the offices of Lady Frances Ryder. It is the same sort of place I went to last summer before I went to the continent. Later I am stopping with one of the college boys at his home in Yorkshire. Then I may go to Devon with Borsch until about Aug. 4. I'm coming up to Oxford then to do some work for my oral examination, which is set for Aug. 8.

Aberdeen is a very nice city of some 200,000 I should say. All the buildings are made of granite which gives them a clean appearance. The quarries near here afford work for a good part of the population. Fishing and the sea employ the others.

I think I've seen more drunks here than in any other part of Europe. There's no doubt about it—the Scots love their drink. The past two nights, Friday and Saturday, the streets have been filled with drunken, reeling men. I've never seen anything like it.

I suppose tomorrow, the Glorious 4th, will be celebrated with great gusto in the States. I think there will be some sort of ceremony in London. I know there are baseball games today.

Tell sister I'm going to write her soon. I must also write grandmother. I should have some letters tomorrow when I get to Meigle. I haven't been able to get any since leaving Oxford as we haven't stopped long enough.

It has been terrible weather since we left Oxford. Except for today it has rained steadily and an overcoat was a necessity. Yesterday my feet got numb and I had to ask for a fire. Can you imagine such on July 2?

Hope the summer is fine at home and that farming is progressing.

Love, Wilson

Writing from London, after his travels in northern England and Scotland, Wilson Lyon described a very happy week visiting the family of an Oxford friend, George Fearnley*, at Ben Rhydding, in Yorkshire. Twelfth century Cistercian Kirkstall Abbey, where he saw the miracle play *Robert of Sicily*, had been extensively restored in the late nineteenth century. Lyon also mentioned a brief return visit to Edinburgh. Craigmillar Castle remains today one of the best preserved medieval castles in Scotland. Hollyrood House is the official British royal residence in Scotland.

In London, his activities included museum going, interspersed with more relaxing and spectacular entertainment. The latter included the film *Ben Hur*, reportedly the most expensive ($3.9 million) silent film ever made, and *The Desert Song*, a lush romance set in Morocco, with music by Sigmund Romberg, and Oscar Hammerstein II as one of the three writers of the book and lyrics.

Laying out his plans for the rest of the summer after taking his oral examination (*viva*) in Oxford, Lyon announced definitively that the subject for his B. Litt. thesis would be Napoleon and the sale of Louisiana to the United States. It was a topic that bridged his interest in modern European history with his interest in the historical heritage of his native South.

The query about the light plant provides a reminder that Heidelberg still had no electric power in the summer of 1927. The reference to diamond prices is explained in an August 18 letter to Girault Jones when he mentions visiting a factory where diamonds were being cut; his mother had perhaps suggested that he make such a visit.

20 Kensington Garden Sq., London
Sunday, July 24, 1927

Dearest mother:

I'm behind in my writing because I never got a spare minute during the time I was in Yorkshire. We were on the go so much that I never had any time to myself.

I'll try and go back and rehearse events of the past week or so. After leaving Meigle, Frank and I stopped for a day in Edinburgh. We visited Craigmillar Castle, passed Holyrood, and took a drive about the city—seeing the places we had missed on our first visit. Frank and I parted there. He went to Oxford for his oral examination (the results are out in law and I see he got a second class) and I went to spend a week at Ben Rhydding, Yorkshire with George Fearnley, an English friend at St. John's.

Ben Rhydding is a residential town in a pleasant valley (called a dale there) above which rise the moors—barren, rocky hills, grazed by hardy mountain sheep. The section is very beautiful and the air was that of the mountains. The river (the Wharf, a small stream as things go at home) was as clear as crystal, and looked as if trout fishing might be good.

Mr. Fearnley is a druggist (they call them chemists here) who owned three stores in the neighboring towns of Otley and Guisley. His home was very modest, of course, in comparison with the palatial luxury of Ruthven. Everything was very homelike. I was accepted as if I had been an Englishman and a family friend of long standing. The home atmosphere was every bit as carefree and easy as it would have been in America. In fact, one might almost have imagined himself in the States—except for differences in eating habits.

The night of my arrival we went to a miracle play *Robert of Sicily* in the ruins of Kirkstall Abbey on the outskirts of Leeds. By the way, if you wish to see where I was, Ben Rhydding is about 25 miles from Leeds. The play was very impressive when viewed from the great nave of an ancient abbey.

Last Sunday a friend of George's drove us to his father's home in the Lake District. Joe should be interested in this trip, as I suppose she has been studying about Wordsworth, Coleridge, and the Lake School of English poetry. The day was perfect for the drive. We got off early and arrived in the lakes for lunch, and it was one of the best lunches I've tasted for many a day. The cottage and garden of the Drury family were charming. It is a place which they only use on weekends when they come up from Manchester, where their business is. The gardener, of course, is there all the time, and the place was a mass of flowers and fruits. From the top of a neighboring hill we could see out to the sea and then to Coniston peak in the other direction. After lunch we drove around Lake Windermere, the largest of the lakes, and took tea at Bowness. It was a great drive and enabled me to visit a district I had always hoped to see.

Monday we went for a picnic to Bolton Abbey—another memorable Gothic ruin. After lunch we roamed over the abbey and took a ride through the grounds.

It was very lively at the Fearnleys, for George's 18 year old sister, Kitty, was the life of the place. She and Mrs. Fearnley together never let things lag. Kitty and I went to a dance one evening at one of the hotels. George had to stay at home with his Irish cousin, Edith, who didn't dance.

I left Ben Rhydding Thursday morning and came here via
Leeds. The whole journey took some six hours but much of
that was lost in waiting at Leeds. The run from Leeds here
was 4 hours. The distance is about 175 miles. As this was not
a train deluxe, you see that the English trains on the whole
are faster than ours.

The place I am stopping here is a favorite resort of mine
and one at which I have stopped several times before. It is
quiet, very comfortable, well located, and cheap (approximately $2.00 a day for room and three meals). That perhaps
sounds none too cheap in comparison with Miss. prices, but it
is by far the best value I know in England. Mine and Frank's
hotel bills in the North were far over $5.00 a day. That trip
has almost wrecked my finances. Although I was visiting
over half the time, the month cost me over $125.00 (£25).
My only hope to pull through the vacation with my money is
to hurry over to France and settle down. What's more we
were as economical as possible, and we took every short corner possible.

Borsch (Illinois) and I have been invited to spend a week or
ten days (July 25-Aug. 2) with Mrs. Baker at Crewkerne, Somerset. I am going down tomorrow afternoon. Somerset is one
of the Southwestern counties and is next to Devon, which it
joins, perhaps the most beautiful county in England. Borsch is
in Cornwall so we will meet in Somerset. After leaving
Crewkerne I think I'll go back to Oxford until my *viva* is over,
Aug. 8. Then Borsch and I are going to make a short trip in
Holland and down the Rhine in Germany and I am going to
come back to Nancy, where I was Xmas. I'll be there and Paris
until term begins at Oxford. I am going to do research in the
Ministry of Foreign Affairs in connection with my B. Litt.
thesis. I believe I told you that my subject was *Napoleon and
the Sale of Louisiana to the U. S. A.* Our examination results are
out on Aug. 13. I'll let you know at once how I came out. I am
expecting a second. I shall be surprised if I do better and very
much disappointed if I do worse. Most of the Rhodes men in
my class have gotten seconds. Only one has a first but several
unfortunately have thirds.

I found Ed Ham of Trinity College and Maine here when I arrived. I thought I had told him goodbye the day I left Oxford. We went to the theatre that evening, and he sailed for New York yesterday. He is teaching at Harvard next year.

Hope French, an American girl I knew at Oxford, and I did a day's touring together Friday. We went through the Tate Gallery, lunched at the Cheshire Cheese (a famous old inn where Dr. Johnson used to dine), visited St. Paul's Cathedral, and the Guildhall. In the evening we saw *The Desert Song* at the Drury Lane theatre.

Yesterday I went through the Egyptology, Oriental, Greek, and Roman rooms of the British Museum. I suppose their collection of Egyptian and Oriental statues, mummies, sculpture, relics, etc. is undoubtedly the finest in the world. Sister will be interested to know that I saw the Rosetta Stone, a column from the Temple of Diana at Ephesus, and parts of the Mausoleum at Halicarnassus.

Yesterday afternoon I saw the film of *Ben Hur*. I don't think I ever saw a better picture. If it comes to Laurel you all should see it. The chariot race is the finest thing I ever saw on the screen. It has been running steadily here at the Tivoli, London's leading movie house, for nearly nine months.

Last night I saw an awfully funny American play *Abie's Irish Rose*. It has been running for well over four years in New York. It is the story of a Jewish boy who marries an Irish girl. The parents of both are furious. There is the rabbi and the Roman Catholic priest, a humorous Jewish couple, and the fighting Irish father pitted against the Jewish father with his detestation of Christians. They finally make up on Xmas eve, and ham is served while an Xmas tree brightens the dining room of the young couple.

I am well and enjoying the summer. I am happy in the thought that another year shall see me home. My how strange it will all seem after three years away! We must do something to celebrate the family reunion.

By the way, I'm still waiting for those pictures of the house. What ever happened to the light plant and is there a chance of water works? I will look into diamond prices.

Had a letter from Hattie May the other day. She seems to be enjoying summer school in Chicago. In fact I've had about three letters in the last six weeks, and I'm ashamed to say I've only written one. Everything is all off, but I think we shall continue to be good friends.

I hope to hear from you tomorrow when I get to Crewkerne. I haven't had any letters in over a week.

Hope the weather has been good for crops and that you are all well.

Love, Wilson

Writing home from Oxford the afternoon after his *viva*, Wilson Lyon described his time in Somerset. Wayford, the home where he stayed, had gardens designed by Mrs. Baker's brother, Harold Peto, a distinguished architect and landscape designer, known particularly for Italian-style landscapes. The gardens at Wayford Manor remain open to the public today, and are considered one of the showplaces of Somerset.

SPU (Southwestern Presbyterian University), the teaching home of the former Rhodes Scholar who came to visit the Bakers while Lyon was there, had moved its campus from Clarksville, Tennessee to Memphis in 1925, and shortened its name to Southwestern.

The tribute to his parents that Lyon includes in this letter is particularly moving because of the context in which it appears: all his B. A. examinations are behind him, he's having a non-stop series of dates with English and American women, and is about to leave for a trip to Holland, Germany and France. Instead of merely regaling his parents with tales of his happiness, he takes time to let them know that he can never forget that without their personal sacrifices and support, none of this would have been possible for him.

He also notes receiving the absentee ballot for the Mississippi Democratic gubernatorial primary. In 1902, Mississippi Democrats joined the growing ranks of Democrats in other Southern states that abandoned nominating conventions, and replaced them with primary elections. Since Republicans had no political power in the South in the 1920s, the Democratic primaries, often requiring a run-off as they did in 1927, usually determined who would hold state offices.

The cablegram to which he refers near the end of the letter was a birthday cablegram for his father.

St. John's

Aug. 8, 1927

Dearest mother:

I really intended to write you every day at Wayford, and never seemed to get to it. You must forgive me. The card to sister at least let you know I was happily situated among friends. All in all the people at Wayford were the most delightful and most cultured society I have ever moved in. The people we met were charm itself. Nearly everyone was a watercolor artist, and most of them had been all over the world.

We were received with open arms and became at home at once. It was the most delightful English home I have ever stopped in. Mr. and Mrs. Baker were saintly people. They were deeply interested in the people of the village and there was a distinctly religious atmosphere about the home.

The house, begun in 1300, was as interesting as a museum. One rarely ever finds such an antique place still used as a residence. The garden was Italian—one of the few I've seen in England.

Curiously enough, while we were there an ex-Rhodes scholar, now a professor at SPU, came with his bride. He had visited the Bakers when he was at Oxford.

We got a number of trips in Somerset, Dorset, and Devon while we were at Wayford. One day we went down to Exeter to see the cathedral and guildhall. The day before we left we took a long drive to the ruins of Glastonbury Abbey and then on to Wells cathedral. Borsch and I spent two days at Winchester and Salisbury on the way back. On the whole I prefer the English cathedrals to those of any country I know.

I came up here from Winchester Thursday and Borsch went to London. Since arriving I've hardly stopped a minute.

I've been running around with girls a good part of the day and night. Marjorie Dance*, an English girl who interests me tremendously, was up for her *viva* and we had quite a glorious time rambling about Oxford and going on the river. Then there was Hope French, an American girl, and I also met the daughter of the Dean of the Medical College at the University of Chicago. The weekend has thus been quite a gay event for me. Yesterday I lunched at the home of Mr. and Mrs. Buckler and later carried Miss Tieken (Chicago) back for tea there. We had a most enjoyable tea and some delightful music afterwards. You and sister might be interested to know that at the moment I'm engaged in reading a little book on music. I'm trying to do a bit of literary browsing and self-culture this summer before I hit my B. Litt. I'm reading books on painting, architecture, Russian, German and French literature, and the drama—as well as a number of French novels and a volume of French verse.

You know, mother, I myself can hardly realize how much I have learned here. My travels and Oxford have fitted me to take a place with credit in almost any intellectual society one meets here. The value of the past two years has been inestimable. When I think of what all my education has meant and will mean to me, I feel more and more grateful to you and father who have made it possible for me to move into that fuller world so far removed from anything any of my schoolmates will ever know. When I think what might have been my fate had I not had sacrificing parents like you and father, I am unable to thank you enough. You have given me advantages better than those enjoyed by boys of far richer parents. I have had the best that the world affords, and I hope I can in some way repay you.

I had my *viva* this morning. It was merely formal and lasted less than two minutes. They had evidently determined my class beforehand. It very probably means I shall get a second. I should do better than a third and I hardly think I can do as well as a first.

After a visit to the dentist tomorrow I am going to London to rejoin Borsch. We are going for a short trip in

Holland and Germany, and then I am coming back to Nancy for about a month. I must settle down or I won't have enough money to complete the summer. Even now I don't see how I'm going to make it. I have been very economical but travel here is very expensive.

I have been in my old room in college and it has been very pleasant. Everything was just as I had left it. During the summer the servants will move all my things to my "digs". It is rather nice not to have to worry at all about the removal of your possessions.

Am glad father got the cablegram on time.

I received the ballot and appreciated it very much. It was too late to return the vote in time for the primary. You must send me the results.

Our examination results will be in the *Times* Saturday morning.

Love, Wilson

Writing to his mother from Amsterdam, Wilson Lyon's letter described his traveling schedule for the remaining vacation weeks and sent back the news that he had received a second class for his B. A. work.

John Hill, whose tragic stabbing death is mentioned, was the uncle of Mansel Hill, a close friend and classmate of Lyon at Jones County Agricultural High School. Hill was in charge of the commissary at the Gilchrist-Fordney lumber camp at Dushau, Mississippi. His youthful white killers were intent on revenge because they felt Hill had been responsible for their being accused of a series of thefts. The crime is a reminder that poverty and rural isolation could lead to sudden and irrational violence in Jasper County, whose small communities were in many ways reminiscent of communities on the American frontier.

This particular letter is also of interest because of Lyon's comments on the current state of Mississippi education, as he worries about the effect of politics on education at Ole Miss if Bilbo is elected governor.

Hotel Van Gelder
Damrak 34, Amsterdam
August 18, 1927

Dearest mother:

Borsch and I have been in Holland now just a week today, and
I think we are leaving Amsterdam this afternoon. We aren't
quite certain, however, and I am waiting for him to come in
so we can decide. Our plans are for him to go to Denmark to
visit a Danish friend and for me to go down the Rhine into
Germany. Unless he gets a letter this morning he may come
with me. Anyhow my plans are quite definite no matter what
he does. I am going to stop perhaps at Utrecht and Arnhem
and then go into Germany. I'll stop first at Cologne for a day
or so. From Cologne I am going to take a boat and go down
the Rhine to Mainz (that is the famous trip one always hears
of). Since I will be going up stream it will take longer but the
fare is also cheaper so there are compensations. I am then
stopping at Frankfurt, Heidelberg, Baden-Baden (perhaps)
and Strasbourg. My tutor and one of my English friends are
at Strasbourg and I will be delighted to see them as well as
the town and the cathedral. From Strasbourg, Nancy is only
two hours, and there I am going to stop with Madame Hodez
for about a month. She is not the lady with whom I stopped
at Xmas but the family that had us over for Xmas dinner,
dances, etc. They were kind enough to ask me to stay with
them, and I decided it would be better than Madame
Desch's—where I was Xmas. I've given you these details so
you can follow my route on the map.

We had a very good passage from Harwich to the Hook of
Holland. The boat was the best I've been on since I crossed
the Atlantic. We had a two-berth cabin, something very
extraordinary on a short distance passage. We stopped first
at The Hague where we were nearly two days. It reminds me
very much of Geneva—there is somewhat the same international atmosphere. The Hague is in no degree a commercial
city but is the capital and general cultural center. The buildings and streets are delightful. One meets universal courtesy,
and practically everyone you come in contact with speaks

English (all the policemen and street car conductors for instance). We went to the picture gallery (where there are some of the finest Rembrandts and other things of the Dutch school). The Peace Palace is a very magnificent and very interesting structure. We stopped over at Leyden a few hours on our way to Haarlem. At Haarlem we stayed a day and a half, saw the picture gallery with Frans Hals' things, the cathedral, and made an excursion to Bloemendal—suburb. The Dutch residential houses are the nicest I've seen in Europe.

Everyone seems to be more prosperous here than in any other European country I've visited. They got enormous profits out of the war. Prices, however, are not as high as I had feared. Traveling here is really cheaper than in England, and what you get for your money is much better. In England you pay 5 shillings ($1.25) for a worse dinner than you can have here for 3 shillings (75¢). Dutch food is very good and so are their hotels. They give you the most enormous portions of vegetables I've ever encountered in any country outside of Germany.

After Haarlem we came to Amsterdam where we've spent nearly four days. Two days we were in the Rijks Museum looking at the pictures. It is most tremendous and simply filled with treasures, especially the Dutch school. Yesterday we took a boat trip through the canals and out to the Island of Marken—returning by the Zuyder Zee. We stopped at several towns on the way, saw two Dutch churches, a cheese factory, and plenty of people in quaint native costume. The wide flowing flannel trousers of the men and the head dress of the women were exceptionally interesting. On the trip we struck up with a couple of American boys from New York and later dined with them in Amsterdam.

I got the results of my examinations Sunday at Haarlem. The list was in *The Times*. I got a second class as I predicted. That is quite good and I am well pleased. There were only 12 firsts out of 280 and none of those were Rhodes scholars. Swearingen took three years to my two and only got a third. Drane Lester only did a third last year. So you see I have

done a lot better than my two Mississippi predecessors.
There are four classes you know. I can now go forward with
my B. Litt. in perfect confidence.

I have so far been unable to get sister something for her
birthday, but I am going to send her a gift before long. I am
also going to write her too. Has she been home this summer?
I suppose you've decided about her college by now.

It has been well over a week since I've had any letters. As
I was moving around so much I decided to have everything
sent on to Nancy. I should be there now in about a week.

The Hill stabbing tragedy was awful. I must write Mansel.
He was very fond of John and I'm sure he is very cut up over
it all.

I am rather anxious to hear from the election at home. I
fear Bilbo, if elected, will dismiss Dr. Hume at Ole Miss and
reinstate Powers. That would certainly be a black day for
Miss. education. Powers is an affable old windjammer but as a
university president he is distinctly out of place. I might like
to teach at Ole Miss under Hume but I wouldn't dream of
going there under Powers. Promotion would depend on politics and not on professional merit.

The weather has been foul since we've been here. Yesterday was the only day it hasn't rained. At the moment it
is raining sheets, a real old American rain, not an English
drizzle.

One of the most interesting things here is the shipping.
Every town is intersected with canals. Amsterdam for
instance is really cut into 90 islands—but all connected by
bridges, of course. The bridges are either lifted or swung for
the larger boats. The windmills are really far less numerous
than I supposed. There are no more wooden shoes than you
see in Belgium.

Love to all,
Wilson

In a letter to his sister Josephine, written to her on her twentieth
birthday from "the other Heidelberg", Wilson Lyon sent a detailed

history lesson, travelogue and, most important, advice about what to study in college. She was about to enroll in the Mississippi Synodical College for Women, a two-year Presbyterian college in northern Mississippi at Holly Springs. On her birthday, this letter brought her love, encouragement, and support from her older brother. Its tone is the most mature of any of the letters he sent to her during his three years abroad.

Hotel Wagner, Heidelberg

August 24, 1927

Dearest sister:

I let time slip up on me and here it is your birthday and I haven't decided what gift to send you. I've been on the look-out but I haven't found anything that suited me. But you may depend on receiving something real soon. Meanwhile I'm going to write you that long-intended letter.

You see by my stationery that I have made my pilgrimage to Heidelberg and have laid at her feet the homages, so to speak, of that other Heidelberg. I'm afraid the German Heidelberg wouldn't claim kinship with the American village if it could cross the water and see. I arrived last night from Frankfurt and have spent a fairly busy day visiting the city. I think I've now seen everything worth the tourist's attention. The town is built on the banks of the Neckar river—hemmed in between it and a fairly high range of mountains. On one of the lower mountains rises the castle—a huge red sandstone building now mostly in ruins. The French blew it up in 1688 when they retreated and after it had been partially repaired a stroke of lightning dismantled it in 1764. Its history has been traced back definitely to the thirteenth century and it may be even older. It is not a complete wreck by any means—all of the walls are standing and some of the rooms are intact. One of the inside walls is said to be the best existing specimen of German Renaissance architecture. It is partly Ionic and partly Corinthian. One of the curiosities of the castle is the immense wine barrel (known as the Heidelberg tun). The present one was built in 1751 and holds 43,000 gallons!

A great flight of stairs leads up some 25 feet to the flat platform erected on top. From the castle one gets an excellent
view of the town, the river, and the bridges. The mountains
range on the opposite slopes (vineyards and fruit groves)
with woods toward the top.

The university buildings are only ordinary—but then they
always are in continental universities. Only the English and
Americans seem to care about the beauty of their college
buildings. The French plaster notices on the outside of their
walls as if they were posters of an advertising company.

In the afternoon (after a thoroughly bad lunch, which fortunately didn't cost much), I crossed the river by the old
bridge and climbed up the opposite hills through the vineyards to a road called *Philosophenweg*, which means "philoso-
phers' road" in English, and had a walk—all the time
enjoying a very fine view of the town with the castle above it.
The city is as lovely as can be and I wish you could be here to
enjoy it with me.

My trip down the Rhine was wonderful. I came from Amsterdam to Cologne by train. Had two days at Cologne—
mostly visiting old churches and studying architecture. I've
never seen so much Romanesque architecture in my life.
Romanesque is the period before Gothic, which began to
come in about 1200. Most of these churches are 800 or 900
yrs. old. Compared with them the cathedral, a Gothic structure and a very fine one, is very modern.

The boat trip up the Rhine—Cologne to Mainz—took 13
hours. The day was bad when we started, but it cleared up
after a while and we even had a bit of sunshine. The river
banks become small mountains after Cologne, and they are
fairly dotted with old castles and ruins. The effect is almost
indescribable in its beauty. Some of the steeper hills are
planted with grape vines to the very top. Stone terraces hold
the soil—which must be much stiffer than our Miss. land or
it would all wash off. The towns along the shore were very
beautiful—many of the houses being charming. We had
our lunch and dinner on the boat and got to Mainz (Mayence
in English) at 9 that night. I was there a day—cathedral,

museums, churches, etc. Got a new French visa and groaned very perceptibly at having to pay $10 for it—especially since ten dollars means an awful lot to me this late in the summer. I went over to Frankfurt yesterday and roamed about a few hours between trains before coming here. I saw the room where the Holy Roman Emperor was formerly elected and the room where he was crowned—also Goethe's house.

If you don't mind, I would like to give you a little advice about what to study at college. You can at least avoid some of my mistakes. Unless you like science, let it all go. The great things to learn are languages, literature, and history. I should like very much to see you continue with Latin and even take up Greek (but these are things you can best settle according to your desires). However, begin French your first year by all means. Put that first and foremost among your modern languages. It is far the most important and the one you will find most useful and enjoy the most. I hope during your college course you will have time for other modern languages— Spanish, German, or Italian—but I repeat again, let French be first. Begin it now and keep it up all the way through. In four years you will be able to read it as well as you do English. How often I have lamented that I did not begin it until my junior year! Take all the English you can. I know you read a lot and I hope you will keep it up. I want you to be really educated—so you will feel at home in any society. I often think of sending you books but I hesitate because I don't know exactly what you want. If you ever want anything special, just let me know.

I am leaving tomorrow for Strasbourg where I stop a day—then on to Nancy, where I plan to remain a month studying French and reading on miscellaneous matters as well as my degree. After a summer of moving about I'm ready to settle down for a while, and I think I'll enjoy the quiet. I've brought along a lot of miscellaneous things I want to read, and that will be a good time to get through them. I have my tennis racquet, and I hope to play a lot. It is now my favorite sport, the only thing I really enjoy playing myself. By the way, did you ever play any at home?

It has been so long (nearly 3 weeks) since I had news from home that I'm almost out of touch. I shall be delighted to get my mail day after tomorrow when I get to Nancy. I didn't have my mail sent on this trip for fear it would get lost.

I hope you have had a happy birthday and that I will be able to assist in the celebration of your next.

Love, Wilson

P. S. Write me soon, won't you?

Wilson Lyon's letters describe five weeks happily spent at the end of the summer of 1927 in Nancy at the home of Madame Hodez, whom he had first met during his Christmas stay there in 1926-27. His growing proficiency in French was allowing him to feel increasingly self-confident, both socially and academically. Adding to his pleasure, he notes in an August 27, 1927 letter to his mother, there were two American girls from the University of Delaware who were also boarding with Madame Hodez while pursuing summer studies.

From a historical perspective, his September 10 letter from Nancy is most interesting for its attack on Governor-elect Bilbo's plans for the University of Mississippi, as well as its criticism of the idea of state-published text books for public schools, both plans that were thwarted by the 1928 Mississippi legislature. Of the two unsuccessful 1927 Democratic gubernatorial primary candidates, Martin Sennett Connor (1891-1950) went on to be elected and serve as Mississippi's governor from 1932 to 1936. Albert Anderson (1878-1954), a former member of the Mississippi legislature, did not seek public office again.

Nancy, France
Sept. 10, 1927

Dearest mother:

The letter with the pictures and the election news came the other day. Although the pictures were none too good I was delighted to see that you were all well and looking so fine. The house looked nice with its new coat of paint and the lattice up. When you make the new photos I hope you won't wait so long to send them.

Your next letter will very probably bring news of Bilbo's election. I should think he will get a good part of the Anderson vote in North Mississippi and enough of Conner's South Mississippi strength to put him in. I'm not nearly so much interested in what he does at Jackson as I am in his attitude toward the university. From all I hear Ole Miss is making splendid progress under Dr. Hume, and his removal would be an irreparable blow—especially since it would mean Powers' return. Jug seems to think Bilbo has a bigger graft for Powers—text book publishing, perhaps. That part of Bilbo's platform by the way is absolutely foolish and utter rot. It is a wonderful scheme calculated to get votes by appealing to the ignorance of the masses. If put into practice it will mean inferior books by second rate authors (Miss. has only a handful of men capable of editing decent books) and falsified history. The American school histories are bad enough without taking them still further away from the truth. Mississippi needs enlightenment from without and not a continuance of her present deplorable ignorance. I should hardly think the voice of Bilbo and the electorate qualified to point the way toward a rational learning and a genuine culture.

I am happy to know that Aunt Vera is so much better and I hope her improvement has continued. I am sure she has profited much under your loving care.

Sister I suppose is busy making her plans to leave. Hope she will like Holly Springs and that the year will be profitable.

Everything moves very pleasantly here. Each day I congratulate myself on my excellent situation. The family is far superior to any other I have lived with in France. Madame is charming, from a good family, and extremely well informed and educated. Dedith, her daughter about 23 or 24 years old, is absolutely charming and attractive in every sense. Henri, the son, who is here only for the weekends is also very pleasant, and the two American girls are quite jolly. So you see everything goes well. The Americans have been away in the Alps for a week and I've been alone with Madame and Dedith—which was very good for my French.

I take a lesson every day from the lady who instructed me

at Xmas. I've been reading plays, poetry, and novels in aston-
ishing quantities. My usual routine consists of nothing but
reading and studying except for the afternoon from four to
seven when I play tennis. There is a very good club here, and
I have joined for the month. I am the only English-speaking
person at the club, so I get lots of practice. My work has not
been without results for I am attaining considerable
proficiency. I speak well enough for carrying on a conversation anywhere and always understand. It has been interesting
to go to the Protestant church here and follow the sermon.

Autumn is beginning to set in but the weather has been
good on the whole. It was raining this morning but we have
sun now and I will be able to play tennis.

Love, Wilson

Lyon returned to Paris after five weeks in Nancy to begin research
for his B. Litt. thesis. Much of his correspondence home during
those days deals with his early research efforts and the difficulties
he encountered.

A subject of great historical interest in his letters from Paris is
his first-hand report of the trip he made from Nancy, on Sunday,
September 18, to the dedication of the memorial to war dead on the
battlefield at Verdun. Its descriptions and tribute to the valor of the
French people provide a sobering reminder that less than ten years
had passed since the signing of the armistice ending World War I.

Marechal Petain (1856-1951), French general and political
leader who spoke at the dedication, was a hero of World War I
because of his defense of Verdun in 1916. Paul von Hindenburg
(1847-1934) was German field marshal during World War I and
president of Germany from 1925 to 1934.

14 Rue Stanislas, Paris VI,
September 30, 1927

Dearest mother:

I'm behind again with my writing for it seemed awfully
difficult somehow to get around to writing at Nancy. I had
plenty of time, but inertia seemed to take me.

I had best begin by telling you of my trip to Verdun on Sunday, Sept. 18. It was the occasion of the inauguration of the *ossuaire* (this is a word which has no equivalent word in English—it means a resting place for bones). The bones of thousands of men were gathered off the field and placed in a temporary sanctuary until money had been raised for erecting a suitable monument. The *ossuaire* has a great tower in the center in the form of a *phare* (lighthouse) and this will burn every night to light the surrounding country and to remind eternally of the nation's sacrifices on that spot. A great bell (*le bourdon de la victoire*), the gift of an American, has been placed in the tower and every evening it will sound, calling the nation to the memory of its dead. The speech of Marechal Petain was well chosen for the occasion and contrasted very favorably with the bellicose declaration that Hindenberg recently made at Tannenberg in commemoration of the German victory over the Russians.

The ground about *l'ossuaire* and around the forts is ruined forever. Weeds and grass have come up of course, but the ground is blown into a million irregular shapes—no two alike. Old trenches are still to be seen and old relics such as boots, canteens, bayonets, etc. lie about. Barbed wire is found everywhere. Some twenty-odd villages there have been completely destroyed. In most cases no trace of them exists—the houses were blown to dust. Verdun, the town, in peace times a city of about 25,000 people, is struggling to reestablish itself. Nearly all the houses are new, and the plan of the town has been changed a lot. The cathedral is only partially restored and evidence of the bombardment exists on all hands. As I dined in a very good hotel and enjoyed a most sumptuous meal, hors d'oeuvres, salmon, beef and vegetables, cheese and fruit, I kept thinking that this food had no right to be there, that in Verdun of today it seemed so strange to find such luxury.

One cannot go to Verdun and see what happened there without admiring the French people. Verdun is an expression of France—a nation often wrong, but always warmhearted and above all ready to make sacrifices for a cause it believes to be just. One must know the French, as any other nation for that matter, to appreciate them. When one has lived with them as I have and has seen them in their homes, as well as on the streets, one gets to love them. The average American's opinion of the French is wrong in nearly every respect. He never stops to think that their civilization is not wrong because it is different from ours. He considers them highly immoral as a nation and closes his eyes to our own reputation on that score.

I left Nancy and came here yesterday, arriving about 2:30. The five weeks I spent at Madame Hodez's were the most pleasant I've spent in France and also by far the most profitable. The family and the two American girls were charming. I made enormous progress in the language and learned a lot about the literature. I am quite proud of my ability to speak French, for I really speak well. I mean by that that I can carry on a conversation with educated people on any subject almost as fluently as I can in English. It is an accomplishment that will furnish me much pleasure as well as aid in my studies.

I began my research at the Ministry of Foreign Affairs this afternoon. The great trouble that presents itself is the question of reading the handwriting of the ambassadors and ministers. I am working on Napoleon's sale of Louisiana to the U. S. and I am reading the diplomatic correspondence of the period, roughly 1800-04. Would that they had had typewriters in that day! The ministry is open from 2 to 6 in the afternoons, and in the mornings I plan to work in the *Bibliothèque Nationale* (National Library). I was up at the American Embassy this morning to get a letter of introduction to entitle me to work in the above-named institution. I was struck with the courtesy with which I was received. It felt nice to have the government receive you in a graceful way. They had previously gotten me permission to work at the Ministry.

I am staying in a boarding house for the first time in Paris, for several reasons. This is the first time I've ever stayed as long as a week in Paris, and it is also cheaper and more convenient when you take your meals where you live. Of course, one doesn't have as good things as one finds in the restaurants.

The news of a good cotton harvest and a fair price sounds good. I hope it will mean good times for father.

I'll follow your advice and write sister encouraging letters. I hope she'll follow my advice about her courses.

After two weeks of work here I return to Oxford on the thirteenth (Oct.). It has been a wonderful summer but a most expensive one and my finances are hopelessly ruined.

Hope the new light plant will be more than a flash in the pan. How electricity and water would lighten your work! I'm sure it would halve it.

Love to all,
Wilson

CHAPTER SIX
Looking Toward Home
1927-1928

A week after his October 12 return to Oxford, Lyon received his
B. A. degree in a ceremony which this letter to his parents describes with detail and humor. He wrote from his "digs" in town
where he lived with Thomas Robinson, a Canadian Rhodes Scholar,
whose friendship he would enjoy for many years after their return
from Oxford. His pleasure in their living arrangements is evident.

Jerome Kern's musical *Sunny*, which he attended during graduation festivities with the family of his English friend George Fearnley, had opened in New York in 1925.

In a newspaper column published in the *Laurel Daily Leader* on
October 31, 1925, Lyon described the commoner's gown, which
he exchanged for a B. A. gown at the conclusion of the degree
granting ceremony: "The commoner's gown, worn by all except
scholars, is without sleeves, and is about the length of an ordinary
coat. Two narrow streamers are attached at the arm holes. . . . The
garment . . . is not in one's way in the least, and one soon is uncon-
scious of his academic attire. . . . The gown must be worn at all
times when interviewing a tutor or any official of the college.
Gown must be worn at all lectures and always at dinner in the
college hall."

10 Keble Road, Oxford
Oct. 23, 1927

Dearest mother:

The activities of the past few days consequent on the degree
ceremony have not given me the time I had expected for writing you. The family of George Fearnley, the English boy I
visited in Yorkshire, was here to see him take his degree, and
I have spent most of the past three days either entertaining
them or going to entertainments given in their honor. I am
very fond of them and it was a genuine pleasure to see them

once more. The family consisted of father, mother, a sister of 19, and George. Robinson and I had them all in to dinner at our "digs" the other evening, and I was happy to find that our landlady had done things up in first-class style. It was really a better dinner than we could have had from the chef at the college, and very much cheaper. The last evening they were here they had six of us, George's friends, as guests for dinner at their hotel, and we went to the theater afterwards. They played *Sunny*, an American musical comedy which has enjoyed quite a successful run over here. I had not seen it before and I enjoyed it very much. Yesterday I had Mrs. Fearnley and Kitty out for morning coffee (it is quite a habit here among those who don't take their work too seriously to drink coffee at eleven o'clock). Later I went by and saw them off at the station.

We took our degrees Thursday, Oct. 20, and I am now a full-fledged B. A. of Oxford. That by the way is no small thing—certainly as far as this country is concerned. Englishmen who are B. A.'s have their letters addressed as such, but of course an American wouldn't go that far. Since I now have two B. A.'s, I am B. A. squared, so to speak. You would have enjoyed the ceremony, for it is really very amusing. Practically everything is in Latin. The vice-chancellor sits enthroned with a proctor (disciplinary officer of the University) on each side. He greets the assembled group of doctors and masters when he enters and speaks a bit in Latin. He raises his academical cap and the proctors do likewise. After each set of degrees has been conferred the proctors march to the door and back, looking as serious as possible but yet appearing rather ridiculous to this modern generation. The degrees are conferred by colleges. The Dean of each college is called by an official, and the candidates are assembled on the right of the Dean who takes the right hand of the man closest to him. I happened to be in that position in our group. After the degree has been conferred the student passes outside where his college servant waits with his new B. A. gown. The servant takes the short commoner's gown and helps you put on the new B. A. one. Then you give him one pound for his services and all is over. The college porter also gets one pound as a tip. As the fees for the degree, examination, and gown were over eighteen pounds, you will see that the degree cost me more than a hundred dollars. They don't give you anything about Oxford!

At the moment I have about completed all the formalities for the B. Litt., the degree I am beginning work for. My supervisor* has certified that I am qualified to leave the probationary period, so I will have the necessary residence requirements for the degree by the end of the year. It is going to require a lot of work, but I think I can complete it before I have to come home. I am going to try very hard anyway.

I am very comfortably situated this year. You knew, I suppose, that I was sharing rooms with a Canadian from New Brunswick, a Rhodes scholar of my year and also of St. John's. We have the best rooms I know in Oxford. The furnishings are very nice, the food is very fine, the service is good, the location is very handy, and the price is very reasonable for Oxford. Although we pay about fifteen dollars a week for rooms and four meals a day, that is much cheaper than we had it in college. It is quieter out here, and I think we will find it easier to study.

I have enjoyed seeing McDougal, and we have talked much of Ole Miss and Mississippi affairs. I have felt much nearer home since I saw him. He has changed very much since I knew him, and all for the better. He has made a good beginning, and I think he will get along quite well.

Sister wrote me a very cheery letter the other day. She seems to have made several friends and to have gotten settled. The course she is taking is very good, I think, and about what she ought to have. If her tastes are what I think they are she should find pleasure in the subjects she has. She was encouraged by the sweater and the box of cherries you sent her. I am writing her today and am going to send her some books that I think might be helpful and interesting to her.

I must begin work in earnest tomorrow. So far I've done very little due to the many interruptions that have occurred during the past week.

I note with disappointment that the price of cotton is off several cents, and I certainly hope it is temporary. We have been fortunate in selling so far, I suppose.

I hope you and father are having a restful time at home.

Love, Wilson

Thoughts of home were coloring Wilson Lyon's thinking in a wide variety of ways as he began his final fall term of study. He was attempting to prepare his parents for the fact his first job might be found outside the South.

Always concerned for the well-being of his family, he praised his father for his decision to "hold" his cotton from the market until the price rose. The £10 mentioned was a check he had sent home at the end of the summer to help pay for his life insurance. His father, realizing how much Wilson needed the money, had apparently written him that he did not plan to cash the check.

His own social life continued to be lively, including dates with Marjorie Dance, who had received her Oxford B. A. and was working in London. He urged his mother to encourage Josephine to learn to dance while at college, noting that he had learned "at Jug's", during a house party that was held at the Jones home in Woodville in the summer of 1924. Discussing a gift for his sister, he suggests that an evening shawl from Paris or Italy "would give her something over the other girls", a clear example of his concern for her and his desire to do something to make her more popular.

St. John's College, Oxford
Nov. 13, 1927

Dearest mother:

Your letter which came the other day cheered me up quite a lot. I was happy to know that sister continued pleased at Holly Springs and that father's affairs were going well. It seems that you chose very wisely in sending her there. The distance from home will force her to be more reliant. I am delighted and grateful that she has made some good girl friends.

You must congratulate father for me on the successes of his year at the farm. It seems from your letters that things have gone very well at home. Cotton looks better, according to the London papers and I hope his holding will pay. In this connection I want to thank father again for the £10—which really has helped me very much. I fear I should have been hard put to it otherwise.

I've been having quite a time socially this weekend. The English girl of whom I've spoken before has been in Oxford, and I've been spending a great deal of the time with her. Robinson and I had a dinner party for her and another girl in our rooms last night, and we went to the theater afterwards. Marjorie, for that is her name, was in to tea this afternoon and I have just been to the station to see her off for London. It has been a very pleasant relief from work, I can assure you, to have her here.

A bit on this same line—I have been hearing from Harriet a bit more recently and we seem to be affecting a better understanding than we had in the past. As you know I've always been very fond of her and I shall look forward a lot to seeing her again next summer. I am convinced now that she is more suited to the life I am to lead than Hattie May was. I still hear from the latter, and it looks as if something had happened to end her love for the man at McComb. I'm all in the dark, but her letters give unmistakable evidence that something has happened.

I'm seeing more of girls here than before. The dance club, four times a term, causes you to meet lots of people in itself. Then one meets others. At the moment I have two dance invitations and a tea dance ahead for this term. These are all private affairs and therefore extra to the University Club. In this same line, I think sister ought to learn to dance if there is a chance at Holly Springs. There probably is, as girls dance among themselves at all girls' schools. It is something that is very necessary at times and which always gives much pleas-ure. If I had not begun to learn at Jug's I would have been continually embarrassed here.

It has been a beautiful day—crisp and cold yet with a

bright sun. We have had several days of that sort. The term
has been very good on the whole.

McDougal seems quite happy and is getting along very
well with the English. I think he will undoubtedly like it
and will create a very favorable impression of Ole Miss and
Mississippi.

The time is beginning to approach when I must apply for
a job for another year. I must commence writing soon. I have
little idea of where I'll land and, pending your consent, I may
just as likely land in California as Maine. I would like very
much to come back to the South, and I certainly hope to
eventually, but just at the moment I feel it might be a good
idea to get an idea of some other section of the U. S. My
knowledge of Europe is in many respects superior to my
knowledge of my own country. When I get home I want to
travel and see other sections of the States. What do you
think about my position? Does the place I choose make a
great deal of difference? I should like very much to know
what you think about the whole thing. I think for my own
good it would be best not to come back to Miss. this early in
the game.

It is time I was beginning to think of getting the presents
I am to bring those at home. I want to buy a silk shawl for
evening wear for sister. Do you think that a suitable gift and
what color should I get? I had thought of a green or possibly
a blue. A shawl from Paris or Italy would be something
unique at home and would give her something over the other
girls. About relatives—I don't see how I can afford to bring
things for all the folk at Garlandville, Collins, and Newton. I
see no solution other than stopping with grandmother. Can
you give me a suggestion? I must begin to think of these
things during the vacation, for this may possibly be my last
visit to Paris. I am guided now more by my thesis than by
inclination. I am going there Xmas because my materials
are there.

I've just bought a pair of rabbit-skin gloves to combat the
cold, and my hands present a hairy appearance like Esau's.
They are certainly good combatants against the cold.

I get the *Daily News* and enjoy it very much. The Sunday one is just enough to keep me in touch but not to require a lot of time to read it.

I've had few letters from America for some time now. I'm afraid I, as well as my friends, have become a very poor correspondent. Harriet says Harold Barber can't write for he is still oblivious to all the world except Annie. I suppose a bachelor should be charitable in such a case. Tomorrow means work in earnest for me. So far I've been slow in getting on with my thesis and term is half gone! I must rush like everything if I hope to get this B. Litt. in.

As time gets nearer I am getting very enthusiastic over coming home. It seems only around the corner now until I will be leaving. August, anyhow, should see me in Heidelberg!

Love, Wilson

By early December, 1927, the fall term at Oxford was almost over and Wilson Lyon was preparing to spend his vacation in Paris, where he could do research for his B. Litt. thesis. His mind, however, was also focused on his family in Mississippi.

The excitement surrounding the impending arrival of electricity in Heidelberg is captured in the newspaper reports that follow, an excitement that must also have been conveyed by his mother's letters. His deep love for his sister is reflected in his suggestion that he would like to help her entertain her friends during the summer of 1928 in their newly-renovated and electrified home. Josephine's recent illness, which he mentions, must have affected her vision, because he acknowledges receiving his mother's request that he not send her books for Christmas.

Aunt Maude, who had apparently been ill, was the wife of Willia Lyon's youngest brother, Thomas Eugene Wilson (1891-1981). Like many other Lyon family members, he farmed in the Garlandville area.

JASPER COUNTY NEWS
November 24, 1927

Heidelberg News:
The Mississippi Power Company is stretching wires and people are having their houses wired preparatory to the electric lights which are promised by January first.

JASPER COUNTY NEWS
December 15, 1927

The Mississippi Power Company promises to light the town up next week.

St. John's College
Sunday, Dec. 4, 1927

Dearest mother:
I was greatly relieved to know that sister did not have to leave Holly Springs, though I was grieved to think her hearing might be worse. I had hoped that perhaps the clearing away of the boils might help her in the end; is there a chance of that? In the same mail with your letter was one from her. She did not say whether she heard any worse than before but said during her illness she had been almost stone deaf.

She seems to have friends and to enjoy Holly Springs a lot. It would be nice if she could have some of them at home next summer when I would be there to help her entertain them. It should be quite possible now that the house has been reworked. In that connection what have you done about the bath? It is really imperative that we equip it if we are to have friends visiting us. I am delighted at the thought of lights in town. Electricity will be a great blessing, for we can utilize it in so many other ways, too. I wish they would put in water too.

Your accounts of father's activities sound very, very good. It seems that I may return home to find the family in easy circumstances! Perhaps we can at last get the much talked of car.

199

What do you think of the new Fords? They seem to be creating a sensation here, and even one good word for a Ford from an Englishman is ordinarily a lot. I see in the paper today that the exhibition in New York has aroused great interest.

Your news of the mild Miss. climate made me homesick. It has been better than usual here this term, but it is cold and misty tonight. I haven't seen the sun for nearly two weeks and then it was only a fitful ray or so.

The son of the family I visited in Somerset last summer (where they had the old house) was up to Oxford to see Borsch and me Thursday. We had a very nice lunch at Lincoln College and afterwards a tea in my rooms. It was a great pleasure to see him again. We have been very cordially invited to visit them again in the spring, and I think we will certainly go. I don't know of a lovelier place anywhere.

I've written to Vanderbilt, University of Virginia, University of North Carolina, Southwestern, and Ole Miss in search of a job. I'm going to get off a lot more letters soon. Maybe I will get some replies during the Xmas vacation. Let us hope so.

I had a letter from Harold Barber the other day, the first for months. He pleaded being a bridegroom as the excuse for his long silence. He seemed to be the prosperous young business man and as happy as could be. They have built a home in Gulfport, I believe. He assures me that he and Annie will always welcome me there. It will be a bit odd to find one's friends married when I am still a gay old bachelor.

Last night I went to a little dance given by the Scottish girls we visited last summer. It was quite good fun.

Term ends Saturday, Dec. 10. I am going down to London then and will stay until Wednesday morning, the day after the football match. I hope to have quite a good time, for I will see my English girl friend and go to the dance being given for the Rhodes Scholars by Lady Frances Ryder. The History professor at Paris could not give me a room in his home, so I will have to look again when I go to Paris. I have several other addresses which I will investigate when I get to Paris. I am very anxious to get in a family, so I can make further progress with my French. This may be my last chance.

McDougal is staying in England for the first part of the *vac* and is coming on to Paris afterwards for a few days. I will show him about there a bit.

I will remember what you said and not send sister books for Xmas. I hope you won't forget to answer my queries about presents for the relatives when I come home. How is grandmother? I wrote her in the summer but haven't heard since. Was glad to hear Aunt Maude was doing well. I've lost out completely on the members of the families at Gar-landville. Has Aunt Vera recovered fully?

I'm engaged in trying to write a chapter of my thesis. I'm to take it to my supervisor this week and see what he thinks of it. If I hope to get through with it I'm going to have to work more than I have so far. I find it far more difficult to apply myself now that I'm doing research.

Love, Wilson

After a brief stop in London, Wilson Lyon spent the Christmas vacation of 1927-28 in Paris, doing research for his B. Litt. thesis. His letters from Paris make clear that research was the order of the day, every day.

His vacation also provided time for friendship; he greatly enjoyed showing Paris to his fellow Mississippian and Rhodes Scholar friend, Myres McDougal. Separated from his closest friend, Girault Jones, by thousands of miles, he used a quote from Balzac in a letter to Jones to describe how important their friendship was to him. Dr. Ware, whose address Lyon had received from Jones, was head of the history department at the University of the South in Sewanee, Tennessee. He was apparently in Paris in the winter of 1927-28.

1 Place de la Sorbonne, Paris
Dec. 19, 1927

Dearest mother:

The weather ever since I've been in Paris has been the coldest I've seen in Europe. The whole continent is in the midst of a gripping frost. There has even been snow at Rome. I landed in Paris more or less in the snow, but there has been none since. Fortunately we've had no rain for a while and things are dry. Paris is quite beautiful with its long icicles hanging on all the fountains and the pools all frozen over—provided one can forget frozen hands long enough to indulge in thoughts of beauty. My rabbit-fur gloves have certainly proved a blessing in all this frigidity. It isn't bad inside here, for the houses are so well heated but it must be arctic in dear old England where everyone despises steam heat and prefers immense icy rooms.

The rugby game was excellent—though we lost. However, one never takes games very seriously here so it doesn't matter. I hardly thought of the defeat a second time. Their team was considerably better but we really lost on penalties, which give the other side a free chance for a goal in English rugby. We lost 6 points that way. The score was 22-14 for Cambridge. I enclose the write-up from *The Times*. It might interest father, though I fear it will be more in the nature of a puzzle. By way of explanation, a *try* is a touchdown and counts 3. A *converted try* means a touchdown after which the goal is scored and counts 5.

I went to a session of parliament last Monday afternoon. It was my first visit and I enjoyed it very much. The Prime Minister and several of the ministers spoke during the time I was there. There was not a debate on, and they were answering questions proposed by the members of the opposing parties. Everybody seemed to be in a rather jovial mood, and laughing was the order of the afternoon.

The dance given by Lady Frances Ryder was very good indeed. Things were quite informal and in some ways it seemed more like the University affairs at home than anything I've met over here. During the course of the evening I danced with girls from nearly all the British dominions.

I came over here the day after the rugby game. Ran into a South African Rhodes Scholar on the train and we made the journey together, coming third class all the way.

I am quite well situated. I have a room in the Select Hotel

for 400 fr. ($16.00) a month and I take lunch and dinner with a family very nearby for 625 fr. or $25.00 a month. For breakfast I get some chocolate and a *croissant*, a sort of bread, in an adjacent café. This means that I live quite comfortably at a reasonable price—cheap in fact for Paris. The family is extremely nice, and I am in a good position to make further progress with my French, which, if I may say so, is becoming very good indeed for an American.

I spend my morning at the National Library (*Bibliothèque Nationale*) and the afternoon at the Foreign Office, I'm getting quite a lot of work done and am quite encouraged with the prospect of my thesis.

I've just finished getting off Xmas cards to friends in England. A week from today and it will all be over. I don't suppose it will make much difference so far as I'm concerned. Xmas isn't much if you aren't at home.

Love to all and a happy new year,
Wilson

Hotel Select, Paris
January, 1928

Dear Jug:

This letter must be brief but I'm so far behind with our correspondence that I must send something—even a few lines— to show that the night life of Paris has not swallowed me up. I've just received your Xmas card and the address of Dr. Ware. I plan to look him up *tout de suite*. I am very grateful for this remembrance on your part, for I stand sadly in need of aid on the other side. While I'm on this subject I might add that all I have in prospect is a nibble from Vanderbilt. They wrote me and asked for detailed information. I hope to goodness something comes of it, for offers aren't rolling in by the score. There is nothing at Ole Miss or SPU—which does not grieve me to tell the truth, as I don't think either would be any too good to start with. I would undoubtedly do better where I can start with a clean slate. You are to be at Lumberton! Did you tell me there was a marvelous rectory there or was it Winona? Anyhow we'll be *tout près* next summer and Xmas—if you aren't going to Woodville, which I can't understand. I hope we shall have occasion to spend many days together and rediscover what we've become since the days of West Gordon. Fundamentally I don't think either of us has changed such a terrible lot. I'm counting on you spending that week or longer with me next summer. It won't be exciting but I have a small library and we can talk—after all what we both enjoy more than anything else.

I suppose you've had a *joyeux Noël* indeed—a date with Virginia every night, etc. I should not be surprised to hear the great news from you two any time. If she doesn't give you the eternal *Oui*, she is making the greatest mistake possible. She'll never find another so faithful, so understanding, and devoted. To compare your past and future with mine, for example, is enough to show what a treasure you offer her. Your remarks in answer to my last letter were well placed. I understand fully the truth of what you say: Only love that is powerful enough to sweep away all obstacles is strong enough for marriage. Yet I may say in defense of myself that I don't think you can appreciate the mind of a three year exile—who has lost touch with nearly all things American. What induced me to speculate so was the eternal questioning about all things back home that wracks the mind of every Rhodes Scholar who doesn't return for the summer vacations. You must admit that it is a bit difficult to feel the *chaleur* if *le soleil* has been gone for nearly three years. You can't feel like you did when you sat on a bench with your girl under an Ole Miss oak, caressed by a moon such as only the South can produce.

Besides, the rupture with Hattie May has affected me perhaps more than I realize. It makes me hesitate and question and unconsciously I withhold what before I gave freely. I must be very much in love again before I will be able to subordinate everything to her—as you certainly know I did to Hattie May. This isn't belated weeping, Jug, but an admission. Hattie May and I are through, I suppose, but I have never loved another as I one time did her.

My position *vis-à-vis de* Harriet is better than it has been for years. Whether we can ever be lovers or only the best of friends is a question which only time can tell. One time in the past I was not quite frank with her. I am determined to retrieve my reputation and try to prove that I am really better than I seemed.

I had not intended to write so much on this subject, but it seems we both come to it inevitably. I might add that only a supreme struggle and a sacrifice of my heart have kept me from being head over heels in love with the English girl I wrote you about. It was not so passing as I thought when I wrote you, for circumstances willed that we should see each other a number of times this winter. It was as you say a case of being *swept over* at once. It is a hard struggle, Jug, old man, but I'll get home unattached. I see only too well the folly of anything else. By the way, she is like Virginia in many ways—only more brunette.

Pardon my out-pourings, but I hope you won't mind the invocation of the good old "after light" bull parties in Gordon. One must talk and there are few people to whom one can say everything. I've been reading a novel of Balzac's today and I ran across the following: "You will have only two or three friends in life, attach yourself to them." After all one doesn't have but two or three friends in the deepest sense. I'm sure I shall never have another that has meant as much to me as you. Our friendship has been one of the greatest things in my life, and I hope I shall always conserve it.

I've had quite a good vacation here. I have a room in the hotel and take my meals with a French family nearby. I've made considerable progress with the French and have progressed in knowledge of the people, the country, *et surtout de Paris*. Have been to the theater several times, *à la Comédie Française, à l'opera*, etc.

Mack came over for the last two weeks of the *vac* and is here with me now. It has been a great pleasure to trot about with him, to aid him with the French, and to recall remembrances of former happy experiences. I believe he said he wrote you some time ago. We often talk of you and he speaks of you in the highest terms imaginable. As I said before, our former fears were useless. *Tout va bien.*

I have been working steadily here and have made good progress with my thesis. I hope to finish the materials here this week. We go back to Oxford the latter part of next week.

I was down at Chartres the other day and I thought how much you would have enjoyed it. I think the workmanship is the best I know. The glass certainly is. What a story those Gothic cathedrals tell! I'm stopping to see the cathedral at Amiens when I go back to England.

Write soon and tell me about your Xmas and your plans for next year.

As ever,
Wilson

After Lyon returned to Oxford from Paris, with research results in hand, his supervisor, R. B. Mowat, urged him to expand the scope of his research by a visit to the Spanish archives in Madrid to review their holdings. Encouraged, he began making tentative plans for the trip. With less than six months remaining before his return home, completing his thesis and finding a teaching job were his primary concerns and this letter documents his ongoing efforts in pursuit of both goals.

His father's walk from Paulding to Shubuta, on which he comments at the end of his letter, would have been more than twenty miles. In saying he hoped that such walks would not be necessary in the future, he was obviously alluding to his hope that the Lyon family would soon be able to purchase a car.

The family's silver was primarily limited to serving spoons and teaspoons, hence the reference to possibly supplementing it with purchases abroad, as his mother seems to have requested.

Cousin Beulah, to whose death he refers, was the wife of Rufus Lyon's first cousin, Eugene Lyon. Jonathan Lyon, a brother of Wilson Lyon's paternal grandfather, was Eugene Lyon's father.

His own life continued to be one of increasing sophistication, as this letter indicates, with its references to attendance at popular operas in Paris, as well as a grand ball given at the Paris Opera House. Paul Painlevé (1863-1933), minister of war, whom he recognized at the ball, was an engineer and mathematician who was personally very instrumental in the design of the fortifications along France's eastern border after the end of World War I— named the Maginot line in recognition of André Maginot who raised funds for their construction. The president of the Republic was Gaston Doumerge, whom Lyon had heard speak at Oxford the previous spring.

Each of the Christmas books that came from Harriet Jackson and Hattie May Benjamin reflected their sense of the current state of their relationship with Wilson Lyon. Harriet's gift, *The Story of Philosophy* (1926) by American Will Durant, was a highly popular introduction to philosophy, and an appeal to Lyon's intellect. Hattie May's gift of *Heloïse and Abélard*, a novel of illicit love and heartbreak by Irishman George Moore, may have been a way of commenting on the star-crossed nature of her own romance with Lyon. He certainly does not seem to have taken offense at this gift, detailing the story of a medieval philosopher and a nun caught in passion.

Oxford, England
Wednesday, Jan. 25, 1928

Dearest mother:

I've been in Oxford several days now, having arrived Saturday. I left Paris Thursday and stopped at Amiens to see the cathedral that afternoon. I went on to London the next day and came up here Saturday afternoon. I spent the morning in London getting my admission card to read at the Public Record Office.

I found two letters from you when I returned. I was grieved to hear of Cousin Beulah's death. It seems that many have passed away since I left. Things will seem much different I imagine. It is a blessing that none of Cousin Beulah's children are very young.

Sister wrote me from Holly Springs. She seemed to be settled and contented. I judge she wants to go to summer school. I should think it would be wise to allow her to stay at Holly Springs if she wishes it. She says the summer term will be over by the time I arrive.

My last few days in Paris were very busy as well as very pleasant. We went to the opera twice; they were playing *Le Chevalier à la Rose* of Strauss and *Thaïs* of Massenet. On Tuesday night before I left I went to a great ball at the opera given by the *École Polytechnique* (Polytechnical School). The President of the Republic was there, and the building was lighted up in gala fashion. The *Garde Républicaine*, the pride of the government police force, stood guard on the great staircase. The President entered the main room as they played the *Marseillaise* and made a circuit, accompanied by certain dignitaries, among whom I recognized M. Painlevé, the minister of war. All the seats had been removed from the room, and one danced on the stage and in the corridors as well. Some nine orchestras were scattered about the immense building. It was a great spectacle and I enjoyed very much the idea of spending the evening with the *élite* of Paris. I had received my ticket through the brother of Madame who is president of the Paris Chamber of Commerce.

Sunday I went to Fontainebleau to see the chateau, a former palace of the kings of France. The present building was erected by Francis I, in the sixteenth century, and has been the scene of many historic events. Napoleon signed his first abdication there and said farewell to the guards. The furnishings are the finest imaginable, and their value is incalculable. The *Grande Salle des fêtes* is perhaps the finest room I've ever seen.

I purchased another large reproduction in Paris for the living room. It is also by Corot and will go well with the one I sent you. I also acquired a large colored etching of a market scene in Southern France as well as a small etching of a scene at a hotel in Provence (Southern France, the region on the Mediterranean). I had them packed well and will leave them that way until I come home. I'm glad you liked the picture I sent. In addition to the things I have already I'm going to get a number of etchings of Oxford and familiar places on the continent. Among the pictures I have framed in my room are two that are exceptionally good.

I found Xmas presents from both Harriet and Hattie May

when I returned. Harriet had sent me Durant's *The Story of Philosophy* and Hattie May a two volume novel of George Moore *Heloïse and Abélard.* Both are very valuable and well chosen gifts.

Robinson received 8 pounds of candy from his Canadian girls, with the result that we have been gorging ourselves for the past few days. We laughed over the radical differences of our respective gifts. I also received a very lovely picture of an American girl I knew here who is now teaching in Hollins College, Virginia.

My supervisor advises that I try to complete the first draft of my thesis this term, so I can do some more research next vacation and then finish it in the summer term. I want to get things in shape to go to Spain if I can. There are probably some documents there I should consult, and then I want to see the country before I return. Borsch and I are talking of making the trip together. It will be a bit expensive, but I think I ought to go if it is at all possible.

Robinson and I are going up to London tomorrow to work in the libraries on our thesis. On Thursdays and Saturdays we can get a cheap return ticket for eight shillings, one half the ordinary round trip fare.

Mr. Costin, my tutor, has sent a very good recommendation to Vanderbilt for me, and I'm hoping it may be of service. I'm going to meet some American professors at London tomorrow, and that may lead to something. There are several American historians working in the Public Record office.

Father must be young indeed—younger than his son if he can walk from Paulding to Shubuta. Still I hope we can arrange so that such walks won't be necessary in the future.

I'll look into the silver prices, my money, etc. and we can discuss the matter before I leave here. I don't think we ought to put money in cheap stuff. The best will last always and will certainly be cheaper in the long run. We would probably do better to get the salad forks at home, as they don't use them here as we do.

Lots of love,
Wilson

In January, 1928, Theodore Bilbo was sworn in as governor of Mississippi. A political furor surrounded the beginning of his term when, in his inaugural address, his proposals included moving the Ole Miss campus from Oxford to Jackson. Wilson Lyon strongly disapproved of this idea and his letter home on February 5, 1928 expresses his vehement opposition, an opposition rooted in the university's history. During the Civil War, the university was closed as students scrambled to enlist, forming their own military company with the governor's sanction. Most of the university's buildings, including the Lyceum building, were used as military hospitals during the war. The Confederate cemetery was the burial site for some of those, wounded in the Battle of Shiloh, who died in the campus military hospital. As a result, the Oxford campus was an historic site, and certainly a symbol of Mississippi's loyalty to the Confederacy. Lyon alludes to this in his February 5, 1928 letter when he states that the university "has an atmosphere and a spirit, all her own, relics of the Old South which she can never have in Jackson."

In his February 5 letter home, Lyon also noted that for the university the "one and only trouble has been lack of appropriations and the eternal curse of state politics." This "eternal curse of state politics" had been defined and decried in a letter by Louis Meredith Jiggetts, published in *The Mississippian* on January 11, 1924 while Wilson Lyon was editing the paper. Jiggetts, a Rhodes Scholar (1920-23), had returned to Ole Miss for a law degree in 1923-24. He called on students to ask the legislature to set aside a certain percentage of the state tax levy for higher education instead of merely appropriating funds "from time to time", a phrase that had particular meaning since the legislature met only every other year. He also protested the fact that the governor alone appointed the trustees of the university, giving him great control over the conduct of university affairs. These facts provided the background for Lyon's opinions.

Lyon was enjoying his annual Christmas gift from home as he wrote. The cake was a fruit cake, which Willia Lyon continued to send annually to the Lyon family every year until just shortly before her death in 1962.

St. John's College, Oxford, England
Feb. 5, 1928

Dearest mother:

I have been much distressed by all the talk about moving the University. I oppose the measure with all my power, for I feel that to move Ole Miss would be to destroy all she has accomplished and stood for during the past eighty years. She has an atmosphere and a spirit, all her own, relics of the Old South which she can never have in Jackson. The one and only trouble has been lack of appropriations and the eternal curse of state politics. All the university needs is a freedom from interference by politicians and a continuance of the wise administration of Dr. Hume. It looks like she will receive neither. I am voicing my protest by writing letters to our representative and our Senator. I also plan to get off a letter of protest to the *Daily News*, which screams for anything that might be brought to Jackson, at no matter what cost.

I read Bilbo's letter with much interest. I must confess it is a very able document—miles ahead of Murphree's ridiculous utterances at the Calhoun County Fair (what he said about Miss. was all right, but his manner of saying it was deplorable). Bilbo's speech sounds a bit more like propaganda than a program to be accomplished. He flings millions around in the way that former legislators did hundreds. I distrust his book scheme, but I'm willing to let him try it. But where does he propose to raise the $60,000,000 for roads? Certainly I am for the roads if he can finance them, without graft. And one smiles with incredulity to hear him talk of appropriating twelve or fifteen million dollars for the University when previous legislatures quibbled over appropriating $300,000 for two years. I wish they would, but I doubt it. Theodore sounds good, but even Mack, an ardent admirer, admits he is absolutely untrustworthy when there is any need for him to be. (Please pardon this long ramble, but I'm wrought up over the proposed sacrilege to Ole Miss).

The pecans arrived safely a few days ago, and I have been enjoying them and the cake immensely. Mack and Robbie have likewise found them to their liking.

So far I have nothing to report in regard to a job for next year. I should like very much to have a reply to some of my inquiries. However, it is still a bit early.

I found my financial situation fairly sound on checking it over, so I'm having a new overcoat made. As I haven't had one since I've been here I have become a bit seedy. The new one is a dark blue, which makes it proper for evening wear and is of the best cloth procurable. I shall bound immediately from seediness to the height of fashion. I am also going to buy a couple of suits before I return. One gets tailor-made things here cheaper than ready-made at home, and the cloth is far superior. I hope to bring home enough clothes to last for quite a while. Heidelberg will never have seen such cloth. It would cost nearly $100 a suit tailor made at home, while the price is less than $50 here.

I have been thinking quite a lot today about coming home. It will be great to feel the Miss. sod and breathe the home air once more. One becomes acclimated and Anglicized, but there is always just one little feeling that always escapes.

The amount of sunshine we've had the past week has been truly extraordinary for this country. It has been all the more welcome, however, for that very reason.

I am learning Spanish on the side. If I possibly can I hope to go to Spain at Easter for the trip and to consult some Spanish documents at Madrid and Seville. I am making good progress with the language. After Latin and French it is fairly simple. My French training is proving invaluable.

Your mention of flowers reminded me that you were on the threshold of a glorious Southern spring. Would that I were there to greet it! I fear the summer heat is going to seem severe after England.

Lots of Love,
Wilson

There was much to celebrate when Wilson Lyon wrote to Girault Jones on March 4, 1928. Bilbo's plans for moving Ole Miss to Jackson had been defeated; Lyon's own plans to travel to Spain for research and sightseeing were being finalized. Most important, however, prospects were looking bright for a job at Sophie Newcomb in New Orleans.

The letter contains a delightful description of the surprise meeting of Myres McDougal and Marjorie Dance, Lyon's English girl friend. French playwright Romain Rolland (1866-1944), whose historical/philosophical drama Wilson Lyon and Marjorie Dance attended during the weekend, had won the Nobel Prize for Literature in 1915. He was a life-long pacifist, and his work reflected the search for a world where his concepts of truth and social justice could prevail.

St. John's, Oxford
March 4, 1928

Mon cher Jug:

This is later than I had intended. My first impulse was to answer your letter immediately, but one never seems to do anything quickly here. It's the Oxford habit that has permeated into my bones.

Life has been rather quiet for me, as most of my time is spent on my thesis. I've been sticking to it rather close, as I want to try and get the first draft of it nearly finished this term. My supervisor has seen half of it and doesn't seem displeased, which was encouraging. Since his favourable report, however, I've had the usual attack of inertia that follows any slight praise. I think I shall be very sparing in encouraging my students! Napoleon and Louisiana are getting on so-so however, and I yet have hopes of getting the degree.

Socially I've been out to a number of dances (I find it quite the best way of amusing oneself). In addition to the University dances I get to occasional affairs given by my girl friends. Marjorie was up for the University Dramatic Society's production of Rolland's *The Fourteenth of July*. That was quite a good weekend indeed, all of which goes without saying I was quite amused at Mack while she was here. She came in to tea with me, and as I was upstairs at the moment no one was in the sitting room. Mack bounded in to see me too, and the two of them stood facing each other. They managed to pass a few words, but both looked embarrassed when I descended. She confessed to me afterwards that she had understood hardly half the things he said! He was rather swept off his feet by her attractiveness (he has assured me that she is far more attractive than any of the girls I ever went with at Ole Miss). I'm sure he thinks I'm holding out on him and that I really am head over heels though I've tried to convince him I'm not.

I seem to have slipped around to girls without really setting out to approach the subject so quickly. It seems however one of our main sources of conversation, so I might as well continue in that strain. For myself there is little to say. As you know my fondness for Marjorie must remain curbed to a reasonable point, and my friendships with the numerous girls I take tea with are merely platonic or dancing acquaintanceships. I am rather expecting the coming of spring to sweep Hattie May into the matrimonial fold. It was about that time that she broke off things last year. . . .

We have only two weeks of the term left, and then come our six weeks for Easter. I am going to Spain, primarily to look up some documents in the Spanish archives at Madrid and also to see the country. Borsch and Gray, Illinois and Minnesota respectively, whom you will recall as my time-honored travelling companions are coming along. They plan to spend most of the time at Granada studying, so I may stay on alone at Madrid until I can finish my documents. We take a boat from Southampton to Vigo. It is two days on one of the South American liners. From Vigo we go by rail to Madrid, then to Toledo, Cordoba, Seville, Granada, Valencia (perhaps), Barcelona, and into France. We are stopping at Carcassonne and Toulouse on our way to Paris. There we have a last look at the Champs-Elysées, and then we cross the channel for the last time for heaven knows how many years. I've been boning up on Spanish by myself this year until I know far more of it than I did of French when I left the States. It is surprising how much one can do on the side if he tries and how little we really do at home with foreign languages. Oh, it's quite natural, of course.

This trip is going to be as expensive as blazes, but fortunately, due to reasonable living, I am not badly off. I should have quite enough money to see me home, and I've gotten into the pernicious habit of thinking that it is incumbent on me to spend all my income. It is a bad sign, and I hope I can conquer it.

I'm trying fast and furiously to get a job. I saw Dr. Ware in Paris, but he said they had arranged all their plans for the coming year. Anyhow he didn't think Sewanee a very promising place from a monetary point of view. You will fall over when I tell you that I have been approached by Newcomb, and the salary is $2,800. I'm expecting a letter almost any day which will decide things. Keep this under your hat, as I don't care to let it out until it is definite. I haven't even told the family. Among the other irons I have in the fire Vanderbilt and Yale are not unpromising, but I shall accept the Newcomb position if I can get it. This business of corresponding on urgent matters at a range of three or four thousand miles is a bit tedious.

If I should go to New Orleans we should be able to see quite a lot of each other. The nearness to home and those I know best is one of the best arguments in favor of that job, not to mention the salary which will be increased to $3,000 the second year! I could save enough in two years to enable me to get my Ph. D. The necessity for that degree is at the moment the pet aversion of my young and uneventful life.

The weather here has been as good as Mississippi can be during the past two weeks. It is really unheard of in this country. I suppose it is compensation for the winter we had last summer. Tonight there is a full moon, and I must confess that the call of romance stirs even my aged bones. It is just as well that temptation is not in my way.

No doubt you too rejoiced at the decisive vote which the legislature gave against the proposal to move Ole Miss. I got an exaggerated notion of the movement over here, and I bestirred myself to the point of writing my representative and my senator. The action of the legislature means Hume stays until he wishes to quit, I suppose. I am glad to see he has reinstated dancing, and I believe the new regulations will keep down the orgies of our former years. I think we alumni are greatly indebted to the Chancellor for the decisive walloping the legislature gave Bilbo. His remark about changing the colors of the institution was a stroke of genius and one of those statements that would have been worth precious stones as a campaign slogan.

Mack has just been in for quite a long session, and we spoke of you. He sent his best and expressed a great wish to see you. He was taken into the Masonic lodge last night, and made the best speech of the evening, so my tutor says.

I must try and get off some letters I've owing since the mind of man runneth not to the contrary (as Dean Lewis would say). Yes, I am coming home early in July. It will be a grand and glorious feeling!

As ever,
E. W.

His trip to Spain in the spring of 1928 broadened Wilson Lyon's knowledge of European people still further. This letter, written as the steam packet *Andes* sailed toward Coruña, is noteworthy for its picture of Eastern European immigrants, bound for South America, boarding the ship at Cherbourg. Lyon's descriptions mark him as a sensitive observer, able to empathize with the sacrifices required of the poor who search for a better life.

Royal Mail Steam Packet *Andes*
Saturday, Mar. 17, 1928

Dearest mother:

I am on board the S. S. *Andes* enroute between Southampton and Coruña, where we land in the morning about 9:30. The *Andes* is bound for South America and is only stopping an hour or so at Coruña and Lisbon before going to Rio de Janeiro and Buenos Aires. It is about the same size vessel we came on, but it has three classes instead of the one. We are in second, which is quite good. It was very interesting last night to see the immigrants for South America coming on board at Cherbourg, France, where we touched just at night fall. They were principally from Eastern Europe, Poland, Hungary, etc. As Cherbourg harbor is not deep enough for large vessels to go inside, the passengers were brought out on tenders, third-class passengers being embarked from a separate tender on the opposite side of the boat from the 1st and 2nd classes. There they were, hundreds of them, in every form of European dress from a black fez to the Hungarian woman's head cloth. Infants in arms and septuagenarians were in that crowd of hopeful human beings—all thirsting to find riches and prosperity across the sea in a new world. The baggage ranged from tennis racquets (a strange article in that crowd) and tied-up sheets of clothing to the weirdest and most ancient trunks. As I looked over the rail at the huddled and pushing crowd I could not help but think of the struggle and sacrifice represented by each passenger there. No doubt the trip had been made possible only after years of saving, in many cases by more than one individual. Their embarkation was a sight which I shall not soon forget.

The sea is very rough indeed today, and I have been feeling tough. However I've recovered now and I feel quite well. We came on board at noon Friday and we land tomorrow, Sunday. After that comes a 30-hour train ride in third class to Madrid. The Spanish trains are the worst in Europe and no doubt we will have a slow time of it. I understand that one must be prepared to feed the bugs and vermin of all descriptions.

I have letters to a number of people in Madrid, and I hope to be able to gain access to the archives I want to see. I should be there some time, if I get the permissions I expect. Then I am going on to Seville, where I hope to consult the dispatches from the Governor of New Orleans. My supervisor has seen a good part of my thesis and he seems to be pleased with what I've done. That pleased me a lot, but I fear his reports are too good. I am with Gray and Borsch, whom you will recall as old travelling companions. They are not staying so long in Madrid, but I am joining them later in Granada if I can finish with my work in time. The towns I

217

hope to visit are Coruña, Madrid, Toledo, Cordoba, Seville, Granada, and Barcelona (perhaps). We are stopping at Carcassonne in Southwestern France and then on to Paris—all on our way back.

Robinson, my roommate, is going to Lady Astor's dance and is dining that evening with the Prime Minister. Later he is going to travel in Germany, where he has never been. He has finished his thesis and he will be carefree next term. But he has been working on it since he came over, so he should be through by now.

The last week at Oxford was rather a rush. We had to get up at 6 yesterday morning in order to get our train for Southampton. I can't remember having been up so early in months.

I've forgotten to add that Mack and Belsheim*, North Dakota, have gone off to Egypt, the Holy Land, Constantinople, Greece, and the Balkans. They took a boat at Naples for Alexandria. They will return by train from Athens. They managed to get a leave of absence entitling them to take off a week from each term. I imagine Mack will be bankrupt for the rest of his Rhodesian days.

I wish I could report some news about a job, but so far I'm without a thing. I'm beginning to get worried, though I know it is yet too early for the appointments to begin to come in. There have been no further answers to my letters. I registered with a couple of teachers' agencies and they should be able to do something for me if worse comes to worse.

I was surprised as well as delighted to hear of Ole Miss winning the basketball championship. I never realized that our team was that good. It is a bit of a joke on A&M who won four games from us before-hand.

I am going to get the shawl for sister on this trip. I can't say whether I'll get it in Spain or France, it depends on the prices in Spain.

It is getting late, and I will close.

Love to all,
Wilson

Wilson Lyon's personal and intellectual growth as he neared the end of his three years abroad is clearly revealed in letters he wrote home from Spain in the spring of 1928. Most striking was his ability to gain access to the archives in Madrid, a complex process all conducted either in the Spanish he had taught himself or in the French which he had worked on improving during a series of Oxford vacations. It seems clear as we read his description of his first meeting with the great diplomatic historian, Samuel Flagg Bemis*, who was also doing research in the Spanish archives, that he probably had no idea of Bemis' prominence or knew that he had recently received the Pulitzer Prize for his historical work, since he notes neither distinction in his comments to his mother.

Hotel Continental, Madrid
Sun. March 25, 1928

Dearest mother:

I have been in Spain a week today. We landed last Sunday morning at Coruña about 9:30. The harbor there is almost a land-locked bay, and the city sets back on the hills. The slopes wore a coat of green and the palms in the city square told us we were nearer springtime than we had been in Oxford. We got a hotel boy who called himself Antonio to show us "the ropes" in regard to baggage and the station and then to take us for a walk about the town. Coruña contains nothing of interest to tourists, but it is a beautiful town and seemed an attractive place in which to live.

At 2:30 we mounted in a third-class carriage bound for Madrid about 500 miles away. Some 19 hours later after a night spent trying to sleep in a sitting posture on a hard board seat, we arrived in the capital. The trip was not without its interest and nothing like so tiresome as I feared it would be. For some time after leaving Coruña the landscape was a series of low mountains and fertile valleys. Then some time in the night we got into the barren plain of Castile, an apparent desert where it appeared that neither man nor beast could possibly find sustenance. The only trees were a few shaggy pines not much higher than one's head. But some towns did exist in spite of the sterility of the soil. About breakfast time we passed Avila, a walled city looking like it might have jumped straight from the Middle Ages. From the train we could see the grating of the up-drawn gate. As a matter of fact it slipped on us unaware. Had we known as much then as we do now I'm sure we would have stopped.

In Madrid we got very comfortably settled in the hotel named above on the stationery. Prices are higher than in France but much cheaper than in England. Full *pension*, i.e. three meals and room, costs me exactly $2.38 per day. Such meals—there are no people in Europe who serve as much as the Spaniards. Breakfast as in all continental countries consists of coffee, tea, or chocolate and rolls and butter, but lunch and dinner compensate for anything that may be lacking in the morning. Here is a typical Spanish menu of the kind we get twice a day and the kind you will get in any real Spanish hotel. One begins with hors d'oeuvres, if it is lunch, or soup, if it is in the evening. Then come the following courses: two eggs done to choice, a meat or some sort of meat dish, a fish course, a meat course with salad or a vegetable, cheese or pastry, and a basket of fruit with two or three varieties to choose from. You don't receive a dainty helping but your plate is heaped up each time. So don't be surprised if I become heavier than my usual 137 pounds. I might add that their cooking is good, too. Their hours of eating are, however, a bit disconcerting. Lunch is from 1-3 (all right) but dinner is from 8-10 (too late in any case). That means that the music in their cafés does not begin until about 11. From one to three in the afternoon all business houses are closed, and life is more or less at a stand still.

Madrid is a very fine modern city—one of the most up-to-date and well arranged cities in Europe. It has no monuments of antiquity but from the point of view of the *Madrileños* (Spanish for citizens of Madrid) it must be a very fine city indeed. The government edifices are magnificent, the streets are capacious, and there is an air of progressiveness about the whole general appearance of things. I was much surprised to find a very good subway system—which however to me seems hardly justified by the size of the city. But perhaps it is the subway that has reduced traffic overhead. At any rate the underground trains are usually filled.

The great incentive of a visit to Madrid is the Prado Museum, one of the world's greatest picture galleries. The great treasures of the gallery are the pictures of Velasquez, Murillo, Goya, and El Greco. Those of Velasquez to my mind are by far the best in the museum. Here in three rooms is gathered all the best work of this famous painter and master of color. One could never tire of looking at them.

Wednesday we all (Borsch, Gray, and myself) went to Toledo, about 50 miles to the South. This, the guide books say, is the most interesting city in Spain, and though I haven't seen the others I can well believe it. Toledo is a monument to the mingling of Christian (Castilian) and Arab cultures in the formation of the Spanish spirit and Spanish art. In the same city is a wonderful thirteenth century cathedral and a small mosque. The city is perched high on the rocks above the Tagus river, and must have been a very strong fortification in the Middle Ages and before. One approaches the gates over a long bridge and gets a memorable view of the city. The streets are nearly all too narrow for any sort of vehicle to pass, and they make such a labyrinth that the stranger can find his way only by the greatest difficulty. We decided to save time and trouble by getting a small boy to guide us about. He was admirable and we decided the 30¢ each was well invested. Toledo was the home of El Greco and his finest paintings are to be found in the churches there and in his home, which has been made into a national museum.

Here in Madrid I've been having some interesting experiences trying to get permission to see the papers I want in the government archives. I found no one here knew how to go about getting what I wanted. The American Embassy that I had written several weeks ago had done absolutely nothing. I set to work with interview after interview until I located what I wanted and found I would have to secure permission from the Minister of Education to see it. I went to see him

and got an authorization, but when I presented it, the director of the archives refused to produce the documents I
wanted and sent me back to him. The Minister of Education
has now written a letter to the Minister of Foreign Affairs
for me, and I am going back Tuesday. I think perhaps I'll get
through this time; there is no reason why the foreign office
should refuse to let me see this correspondence. I've had to
do a lot of talking in Spanish, and I've come off very well
indeed if you consider that I've learned all my Spanish by
myself without one single lesson from anyone. I spoke to the
minister in French and occasionally to other officials in it.
Practically no English whatsoever has passed in any of the
conversations. If I get what I want it will be no small
achievement, and I think I will have just reason to congratulate myself.

Borsch and Gray have gone on to Granada, via Córdoba
and Sevilla. I will join them in Granada as soon as I can read
the documents here and in Seville. We are stopping at
Granada in a boarding house almost within the grounds of
the Alhambra.

It looks very much as if I am coming to Sophie Newcomb.
The head of the history department writes me that he is pro-
posing my name to the Dean for appointment and if it is
passed I shall be elected. He has promised to let me hear as
soon as possible. While that is not a definite appointment, it
looks very much like I shall get the position. New Orleans
and $2,800 will not be bad for a start!

I struck up with four other Rhodes scholars in the Prado
this morning, and we arranged to go out to Escorial tomorrow to see the palace, churches, etc. It was built by Philip II
who is buried there.

Yes, it was Harriet's father who married. She styled his
wife as "an old friend of the family".

Love, Wilson

Hotel Continental, Madrid
Thursday, April 5, 1928

Dearest mother:

I'm feeling quite lively this evening because I have at last
secured permission to see the documents I want to consult.
The letter just came this afternoon. The two weeks of waiting were beginning to get on my nerves and I feared I would
never get a reply. The Spanish nation has no reputation for
speed.

I spent part of the afternoon talking with a professor from
George Washington University who is here having documents photographed for the Library of Congress. He is having the same difficulty I had. He has done a lot of work in the
field I'm on, and he showed me up so badly that I came away
feeling rather blue. One of the secretaries of the American
Embassy gave me Professor Bemis' address.

This is Holy Week and all over Spain, especially in the
South, celebrations are in progress. At Seville especially they
are gorgeous, and thousands of tourists go to see them.
There are parades of monks and priests in costume dress
bearing images of Christ on the cross. Here in Madrid there
are no processions, and the only sign of Holy Week is the
constant going in and out at churches and the absence of theater programs. Today there were many girls in the streets
wearing their *mantillas*. The *mantilla*, as you probably know,
is a high comb over which a lace veil is draped. It is worn in
place of a hat. They are very beautiful, and the Spanish girl
so dressed has all the charm tradition ascribes to her. If Spain
were great in proportion to the beauty of her young women,
she would be among the leaders of the world.

It is beginning to get warm even here in Madrid. On
account of its high altitude Madrid does not have the early
spring one would expect. The city is situated on the great
plateau of central Spain, and snow-capped mountains can be
seen in the distance. To the South however lies the fertile and
sunny province of Andalusia. I envy Gray and Borsch the
sunshine they are enjoying at Granada.

I've been spending the past week rewriting part of my

223

thesis and have got the first chapter in final form. There are six others to do. I've got all but one of them written in some form, so I'm well on the way. I'm not too happy about this thesis—principally because of the subject. I fear it will be impossible to make an original contribution on the subject, and that may give the examiners a chance to fail me. At any rate I'll be happy to finish with it. My plans are to submit it about the middle of next term.

I've become more accustomed to the Spanish meals and manage to get along fairly well with them. I marvel at my ability to put away the eight courses twice daily. However as they don't have tea and as breakfast is no more than coffee and a roll it isn't so difficult after all. I'm afraid papa would not find their system to his liking, as I remember he always likes a good breakfast.

This is cotton planting time at home I suppose and to think I'll see the cotton growing this year! I've been thinking lots of home here in Madrid and I am looking forward eagerly to the time when No. 3 shall drop me and my bags at Heidelberg. I've thought it all out many times during the past three years!

I've got separated from my letters, and it has been some time since I heard from you.

Love to all,
Wilson

Back in Oxford, Lyon continued work on his thesis. Still without word of any sure job for the fall of 1928, his need for a network of American contacts was very clear to him—hence his decision to join Beta Theta Pi at the invitation of the Ole Miss biology profes- sor, presumably Professor Thatcher, whom he had met in Paris in the summer of 1926. He had been nominated by Chancellor Hume, whom he greatly admired.

The allusion to his sister's trip to Tennessee, at the end of this letter, has a poignant sequel. In the summer of 1995, Josephine talked about the trip. She went home for the weekend with a college friend whose family had a sheep farm. The trip meant so much to her that almost seventy years later, she could still remember what she wore—a lavender coat with a white fur collar.

St. John's College, Oxford
Sunday, May 6, 1928

Dearest mother:

I'm afraid it has been a long time since I wrote you, but the days slip by very quickly when one is on the move. I have been in Oxford now exactly a week today. We came from Granada to Paris in one jump, making the necessary change at Madrid and waiting four hours at the border station. We didn't go by Barcelona and Carcassonne after all, for we found the train service did not suit us. The ride through the Pyrenees and the Basque country was very beautiful. Night came on at Bordeaux and we saw nothing from there to Orleans, which naturally interested me.

We were in Paris four days, and I have never seen the city more beautiful. It was heavenly with its spring atmosphere. The trees on the boulevards and in the parks were well out, and the weather was almost hot. I did four days of intensive work and unearthed some very interesting and helpful material.

I arrived in London Saturday morning after a night crossing from Dunkirk to Tilbury, a town just below London on the Thames. We were delayed for over two hours by fog at the mouth of the river. I spent the afternoon in the library of the British Museum and went to the cinema that evening with Marjorie (you will remember her as the English girl I often speak of). Sunday we lunched together at a little village just out of London and I came up here in the evening.

After losing a day or so in getting settled I got to work on my thesis and so far I've made gratifying progress. I won't be able to turn it in until June 15 which means I will be late getting an examination. That will probably retard my departure. Just now I can't say when I'll get away but it should be some time in July. I need not say that I will come just as quick as possible.

To date I am without further news from New Orleans or

any favorable offer from any university. If the Newcomb offer crumbles I may be in a bad way. However, I'll wind up with something I suppose, and if I can tide over next year I'll have connections that will aid me. Right now I'm completely out of touch with everything.

For that reason I think I ought to accept the invitation which the biology professor at Ole Miss has just sent me to join a fraternity, Beta Theta Pi. The chancellor nominated me and is, of course, himself a member of the same fraternity. Membership would not only put me in touch with affairs at Ole Miss but would be very valuable to me socially and academically in university circles. There is some expense of course, but it should be amply worth it. What I need above all now is to get in touch with American affairs once more. Do you know anything about Hattie May's engagement or wedding? Jug spoke of it as an "announcement" only and assumed I knew. But as some of my letters were lost, I never got the announcement if she sent one. Of course it is all the same in the end, but I am merely curious. Any regrets that I may have had are of course history now. It was impossible from the first that we could have married, for it will be several years before I will be in such a position and she would have been 27 or 28 by then. These three years have taught me to look much further than I ever could have in 1925. So you may rest assured that the news made no impression other than that of interest. I hope she has married a nice chap and that she will be happy—that is all.

The day has been perfect here. Robbie and I went on the river in the afternoon. There were great crowds of people in punts and canoes, and the people looked very nice in white. If we can just keep this lovely weather no one can grumble.

You seem to have had an awful spring at home. We have done much better here. Farming operations must be in a bad way indeed.

A lady in North Oxford has asked me to join her party for three of the dances during Commemoration Week (something like our commencement). As I will be through with my work then, I was glad to accept. This means I will have a real commem which I otherwise could not have afforded for the tickets for each dance are $10 per person.

I haven't heard from sister in months. How is she and did she have a good trip in Tennessee?

Mack reports a great time in the East but says he is just as happy the trip is over. He plans to spend most of the summer quietly in France, studying and trying to save his money.

I think I'll have enough money to get home safely but that is about all. It may not be too easy to settle down after the easy time we've had here. However I'm eager to try it.

I hope you are all well and that the weather is better.

Love, Wilson

Girault Jones announced his engagement to Virginia Wallace in the spring of 1928, and this letter brought Wilson Lyon's congratulations. Just a year before, he had purchased a graduation present in Brussels for Virginia at Girault's request—a small Venetian leather purse, with two handkerchiefs inside trimmed with Belgian lace. Girault and Virginia would be married on April 22, 1930. Sadly, she died only seven months later of a brain tumor.

In the spring of 1928, as Lyon worked on completing his B. Litt. thesis, Jones was completing his theological studies at the University of the South in Sewanee, Tennessee. He was ordained at his home church, St. Paul's, in Woodville, Mississippi on June 17, 1928.

As he writes, Lyon is clearly looking toward home with great anticipation. But there is much that he hates to leave. This letter captures his growing need to say his goodbyes to all that he has come to know and love during his three years of Rhodes study— whether it is Marjorie Dance, the boulevards of Paris in the spring (the *Boul Mich* is the Boulevard St. Michel), or the many aspects of Oxford life he has come to treasure.

St. John's College, Oxford
May 13, 1928

Dear Jug:

I was delighted to find your picture when I returned not long ago, and I shall treasure it in the spirit with which it was sent.

Mack and I thought you a bit more mature but otherwise we noticed little change. Despite your assertion it seems to me a very excellent photograph.

This letter is long overdue, *mon cher ami*, and I realize fully my delay. But with travel and an unsettled frame of mind I have not been able to seize the right moment for the sort of note I cared to send. To save you further anxiety, I will say at once that the Benjamin "announcement" had nothing to do with it. My regret over her loss came last year, and has long since been over. I accepted the first rupture as final, as common sense told me it was the only way. Is she married or officially engaged? My only information is from your letter. A bundle of my letters were lost in Spain, and if she sent me an announcement it was in the package.

The definite end of my own affair in no way diminishes my joy at your new happiness. I am very glad for you both, for I have always thought you admirably suited to each other. You remember I have always liked Jin immensely and it will be a great pleasure to entertain the two of you in the years that are to come. You have won your inspirer—nothing could be more beautiful. Fortunately you have escaped a disillusionment. Their influence is not too good on one's character, I may assure you.

The role will be reversed henceforth. I, once so valuable in confidences, must be the recipient of yours. Female society I shall seek, it is necessary for my happiness, but I shall try to avoid falling in love too deeply until I am better situated. Next time I want to have something to offer the girl.

I see Marjorie every few weeks, and she is as delightful as ever. I love her, more than she will ever know, but I've repressed myself in the knowledge of the unhappiness anything serious would bring. I cannot ask a girl to marry me whose social position and background would make it impossible for her to be happy with my family and the conditions under which I was brought up.

Nevertheless the moments with her recall old sentiments—long dormant—and make the days sweeter even with the thought of the inevitable end behind. She is coming up for Eights Week and I am taking her to a commemoration ball and I suppose that will be the end.

The question of coming home looms up bright and alluring—despite the fact that I am jobless and appear likely to be so. The Newcomb business is not yet settled and that may save me. Otherwise I have little idea of the future. It is annoying to fit oneself for a profession and then be rejected. However I'm not worrying as there are several alternatives and I will eventually manage I'm sure. Oxford at least should have given me a little *savoir faire* along with *savoir vivre*.

I am now terribly pushed trying to finish my thesis and get it in by June 15. I found some valuable documents in Spain, and that has helped things a lot. My supervisor seems fairly pleased, and I'm hopeful of getting through. As my examiners have to be appointed afterwards and then a date set for the examination, I have no idea when I shall get away. I hope to sail early in July. In all events I shall be home by August 1. I should like very much to be present at your ordination. You have a great advantage in being able to commence directly your work without further preparation.

I trust this will arrive at Sewanee before you leave. You are no doubt now in the midst of the final rush. The weather here has been delightful so far, and I have enjoyed quite a bit of tennis. I hate the thought of leaving these delightful grass courts behind. We really have nothing in America to compare with them. And the river and punting are absolutely *sans rival*. There are few more delightful pastimes than an afternoon on the river with a charming girl or with a very close male friend. I shall miss very much the delightful conversations of Oxford.

My recent journey to Spain was very pleasant, and I could write much—all of which I'll save until we meet. I learned enough Spanish to read quite well and can hold a simple conversation. There is no more courteous or polite people in Europe. I paid my goodbye to Paris by drinking a good quantity of sparkling red Burgundy and feeling very sad over the thought of not seeing the *Boul Mich* again for many years. The city, as was fitting, looked her best. The boulevards were charming with their spring color, and the carefree people in the Luxembourg reminded one of that delightful insouciance which we prudish Anglo-Saxons so woefully lack. *Comme j'aime le quartier latin.*

I plan to sail to Boston and to visit New York, Philadelphia, and Washington on the way home. I am very anxious to examine and study them in the light of what I've learned over here. I'm sure I'm more qualified than I was three years ago.

I hope you are planning to visit me next summer. Mother has already spoken of the pleasure with which she anticipates seeing you again. Except for a trip to Water Valley and an occasional day or so away I shall be there all summer.

It was too bad about Harold's father's death. I suppose you knew of it.

An English friend with whom I stopped in Somerset was up the other day, and all the family are inviting me down again before I leave. I shall take advantage of the opportunity by all means, as I have rarely been in a more charming place.

Any letter arriving by July 1 should be sent here.

Cheerio, Wilson

The last letter we have that Wilson Lyon wrote home before leaving Oxford carried the sobering news that the job he had hoped to get at Sophie Newcomb had not materialized, and no other job appeared to be in the offing. He was obviously bitterly disappointed and concerned, but also determined to put the best face on matters. By July, Frank Aydelotte*, American secretary of the Rhodes Trust, would come to his aid with a college teaching job.

St. John's, Oxford
June 7, 1928

Dearest mother:

I hope you and father have not been worried about my long silence. I have been in such a hurry and rush with my thesis that I haven't had time to think of anything else. After a great effort I have finished it, and I am now recuperating from the ordeal and waiting for my oral examination. The examination has been set for June 19 at 2:30 P. M. The thesis was in fairly good shape and I am hopeful of getting through. My supervisors* thought I would make it anyway, and their opinion should be fairly accurate.

I suppose I might as well begin with the worst. I have no position, and my prospects are none too rosy. The man at New Orleans led me on in a rather unbusinesslike way. After writing me in March that he was going to appoint me, if the Dean consented, he announced in May that the person whose place I was to have was not leaving and that he could not offer me the place. He has offered me a place for year after next and wants me to come to New Orleans to see him this summer, but that doesn't help things for next year. While I did not refuse another offer on account of the Newcomb proposition, I slacked up in my attempts at securing something as that seemed practically assured.

I am not yet completely without possibilities, however. I recently learned that there were places going at the Universities of Missouri and Iowa, and I got in communication with them. Also, President Aydelotte of Swarthmore College and head of the Rhodes Trust in America, whom I met recently, thought he could probably throw something my way before the end of the summer. I shall probably get something before the next session begins, but I doubt if I can get the sort of thing I want. The whole trouble is that I have lost all my contacts on the other side, and universities usually take people they know personally. The University of Mississippi unfortunately does not enjoy prestige enough to be of much assistance, and then, too, the history department has changed completely since I left. I've worried a lot over the whole affair, but I'm sure it will come out all right in the end, so don't you and father bother about it. There are lots of other things to do besides teaching, anyway. I've thought a lot of entering the examinations for the diplomatic service, but we can talk that over when I get home.

About getting home. I can give no dates, but can tell more exactly now. I am staying here for Commemoration (something like our commencement) which is over about June 29. I've asked Marjorie up for one of the dances, and then I've been asked to join a party for three of the others. Borsch and I plan to spend a few days in Somerset where we were last year, and then I hope to sail, about July 7. Frank Gray and I are hoping to get a passage for thirty-five dollars on a cargo boat of the United States Lines for New York. The trip takes nine days, and we eat with the officers. The saving would be about seventy-five or eighty dollars on the price of student third on a passenger liner, and in our present condition that is a lot. I think we will get the place all right; anyhow we will know in a few days. If we don't get that, we are going to book a passage soon, and in either case I can soon tell you the date of my departure from this island.

I want to stop either in New York City or at her home in Troy to see an American girl I used to know here my first year. Then on the way home I want to stop a day or so at Philadelphia, and a few days in Washington. I may go to Boston first, as I mentioned before, but I'm not sure at the present moment. I'm sure you'll agree with me that I should get a glimpse of these great cities of my own country while I'm passing through, and while I can do so with little extra expense. I should be home sometime about July 27 or 28, or thereabouts. It is later than I had intended and later than I like, but it seems that if I do these things I can't get there before. As I may stay in Mississippi a long time when I arrive, I think I ought to profit by my opportunity.

I had a very quiet birthday yesterday, played tennis in the afternoon and went to the movies at night. I can hardly believe that I am twenty-four, but the facts are against me. Once I thought that after passing twenty-one one became very settled indeed, but I feel about as youthful as ever.

I think I will have just enough money to get home, but in case I find I can't make it, I'll let you know. It is very good of papa to offer to help me. I've bought a few clothes for next year and that has crippled me some, but I should just about make it. The expense of applying for permission to submit my thesis and the typing cost over $56.00, and if I get the degree, it will cost about seventy more to take it. They certainly know how to raise revenue here.

The weather has been nice since I finished with the thesis, and I've already managed to get quite a red face and a healthy complexion. The sun isn't quite hot enough to blister one violently here, so one gets rather tanned without too much pain. For England it has been really dry for some days past. The week for the college boat races was perfect, and the Derby, the racing and betting event of the country, was run under perfect conditions at Epsom Downs yesterday. The papers say more than half a million people were there.

I suppose sister is at home now. I had a letter from her some weeks ago, and she was just about ready to leave Holly Springs then.

It is a great thought that only about another month is to be spent before I take passage for home. I cannot tell you how I am looking forward to coming.

Lots of Love,
Wilson

CHAPTER SEVEN
Mississippi Homecoming
and the Years Beyond

In early August, 1928, Wilson Lyon reached home. His homecoming was reported in the *Jasper County News* on August 9: "Mr. E. W. Lyon, who has been attending school at Oxford, England for the last three years on a Rhodes scholarship, returned home Saturday where he was greeted by his many friends. He was accorded a hearty welcome at a reception by the Heidelberg PTA in the home of Mr. and Mrs. Dr. G. E. Eddy. A host of friends and relatives met there to give him the greatest ovation of his life and welcome him back again. Mr. Lyon has won fame in all the schools he ever attended from the primer grades in his home town to the graduating at Oxford, England. Jasper County should be proud to have such a son. I am sure Heidelberg is."

In 1995, Lyon's sister Josephine recalled his return home, remembering that a group of friends was at the station to meet him and that someone drove the Lyon family home, since they had no car. Recalling the party at the Eddy home, she described how "we sat around and talked. Wilson", she noted, "did most of the talking." Dr. Eddy was Heidelberg's town doctor, and his wife was a close friend of Wilson Lyon's mother.

Lyon cannot fail to have noted that a spirit of optimism seemed to prevail in Heidelberg in the summer of 1928. The August 23 issue of the *Jasper County News* reported a new gin in town, a new sawmill, and a new jewelry and watch repair shop. Cotton-picking season was about to begin; in the August 9 *Jasper County News* reporting Lyon's return from England, another brief article noted that the county's first open boll of cotton for the season had been sent to the newspaper's office in Bay Springs.

Lyon was particularly happy that he had arrived home with a job. In his June 7 letter to his parents, he mentioned that in Oxford he had recently met Frank Aydelotte, American secretary to the Rhodes Trust, who thought he might be able to find a teaching job for him for the 1928-29 academic year. "In mid-July he cabled the good news that there was a position at Louisiana Tech in Ruston, which would offer me an assistant professorship with a salary of $2,500 for 42 weeks of teaching."[1] His fear that he might not be able to begin his career in academia right away was relieved. Louisiana Polytechnic was a start, with a salary almost as high as the one he had hoped to earn at Sophie Newcomb.

After the initial excitement of his reunion with his family and community friends, Lyon wanted to see and talk with his college roommate, Girault Jones, who had now completed his training for the ministry and had a small Episcopal church in Lumberton, Mississippi—with mission ministries in Poplarville, Columbia, Wiggins, Picayune, and Tylertown. It was a reunion that would allow each to share personal hopes with the other as they began their professional careers.

In the fall of 1997, Bishop Jones recalled in great detail their visit together during August of 1928.[2] Jones decided that his friend Wilson needed to see Louisiana. Although he had just completed a thesis about the sale of the Louisiana territory, Jones felt Lyon knew little of the area. The two of them set off in Jug's car to tour French Louisiana, with New Orleans their first stop. At the famous New Orleans French restaurant, the Galatois, Lyon spoke to the waiter in French and was delighted to be answered in French. When he asked the waiter where he was from originally, he said "Paris". Obviously Lyon had not yet encountered Louisiana French *patois*, which Jones knew was the hallmark of the true French Louisiana.

All this changed in a restaurant in Thibodaux, the heart of the Louisiana French country, where the waitress, who understood French, would only respond to him in English. When Lyon asked her why she would not speak French with him, she replied, "I speaks only to them that knows it." Wilson Lyon might not be hearing French *patois*, but he had encountered it!

Back in Heidelberg after this trip, he was still very much a local hero. On Friday, August 31, he was the featured speaker at the

1. *The Education of a Mississippian*, p. 13.
2. Conversation with Elizabeth Webb in November, 1997 during her visit with him and his wife, Kathleen, in Nashville, Tennessee.

annual Jones County Agricultural High School alumni banquet in Ellisville. Tickets were $1.00 each.

He spoke at a pivotal moment in the history of the school: the expansion of its program to include junior college work. On June 29, 1928, the school had received full accreditation as a junior college from the Mississippi Junior College Commission. With the advent of consolidated school districts, and the development of improved roads for traveling to public high schools, the secondary programs provided by agricultural high schools around the state were no longer needed in the way that they had been when Wilson Lyon was a high school student just ten years earlier.[3]

By September, Lyon had moved to Ruston, Louisiana, to begin his college teaching career. The September 27, 1928 issue of the *Jasper County News* announced that he had "accepted a chair to teach history in the Polytechnical Institute in Ruston, Louisiana." Unstated in that article, however, were the complications he encountered as he approached his job. In his autobiography he reports that "when I returned home, I found that the vacancy at Louisiana Tech had resulted from political controversy between Governor Huey Long* and the administration of Louisiana Tech. The confusion was such that I could not learn the courses I was to teach before I actually arrived on the campus and met the new head of the Division of the Social Sciences."[4]

The energy that Wilson Lyon had displayed as he worked on his B. Litt. thesis at Oxford, came to the fore again. After meeting with his new department head, he began preparing courses in American history and government, British history, and European history. His course load was twelve hours in the first semester and fifteen in the second semester. Looking back on the experience, he realized how valuable it had been for him. He notes that he was "given a great deal of freedom in organizing my courses" and adds that "the preparations greatly extended my knowledge of history and political science."[5]

3. Richard Aubrey McLemore, "Higher Education in the Twentieth Century," in *A History of Mississippi*, 2, pp. 424–25.
4. *The Education of a Mississippian*, p. 13.
5. Ibid., pp. 13–14.

Lyon had hoped to find a teaching position in a liberal arts college, not a technical college, and therefore began almost at once to look for an appointment for the 1929-30 academic year. For help, he turned to his Rhodes Scholar friends. In the fall of 1928, his Oxford roommate, Thomas Robinson, who was teaching sociology at Colgate, learned that a position was going to be added to the history department in the fall of 1929. He submitted his friend Wilson's name to the department chair. The history department brought Wilson Lyon to Hamilton in the winter of 1929, agreeing to pay his way to the campus, but not agreeing to pay his way home unless they hired him. He got the job and a paid return trip home.

With a job at a liberal arts college his at last, Lyon turned to the task of getting a Ph. D. This was the necessary requirement for full membership in America's academic community that he had complained about on more than one occasion in letters written from Oxford to Girault Jones. Fortunately, he was able to complete his residency requirements for the degree in three summers at the University of Chicago (1930-32), expanding his Oxford B. Litt. thesis into his doctoral dissertation. Getting his Ph. D. through work in the summers allowed him to continue full-time teaching at Colgate during the regular academic year.

While at Chicago, he found the woman with whom he shared his life and dreams from 1933 until his death in 1989. Carolyn Bartel, to whom he was introduced at the end of the summer of 1930, was a native of Richmond, Indiana, and the granddaughter of German immigrants who had established successful wholesale dry goods and wholesale grocery businesses in Richmond. A 1928 graduate of Wellesley College, she had earned an M. A. in history at the University of Chicago and was a copy editor for the *Journal of Modern History*. They were married on August 26, 1933 at the First English Lutheran Church in Richmond. Several Rhodes Scholar friends were ushers, including Thomas Robinson, Reuben Borsch, and Myres McDougal.

Girault Jones offered a prayer at the end of the ceremony. He had served the Episcopal church tirelessly in a series of tiny Mississippi parishes and was living in Pass Christian at the time Carolyn and Wilson Lyon were married. After the wedding was over, he drove Willia Lyon home to Heidelberg in a new black Plymouth roadster, with red wheels, that he had picked up at the factory in Detroit just before the wedding. Rufus Lyon, blind with glaucoma by 1932, had remained at home, with Josephine to care for him.

At the time Carolyn Bartel and Wilson Lyon married, he was a well-established member of the Colgate history department, and had been living outside the South for four years. In 1934, the University of Oklahoma Press published his first book, *Louisiana in French Diplomacy, 1759-1804*, based on the work he had done for his doctoral thesis. He dedicated the book to his parents, Willia Wilson Lyon and Rufus Lyon. This dedication was his public statement that without their support, from his earliest childhood, his educational career could never have developed as it did.

A life in academia required that he continue to publish. Nine years after leaving the continent as a Rhodes Scholar, Lyon returned to northern France in 1937 to do research for a second book. In 1942, the University of Oklahoma Press published *The Man Who Sold Louisiana, The Career of François Barbé-Marbois*, a biography of the man who negotiated the sale of Louisiana to the United States for Napoleon. This time, he dedicated his book to his wife, Carolyn Bartel Lyon, who undoubtedly helped read proof during its preparation for the printer.

However, before the book was set into final proofs, Wilson Lyon's life had taken a dramatic turn. In the spring of 1941, he had accepted the presidency of Pomona College, in Claremont, California. His move to Pomona resulted from the recommendation of his Rhodes Scholar classmate, Paul Havens, who had taught in Claremont at Scripps College and had been a member of the graduate faculty of the Claremont Colleges from 1930 to 1936. In 1941, Havens received a general request, sent to alumni and members of the Claremont academic community, asking for names of possible candidates to succeed Pomona's retiring president, Charles K. Edmunds. In response, Havens submitted Wilson Lyon's name.

Near the end of his life, Wilson Lyon described his being named president of Pomona College in a brief unpublished essay titled "Our Coming to Pomona". His words beautifully capture how much his years at the college came to mean to him:

In the spring of 1941, Carolyn and I were called to a new world. For twelve years I had been teaching European history at Colgate University in Hamilton, New York, and had become chair of the history department. In January 1941, we received a letter from Dr. Burgess, Secretary of the Faculty at Pomona College. He said he assumed we knew why he wanted to see us and invited us to meet him in Utica, New York, for a meeting and a luncheon.

We did so and had a pleasant time. He disclosed that I was under serious consideration for succeeding Dr. Edmunds. Some weeks went by, and we had no word from the College. I learned, however, that my name had been suggested by a fellow Rhodes Scholar, Paul Havens, then-President of Wilson College, Chambersburg, Pennsylvania. I had never been to California, and my friend Paul came to Hamilton to tell me of the merits of Pomona.

One evening in April, I received an exciting telephone call from President Edmunds. Telephone calls from California were something new for Carolyn and me.

President Edmunds invited us to come to Claremont for an interview. Furthermore, he suggested that we fly. Neither Carolyn nor I had ever taken a commercial air journey, and we had two young children to think about. We replied that we would come, but by train.

Dates were arranged, and the first leg of the journey was to go to Richmond, Indiana, and leave our children with their maternal grandparents. This done, we took the train to Chicago, where we boarded the Santa Fe Chief for the trip to Claremont. A more lovely and comfortable trip could not have been imagined. We arrived in the morning, and I shall never forget the sunlight on the eucalyptus trees on College Avenue.

We were lodged at the Claremont Inn, whence we were conducted to meet all the elements of the College. We had meals at Frary and Harwood. We met the Administration Committee of the Faculty.

Our impression of all we saw and did was almost overwhelming. We had never seen a student body of such ability and virtue.

When we met with the Trustees, we were ready to come to Claremont, if called. Happily, the Trustees felt favorably, and after our interview with them, I was offered the presidency. I had conferred fully with the President of Colgate, and I was able to give my decision. I accepted on condition that my decision be withheld from the press until I could return home and give my decision to Dr. Cutten, the President of Colgate.

In September 1941, Carolyn and I, with Elizabeth, 5, and John, 2, arrived in Claremont on the Santa Fe Chief. Thus began my 28 years of happy and rewarding service to Pomona.[6]

He assumed the presidency of the college just three months after his thirty-seventh birthday. At his inauguration, Pomona presented honorary D. Litt. degrees to two of his Rhodes Scholar friends and mentors. Frank Aydelotte, American secretary of the Rhodes Trust, who gave an inaugural address, had helped him find his first job; Bernadotte Schmitt was a professor of modern history at the University of Chicago and had been an advisor for Lyon's Ph. D. thesis. Both men had been Rhodes Scholars, members of the class of 1905.

For almost three decades, Wilson Lyon led Pomona. He presided over the college during World War II, watched the GIs return, built a strong faculty, increased the college's physical plant, and protected academic freedom within the campus community, even during the pressures of the McCarthy era. The story of his academic career at Pomona College is well documented in the *History of Pomona College, 1887-1969*, which Pomona's trustees commissioned him to write in the years following his retirement.

Looking back on the steps Wilson Lyon took as his academic career advanced, it is clear that the Rhodes Trust and Rhodes Scholar friends provided the support and professional contacts that made each step possible. His devotion to these friends and to the Rhodes Trust was one of the central facts of his life, and grew from his gratitude for all that his Rhodes associations had made possible for him both personally and professionally.

6. Personal papers of Elizabeth Lyon Webb.

During his years at Pomona, his educational leadership was honored with twelve honorary degrees by colleges and universities throughout the United States. Most significant to note are those awards that recognized his ongoing connection to the worlds and educational opportunities of his youth. Queen Elizabeth II appointed him Honorary Commander of the Most Excellent Order of the British Empire in 1964, in recognition of his ongoing support of the Rhodes Scholarship program. At the University of Chicago, where he received his Ph. D. in 1932, he was the recipient of the Alumni Medal in 1967. In the same year, he was also the recipient of the annual Honor Alumnus award at Jones Junior College, which, while still an agricultural high school, had prepared him for the University of Mississippi. Eight years later, in 1975, the University of Mississippi itself named him an inaugural member of their Alumni Hall of Fame, fifty years after his graduation.

In 1956, while still serving as president of Pomona College, Wilson Lyon became the editor of *The American Oxonian*, the quarterly publication of the American Association of Rhodes Scholars. Until 1962, he added *American Oxonian* editorial tasks and decisions to the diverse and ever changing administrative responsibilities required of him as Pomona's president. Working with Carolyn, whose skills as a proof reader for the *Journal of Modern History* at the University of Chicago were invaluable, he was able to derive great pleasure in creating a publication that helped keep Oxford and the Rhodes Scholar experience alive for its vast network of American alumni.

The movement between the worlds of his Mississippi home and the wider academic communities of England and the United States, that is a hallmark of the experience reflected in his Oxford letters, continued throughout his life. A stop to visit his family in Heidelberg often concluded a trip he made to East Coast colleges and universities, recruiting faculty for Pomona College.

Over those years, Heidelberg was marked by major changes transforming both the economic and social life of the community. Initially change came slowly, and the prospects for the town's future seemed doubtful. Although electric power had finally arrived at the end of 1927, streets remained unpaved, and there was still no pure water system. The basis for the town's economic life was also disappearing. Many timber areas had been logged over; low cotton prices devastated the agricultural basis for the region's economy.

Then, in 1943, everything changed. Spurred on by the knowledge that a prehistoric sea had existed in eastern Mississippi, developers struck oil in its pressured sands. While Wilson Lyon was studying abroad as a Rhodes Scholar, the *Jasper County News* had reported drilling in the area around Bay Springs, Mississippi, about thirty miles away, but no one was prepared for a strike of the size found in Heidelberg. The Heidelberg field, initially 120 acres that included all the land under the town itself, soon had both a producing oil well, Helen Morrison No. 1, and a producing gas well.

An article in the *Jackson Daily News* on November 27, 1949 described Heidelberg as "the only municipality in Mississippi located in an oil field." By 1949 there were thirty-nine wells producing within Heidelberg's corporate limits, with schools and churches benefiting from the discovery, as well as the municipal government. With oil money the town paved its streets, constructed a sewage treatment plant, and a pure water system—all things that Lyon mentioned as desperately needed in his letters from England in the 1920s. By 1950, oil money also brought a home phone system and natural gas for cooking and heating into Heidelberg's homes.

Wilson Lyon always regretted that his own father, who died in 1942, had not lived to see the coming of oil to the community. His family, however, was able to benefit because they, like many other Heidelberg families, retained the mineral rights on their farm land. Willia Wilson lived until 1962. The economic uncertainty that had always clouded her life, and that had led her son to send money home on a regular basis after he returned from England, was lifted for the last twenty years that she was alive.

A twenty-first-century postscript is needed for this story, because the Heidelberg field has had an almost miraculous history. In 1949, geologists predicted that the oil field would have a life of approximately twenty-eight years, and, as predicted, production began to decline in the 1980s and early 1990s. In 1999, however, Denbury Resources, a Texas-based company that acquired the Heidelberg field in 1997, flooded six of its units, allowing oil production to continue. Now Denbury hopes to extend the life of the field even further by using carbon dioxide to extract oil. The carbon dioxide will be transported by pipelines from major reserves near Jackson, site of some ancient volcanoes. Meanwhile, Denbury is extensively developing gas reserves in the Heidelberg field. It is a harvest that farmers in Wilson Lyon's day could never have imagined.

The community itself has not fared as well, though initially there was rapid growth. Heidelberg, with less than 600 residents when Lyon left for England in 1925, grew to 1,112 by 1970. Population in 2000 was only 840. Today, many of the stores that lined the community's single business street are empty, including a general mercantile store, owned by Allen Mixon, where Wilson Lyon worked in the summers during his years at Ole Miss, even tending the store alone so that Allen could take a honeymoon trip.

As is typical in so many of America's small towns, Heidelberg's downtown merchants have been forced to close, their business lost to a strip of stores that has grown up on the edge of town near Interstate 59. This highway, which has ended the isolation imposed on Heidelberg by the dirt roads of Wilson Lyon's youth, has made it possible for Heidelberg to become a comfortable "bedroom" community for many of its residents who work in Laurel, about fifteen miles to the south. It has also, however, changed the shopping patterns of its residents.

In addition, and most significantly, many of those benefiting from Heidelberg's mineral wealth today do not return that wealth to the community. They are descendants of the original Heidelberg residents who profited from the field, but who themselves now often live outside Mississippi and even outside of the South.

Momentous as it was, the discovery of Heidelberg's oil was not the most dramatic social change that would occur in the Mississippi world that Wilson Lyon knew in the 1920s. In 1928, when he returned home from England, no one would have believed that just twenty-six years later, in 1954, the segregated schools that had started him on the path to his Rhodes Scholarship would be declared unconstitutional by the United States Supreme Court. At the University of Mississippi, whose white students had had their rooms cleaned and their meals served by black janitors and waiters in the 1920s, James Meredith enrolled in September, 1962. Though tragic violence accompanied his enrollment, it marked the beginning of the integration of higher education in the state.

Just as an end to the legality of segregated schools could not have been imagined in 1928, so no one could have imagined that the restrictions effectively prohibiting African Americans from voting would be swept away by the Voting Rights Act of 1965. No longer would the white circuit clerk have the right to register a local hero like Lyon *in absentia,* as he assumed in a letter written to his family from Oxford on February 16, 1926. By 1965, Wilson Lyon's son John, a young attorney with the Civil Rights Division of the Justice Department, was in Mississippi enforcing the Federal Voting Rights Act to ensure that all Mississippians, no matter what the color of their skin, could vote.

Wilson Lyon applauded the end of segregation in the South and was saddened when the end of school segregation in Heidelberg led not to integrated public schools but to the founding of a white academy in the early 1970s. However, when he came home for a visit, he was family, never a critic; an accommodator, never an agitator. To the end of his life, he was one of Heidelberg's most beloved native sons. When he spoke at the town's Centennial celebration in 1984, he named again the teachers who had started him on the right educational path when he entered the white Heidelberg school as a six year old. Though he grew up in a place where educational opportunity for young people was severely limited, he never forgot that it was this place, and his family, whose belief in his abilities had set him on the pathway to educational achievement.

As we read the letters that have inspired this portrait of Wilson Lyon, we picture the settings where they were written and the settings to which they were sent and are reminded of the intense social change and upheaval that both the United States, England and Europe have experienced since they were written. The Confederate monument, dedicated by Wilson Lyon's mother in Heidelberg when he was only seven years old, stands today in a circle in front of the town's community library. But today's Heidelberg, with its racially-integrated library and police force, reflects the dramatic social changes that have come to the community since that day in September, 1911, when the monument was dedicated. The Rhodes Scholarship, now open to women and accessible to those of all races, reflects a similar movement away from the male exclusiveness and white privilege that marked the world of the 1920s.

It is good to reflect on these positive changes in moments when the violence inherent in much of contemporary society threatens to overwhelm us. Wilson Lyon's youthful story gives us hope. It reminds us again that, in a vastly imperfect world, there is still a place for an individual of character and intelligence to make a difference.

From Heidelberg, to Ellisville, to Oxford, Mississippi, and then to Oxford, England, his experiences provided opportunities for personal growth that in turn shaped his professional career. Throughout his life, Wilson Lyon, teacher and college president, worked to actualize his fundamental beliefs: that freedom of thought, possibly first learned as he talked about Darwin with his Grandfather Lyon, was necessary for the pursuit of knowledge, and that informed and compassionate opinion was the necessary requisite for creating a civil society. His education, begun in Mississippi, prepared him for a life of service to America's academic communities, and he treasured every phase of it, beginning with his days in the Heidelberg primary school. Education opened to him the "world of the American University, to which I am so attached" as he described it in a letter to his mother written on September 8, 1926. That world became his true home. It was a home that found its fullest expression in his twenty-eight-year tenure as president of Pomona College.

DIRECTORY OF NAMES

American Ambassador: Alanson B. Houghton (1863-1941)

Manager of his family business, the Corning Glassworks in Corning, New York. Appointed ambassador to Great Britain by President Calvin Coolidge, a post he filled from 1925 to 1929, after serving from 1922 to 1925 as ambassador to Germany.

Astor, Nancy Langhorne (1879-1964)

The American wife of Waldorf Astor, heir to the family fur-trading and real-estate fortunes. Both Waldorf Astor and his father were American ex-patriates, and active in British politics. When Waldorf Astor succeeded his father in the House of Lords in 1919, Nancy campaigned for the seat he vacated, and became the first woman elected to the House of Commons. She was a pacifist, a champion of women's rights, the rights of children, and an advocate for the temperance movement. She remained in the Commons until 1945.

Aunt Vera: Vera Orline Wilson Smith (1881-1933)

Younger sister of Wilson Lyon's mother, Willia, and sixth of the eight children of Thomas E. Wilson and Josephine Yongue Wilson. Educated at the Garlandville Academy, Vera Wilson taught music at a public school near Bay Springs in Jasper County before her marriage to John Campbell Smith in 1908.

The family lived first on a farm outside Collins, Mississippi, and then in Collins itself, moving in part so that the children could attend better schools. In 1926 the family moved to Wiggins, Mississippi, where John Smith managed the pickle factory. Vera and John Smith lost two children between the birth of their son Murray, and their daughter Orline. One, a girl, died at birth. A son, born three years later, died of a respiratory infection when he was less than three. It is undoubtedly these deaths, as well as Vera Smith's own illnesses, to which Wilson Lyon alludes in his letters when talking about his aunt's hard life. She died of cancer in 1933.

Aydelotte, Frank (1880-1956)

A graduate of Indiana University at age twenty, Frank Aydelotte already held an M. A. from Harvard when he was elected a Rhodes Scholar in 1905. At Oxford he studied English literature while in residence at Brasenose College (1905-07), but did not receive his B. Litt. degree until 1913 because he left Oxford after two years to be married, something that was not permissible under the original provisions for the scholarship in Cecil Rhodes' will.

After teaching at Indiana University and MIT, he became president of Swarthmore College (1921-1940). In 1918, he was named American secretary to the Rhodes Trustees, a position he held until 1952. His creative and innovative thinking led to a reorganization of the method for selecting American scholars, and ensured that all who received the scholarship would be chosen as the result of a highly competitive process.

Barber, Harold (1904–?)

Ole Miss classmate of Wilson Lyon who took over his father's real estate business in Gulfport, Mississippi. Barber was circulation manager of *The Mississippian* (1923-24) when Lyon was editor, and was assistant editor-in-chief of the 1925 *Ole Miss*, the college yearbook, where he worked closely with other staff members, including Wilson Lyon, who edited the Athletics Department of the book.

Belsheim, Edmund Olaf (1905-1991)

A graduate of the University of North Dakota, Edmund Belsheim was in residence as a Rhodes Scholar at St. John's College (1927-30). He received a B. A. in jurisprudence (1st Cl.) in 1929 and a B. C. L. (2nd Cl.) in 1930. The following year he earned a J. S. D. at the University of Chicago Law School and then practiced law in Chicago until 1937. During the remainder of his professional career he alternated between practicing law and teaching law at universities in Tennessee, Virginia, Nebraska, and Oregon.

Bemis, Samuel Flagg (1891-1973)

After receiving a Ph. D. in history and international law at Harvard in 1916, Bemis began teaching history at George Washington University in 1924 and became department head in 1925. In 1926 he received the Pulitzer Prize in History for *Pinckney's Treaty: A Study of America's Advantage from Europe's Distress, 1783-1800.* At the time he met Wilson Lyon in Madrid in the spring of 1928, he was on leave from George Washington University (1927-1929), leading the European Mission of the Library of Congress.

In 1934, Bemis left George Washington for Yale University. There he was named Sterling Professor of Diplomatic History and Inter-American Relations in 1945, a chair he held until his retirement in 1960. He received a Pulitzer Prize in Biography in 1950 for *John Quincy Adams and the Foundations of American Foreign Policy.*

While still on the faculty at George Washington University, Bemis reviewed the manuscript for Lyon's first book, *Louisiana in French Diplomacy, 1759-1804,* which was published in 1934. That book had its beginning in the B. Litt. thesis that Wilson Lyon was researching in the spring of 1928, when he and Bemis first met.

Benjamin, Hattie May (1904–1982)

A native of McComb, Mississippi, Hattie May Benjamin, like Wilson Lyon, was active in a number of campus organizations at Ole Miss. During her senior year she was president of the YWCA and secretary of the Associated Student Body. A citation in the 1925 *Ole Miss* notes that "of all the girls at Ole Miss there is none who is as constant, lovable, and true as Hattie May. She is ever ready to give a helping hand to all. A girl who showers love, friendship, and goodness on all who come in contact with her. She has many friends at Ole Miss who will miss her next year." She and her husband, John Egger, spent time together with Wilson and Carolyn Lyon when they returned to Ole Miss in 1975 for the fiftieth reunion of the class of 1925.

Bilbo, Theodore G. (1877-1947)

Bilbo's life in Mississippi state politics included service in the state Senate (1908-1912), a term as lieutenant governor (1912-1916), and two terms as governor (1916-1920, 1928-1932). As governor of Mississippi he was a populist. During his second term, his plan to move Ole Miss to Jackson was defeated, but he exerted political pressure that led to the removal of Alfred E. Hume, the Ole Miss chancellor who had opposed his plan.

Bondurant, Alexander (1865-1937)

A graduate of Hampden-Sydney where he received both B. A. and M. A. degrees, Alexander Bondurant took a second M. A. at Harvard. He joined the faculty at Ole Miss in 1889, where he taught Latin language and literature. While at Harvard, he became convinced of the value of intercollegiate football to campus life. In 1893 he organized the first team at Ole Miss, serving as its coach during the early years when the sport was struggling to establish itself on campus. He also chose red and blue for the college colors—red for Harvard and blue for Yale.

Under Dr. Bondurant, Ole Miss greatly expanded both its undergraduate and graduate Latin curriculum, a subject studied by all Ole Miss students who were awarded Rhodes Scholarships.

Borsch, Reuben August (1903-1983)

A graduate of Illinois Wesleyan University, Reuben Borsch was elected a Rhodes Scholar from Illinois. At Oxford he was in residence at Lincoln College (1925-28) and received a B. A. in jurisprudence (2nd Cl.) in 1927 and a B. C. L. (2nd Cl.) in 1928. He practiced law in Chicago throughout his professional career.

Brown, Calvin S. (1866-1945)

Brown taught modern languages at Ole Miss. Girault Jones reports that "it is said that his family was required to speak a different language at meals . . . I suppose predetermined by him. I know his son was proficient enough to hold a good teaching position on graduation."

Callaghan, Allan Robert (1903-1993)

A native of New South Wales, John Callaghan, whose father was a sheep rancher, was a graduate of the University of Sydney, with a B. Sc. in agriculture. He was in residence as a Rhodes Scholar at St. John's from 1925 to 1928, receiving a B. Sc. in biology in 1926 and a D. Phil. in biology in 1928. On returning to Australia, he had a distinguished professional career in agriculture, holding a number of governmental administrative positions.

Cecil, Lord Hugh (1869-1956)

At the time he spoke at the annual Rhodes dinner in June of 1926, Lord Cecil was member of Parliament for Oxford, a post he held from 1910 to 1937, with an interruption during World War I when he served as a lieutenant in the Royal Flying Corps.

The chancellor [England]: 1st Viscount George Cave (1856-1928)

The honorary head of Oxford University, elected by university graduates and academics. Named chancellor in 1925, Cave, a lawyer, was an Oxford graduate and member of St. John's College. At the time of his election, he was serving as Lord High Chancellor of England, in the government of Stanley Baldwin. He had also served for two years as Counsel to Oxford University.

The chancellor [Mississippi]: Alfred E. Hume (1866-1950); chancellor 1924-30, 1932-35

Born in Beech Grove, Tennessee, Hume studied at Vanderbilt, earning three degrees, including a Doctor of Science, before joining the Ole Miss faculty in 1890 to teach mathematics and astronomy. He was chancellor from 1924 to 1930 and from 1932 to 1935. As chancellor, he made many contributions to the university, adding substantially to its physical plant and establishing its graduate program as a separate administrative entity. His first term was initially marked by severe social restrictions on campus: students could not smoke, drink, dance, wear shorts, or play tennis on Sunday, and were required to go to daily chapel. These restrictions were removed, however, before his term was over. During his second term, he was a guiding presence, helping reestablish the academic integrity of Ole Miss after its reputation had been tarnished by politics during the chancellorship of John Powers (1930-32).

Writing in the *University of Mississippi Alumni Review* in the Winter, 1974 issue, A. B. Lewis provided some personal reflections about Hume. He was often called "Little Allie" because he was very short. Personally, he was courteous, but reserved. He was an excellent teacher, with a first-class mind, and would not accept anything but a student's best. "It was not so much that he demanded the best of you in his classes. It was that you were afraid not to do your best."

Hume is perhaps best known for the steps he took to prevent Governor Bilbo from persuading legislators to move the Ole Miss campus from Oxford to Jackson. In the winter of 1928, he organized a visit of state legislators to Oxford. In a powerful speech, he appealed convincingly to them by presenting the university as a symbol of the state's pride in the sacrifices of its Confederate sons, particularly those students who served in the "University Greys".

The chancellor [Mississippi]: John Neely Powers (1869-1939); chancellor 1914-24, 1930-32

Powers was appointed chancellor of the University of Mississippi in 1914, serving his first term until 1924. During this term, he guided the university through a period of growing enrollment, when much of the physical plant was deteriorating and faculty morale was low. Under him, a number of dormitories and classroom buildings were erected on the campus. He created the departments of music and home economics and established the School of Commerce and Business Administration.

His dismissal by the trustees in 1924 came after the election of Henry Whitfield as governor. Alfred E. Hume was named by Whitfield to replace Powers, just as

Wilson Lyon began his senior year. Hume served until 1930 when Bilbo pressured the trustees to reappoint Powers, who held the post of chancellor until 1932. In his second term, politics were injected forcibly into the academic affairs of the university, leading to contentious faculty appointments and dismissals and a loss of accreditation for Ole Miss by the Southern Association of Colleges and Schools.

Powers' lack of a formal academic degree was undoubtedly one of the reasons that Wilson Lyon, in his Rhodes Scholar correspondence with Girault Jones, expressed the view that he did not think Powers was qualified to be chancellor at Ole Miss. In fact, Lyon was indebted to Powers, since it was he who supported Lyon's initial desire to report news of the university in Mississippi newspapers.

Cole, George Douglas Howard (1889-1959)

Educated at Balliol College, Oxford, Cole was a proponent of the ideas of the Fabian Socialists, a group founded in 1884 and dedicated to social reform through gradual change. They advocated a minimum wage, urged the creation of a National Health Service, and argued in favor of abolishing hereditary peers. Many Fabians were involved in the formation of the British Labor party in 1900, and Fabian ideas and concepts influenced the political policy-making of Labor politicians. Cole worked for the Fabian Society for six years before coming to Oxford, where he became a reader in economics at University College, Oxford, a post he held at the time Wilson Lyon was studying at St. John's College on his Rhodes Scholarship. He was recognized as a distinguished political theorist, economist, and historian.

Costin, William Conrad (1893-1970)

From *The American Oxonian*, April, 1971, 81-82: "With the death of Dr. W. C. Costin on October 6, 1970, St. John's College lost one who, as undergraduate, Fellow, Dean, President, and elder statesman, had been a leader in its life for more than half a century. Born in 1893 and educated at the Reading School, William Conrad Costin was an Exhibitioner at St. John's when he left for military service in World War I. He distinguished himself as a Captain in The Gloucester Regiment and was awarded the Military Cross. Returning to Oxford after the war, Costin received a first class in Modern History in 1920, and was elected to a Fellowship at St. John's in 1922.

"Thereafter, the College was to be his life. As tutor and later Dean, he sought to strengthen its academic life, develop its facilities, and expand its financial resources. Costin was one of those most responsible for the impressive growth of St. John's, particularly after 1945. His lifetime of devotion to the College reached a fitting climax in his unanimous election as President in 1957. Blessed with robust health and amazing energy, he led in expanding the numbers of Fellows, undergraduates, and graduates, and added to the College quadrangles some of the most remarkable buildings in Oxford. As a Fellow he had contributed much to the wise management of the finances of St. John's which made this possible. To Costin, all these interests and activities were but means to the enhancement of learning, the advancement of the College, and of Oxford.

"As a scholar he was indefatigable, publishing works on Great Britain and China in the nineteenth century, and Law and the Constitution in Great Britain after 1660. His labor of greatest love was *The History of St. John's College, 1598-1860,* which he published in 1958.

"To the University he brought the same devotion and wisdom he gave his College. Of the many Oxford bodies on which he served, that which interested him most was the Curators of the Bodleian, of which he was a member for many years. He was an ardent supporter of the Rhodes Scholarships, seeing that St. John's always had a good complement of Scholars and himself making a point of knowing individual Scholars and thoughtfully assisting them in their adjustment to the College and to Oxford. He was a close friend of Sir Francis and Lady Wylie, and he worked closely with their successors at Rhodes House.

"Above all, W. C. Costin was a college tutor and a truly distinguished one. Genuinely interested in people, he sought to know his pupils and he extended his friendship to them. When President, he annually entertained all members of the College in small groups in the Lodgings, the first-year men at breakfast, the second-year men at luncheon, and the third -year men at dinner. His pupils later filled the most eminent positions at home and abroad, and he took great pride in their achievements. As he remained unmarried, they and the College were in many ways members of his family. Lester Pearson, Dean Rusk, and Michael Stewart were among his tutees, and there was a time when a meeting of the Prime Minister of Canada, the Secretary for Foreign Affairs of Great Britain, and the Secretary of State of the United States would have been a reunion of old St. John's men.

"For those of us who knew Costin over so many years, his passing is a deeply regretted break with a much loved past. Our visits to Oxford led us first to his rooms in the College, to the President's Lodgings, or after 1963 to his house at 4 Wellington Place. Our families came to know and love him and through him to share something of our youth. He was for us all the very best of Oxford."

Crone, Neil Louis (1903-1985)

A graduate of Grinnell College, Neil Crone was elected a Rhodes Scholar from Iowa in 1925. He was in residence at Merton College (1925-29) and received a B. A. in physiology (1st Cl.) in 1927 and a D. Phil. in pathology in 1929. After receiving his M. D. from Harvard Medical School in 1931, he had a distinguished medical teaching and administrative career at both the Harvard Medical School and Harvard Business School.

Dance, Marjorie Violet (1905-?)

Educated at County High School, Braintree, Essex, Marjorie Dance matriculated into Oxford University from the Society of Home Students (St. Anne's College since 1952), on October 15, 1924. She received her B. A. in modern history (3rd Cl.) on November 26, 1927. Her father was a nurseryman in Braintree. Her college has no record of her activities after she left Oxford, with the exception of the fact that her married name was Mrs. C. J. Lake.

At the time of her residence in Oxford, the Society of Home Students, formed in the late nineteenth century, housed women who could not afford to live in an Oxford College. Their educational program was coordinated by a female administrator/principal, and they participated fully in the life of the university. At the time of Marjorie Dance's residence, tutors of the Society of Home Students specialized in the humanities. Today the college, now named St. Anne's College, offers opportunities for study in the sciences and social sciences as well. It is now a coeducational institution.

Fearnley, George Martin (1906-1937)

George Fearnley studied at The Grammar School in Ilkley prior to matriculating at St. John's College on October 11, 1924. He received his B. A. (4th Cl.) in jurisprudence on October 20, 1927, and his M. A. on June 23, 1932. (The Oxford M. A. was a purchased degree and required no further study). While in residence at St. John's he was a member of the college debating society, which is probably where he and Wilson Lyon first became acquainted. In 1926-27 he also played on the college rugby XV.

His professional career included work for the Manchester Corporation, where he began in 1931, and became Prosecuting Solicitor by 1935. At the end of his life he was working as Deputy Town Clerk in Exeter. His untimely death was caused by acute appendicitis.

Gray, Franklin Dingwall (1904-1990)

A graduate of the University of Minnesota, Frank Gray was in residence as a Rhodes Scholar at Hertford College (1925-28), receiving a B. A. in jurisprudence (2nd Cl.) in 1927 and a B. C. L. (2nd Cl.) in 1928. He practiced law throughout his professional life in Minneapolis, a partner in Gray, Plant, Mooty, Mooty, and Bennett. He and Wilson Lyon maintained a close friendship throughout their lives, and their families traveled together to Oxford for the fiftieth anniversary of the founding of the Rhodes Trust in 1953 and the eightieth anniversary of the founding of the Rhodes Trust in 1983.

Halasz de Dabas, Michael (1906-?)

Almost no information, beyond that provided in Wilson Lyon's letters, remains about Michael Halasz. In the matriculation form on file in the Oxford University Archives, he stated that he studied at Pazmany Peter University in Budapest. He was the first son of Maurice Halasz de Dabas, who was part of a family of large landholders, and a member of the Hungarian Parliament. Michael Halasz matriculated from Hertford College at Oxford on October 10, 1925, but there is no record of his having sat for any examinations.

The reasons for Michael Halasz studying at Oxford are never made clear by Lyon's letters, nor is his course of study identified. World War II, and the postwar takeover of Hungary by a Communist government, led to the confiscation of the Halasz landholdings. For some time, according to Ellen Gray, Michael Halasz worked in Hungary as a bricklayer. He may eventually have gone to England. His

1946 letter to Wilson Lyon, referenced in Chapter Three, describes the devastating losses that the Halasz family experienced during the postwar period.

Ham, Edward Billings (1902-1965)

A graduate of Bowdoin College, Ed Ham was elected a Rhodes Scholar from Maine in 1923. He was in residence at Trinity College (1923-27), receiving a D. Phil. in French literature in 1927, after taking a year's leave of absence to complete an M. A. at Harvard. He taught briefly at Harvard, Princeton, and Yale before moving to the University of Michigan where he taught for twenty-two years in the Department of French (1941-63). The last years of his life (1963-65) were spent teaching at Alameda State and California State College.

Hart, John Lathrop Jerome (1904-1986)

Hart graduated from Harvard in 1925. At Oxford he received a B. A. (2nd Cl.) in jurisprudence in 1927, and a B. C. L. (2nd Cl.) in 1928. An avid outdoorsman, he was active in both the mountaineering and ski clubs while at Oxford. His professional career was spent as a lawyer in Denver, Colorado.

Havens, Paul Swain (1903-1980)

A graduate of Princeton, Paul Havens was a Rhodes Scholar from New Jersey, in residence at University College (1925-28). He received a B. A. (2nd Cl.) in English language and literature in 1927, and a B. C. L. (2nd Cl.) in 1928. He was assistant professor of English at Scripps College, in Claremont, California, and a member of the graduate faculty of the Claremont Colleges from 1930 to 1936. In 1936 he became president of Wilson College in Chambersburg, Pennsylvania, where he remained until his retirement in 1970. It was he who, late in 1940, suggested Wilson Lyon to the Pomona College Board of Trustees as a possible candidate for the presidency of Pomona College.

Jackson, Harriet Jemima (1904-1998)

Harriet Jackson, the daughter of a doctor, was a native of Water Valley, Mississippi. Entering Ole Miss in 1921, she took just three years to complete her B. A. and graduated in 1924. She received an M. A. in French from Ole Miss in 1936. In 1949 she joined the faculty as assistant dean of women and instructor in modern languages, and was promoted to assistant professor of modern languages in 1957, a post she held until her retirement in 1970. At her death she left $345,300 to the university, to be divided evenly among the School of Medicine, College of Liberal Arts, and Friends of the Library. The gift reflected her lifelong devotion to Ole Miss and its students.

Jiggitts, Louis Meredith (1899-1945)

Elected a Rhodes Scholar from Ole Miss in 1919, Jiggetts was a resident of St. John's College (1920-23), receiving a B. A. in jurisprudence (2nd Cl.) in 1923. Returning to Mississippi, he was awarded a law degree (L. L. B.) in 1924 at the Ole Miss Law School. He practiced law in Jackson, Mississippi from 1924 to 1940, serving as city prosecuting attorney from 1926 to 1928. From 1928 to 1940 he was the Mississippi State Supreme Court reporter, and was a lecturer at Jackson School of Law from 1932 to 1940. He died as a result of injuries sustained in the Pacific theater in World War II, and was awarded a Bronze Star for his war service.

Jones, Girault McArthur (1904-1998)

Girualt Jones, Wilson Lyon's closest Ole Miss friend, grew up in Woodville, Mississippi where his father, Ackland Hartley Jones, practiced law. He was the oldest of nine boys; the family later adopted a girl. After graduating from the University of Mississippi in 1925, he received a degree in theology from the University of the South in Sewanee, Tennessee, in 1928 and was ordained an Episcopal deacon in June of 1928. His first wife, Virginia Wallace, whom he married in 1930, died of a brain tumor seven months later. In July, 1935 he married Kathleen Platt, who was an Episcopal student worker at the Florida State College for Women.

Jones began his ministry in Mississippi, becoming rector of Trinity Church in Pass Christian in 1931. In 1936 he moved to Louisiana, where he served as rector of St. Andrew's Church in New Orleans and was also the Episcopal chaplain at Tulane. In 1949 he was appointed the seventh bishop of the Episcopal Diocese of Louisiana, a post in which he served with distinction until his retirement in 1969.

The University of the South was blessed with Jones' leadership in a variety of ways throughout his long life. He served three terms on the university's Board of Regents, and was elected sixteenth chancellor of the university in 1967. From 1981 to 1982 he was interim Dean of the School of Theology at Sewanee. Jones and his wife retired to a home in Sewanee, which he named *Meanwhile*, a reminder that this earthly home of ours is just a temporary home until we find our true home in eternity. The spirit of joyful realism suggested by the name epitomizes all that made Girault Jones the caring and compassionate leader and friend that drew Wilson Lyon and so many others to him throughout his life.

Jug

Nickname for Wilson Lyon's college roommate, Girault Jones. For full biography, see above. A full explanation of his nickname can be found in the prefatory material for the letter Wilson Lyon wrote to him on July 12, 1926 from Vienna.

Kerr, Philip Henry, 11th marquess of Lothian (1882-1940)

Kerr had been named general secretary of the Rhodes Trust in June of 1925, just three months before he spoke to Wilson Lyon and his American Rhodes Scholar classmates in New York. From 1905 to 1910 he had served as a colonial administrator in South Africa. Returning to England, he allied himself with the Liberal Party, and was Prime Minister David Lloyd George's private secretary (1919-21) and an active participant in the Paris Peace Conference (1919) that concluded World War I. He was a great proponent of the idea that Britain and the United States, working together, could insure international peace. In the context of this belief, he felt that it had been Rhodes' intention to use Rhodes Scholarships to encourage unity among all "English-speaking races", creating leaders across the globe who would work together to prevent war. Kerr proved to be an effective administrator of the Rhodes Trust. The decision to increase the Rhodes annual stipend to £400 came after he had done a complete review of the financial status of the Trust. He served as General Secretary until 1939, when he resigned to become the British ambassador to Washington.

Leighton, Lawrence Brock (1904-1966)

Leighton graduated from Bowdoin College in 1925. At Oxford he was a resident of Trinity College (1925-28) where he read philosophy and ancient history but did not take a degree. Returning to the United States, he received an M. A. in classics from Harvard in 1933. His professional career was spent as an instructor, lecturer, or tutor, in classics and literature, at a variety of East Coast colleges and private schools.

Lester, Walter Hugh Drane (1899-1941)

A graduate of Batesville High School, Drane Lester received both a B. A. and an M. A. from the University of Mississippi before being named a Rhodes Scholar in 1922. During a year's leave of absence (1924-25) he returned to the University of Mississippi where he earned a law degree. In 1925, when he and Wilson Lyon sailed on the *Lancastria*, he was bound again for Oxford to complete his studies in law. He received a B. C. L. (3rd Cl) in 1926. With two years' experience of Oxford life, Lester was a reassuring companion and guide for Wilson Lyon as he took up his Rhodes Scholarship in the fall of 1925. After leaving Oxford in 1926, he returned to Memphis, where he practiced law before joining the FBI in 1932, where he was a special agent, supervisor, and inspector at the time of his death in an automobile accident.

Lewis, Arthur Beverly (1901-2000)

A. B. Lewis entered the University of Mississippi in the fall of 1918, after graduating from Jackson High School. At Ole Miss, he studied under many of the same professors who taught Wilson Lyon, particularly Dr. Alfred Hume in mathematics, and Dr. Milden in Greek and Latin. He, Jug Jones, and Wilson Lyon were close friends during the years they spent together on the Ole Miss campus. He majored in physics, completing his B. A. in physics in 1923, and his M. A. in physics in 1925. He also served as an instructor in physics during the 1924-25 academic year.

As Wilson Lyon left Mississippi to study at St. John's College in Oxford, A. B. Lewis went to Washington, D. C. where he began work at the National Bureau of Standards in the summer of 1925 and enrolled at Johns Hopkins. There he received his Ph. D. in physics in 1930 and married Alma Gochenour later that month. A love for Ole Miss and the desire to teach led him back to Mississippi in the fall of 1936 as an associate professor of physics and mathematics, with a half-time appointment in each department. In 1941 he was named professor of physics and astronomy, becoming chairman of the Department of Physics in 1952. In 1957 he was named dean of the College of Liberal Arts, a post he held until his retirement in 1969. He continued to teach part-time for two years after his retirement, remaining in Oxford until his death in 2000. The physics building at Ole Miss is named Lewis Hall in his honor.

Long, Huey (1893-1935)

A radical social reformer and populist, Long was governor of Louisiana from 1928 to 1932. He assumed almost dictatorial control over state affairs during his time in office, and his meddling in the affairs of Louisiana Polytechnic at the time Wilson Lyon was hired was just one small example of this tendency.

McDougal, Myres Smith "Mac" or "Mack" (1906-1998)

A native of Booneville, Mississippi, Myres McDougal was a graduate of the University of Mississippi where he received B. A. and M. A. degrees in political science (1926) and a law degree (1927), before being named a Rhodes Scholar in 1927. He received a B. A. in jurisprudence (1st Cl.) in 1929 and a B. C. L. (1st Cl.) in 1930. During his distinguished professional career at Yale University, he redefined the study and teaching of international law, and was an internationally acclaimed legal scholar.

In 1923, McDougal joined the staff of *The Mississippian* when Lyon was editor. He wrote a weekly column titled "Did You Know" that provided vignettes of events in the history of the university.

In a letter written to Wilson Lyon's widow, Carolyn, on May 7, 1991, McDougal recalled his friendship with Lyon, which dated from their high school days on the Mississippi stock judging team: "The thought of you brings back many happy memories that you are too young to share, of when Wilson and I were boys in Mississippi, judging livestock at A&M, while planning for a very different career at Ole Miss. I subscribe entirely to the thesis that early friends are the best friends. Certainly I had few to whom I felt closer than Wilson. He did much for me."

Milden, Alfred W. (1868-?)

Professor of Greek language and literature (in translation) at Ole Miss. Both Wilson Lyon and Girault Jones studied with him. Jones remembers him fondly as "an excitable little man" and notes that "he made the dullest of us come alive". In addition to his teaching, Dr. Milden served as Dean of the College of Liberal Arts from 1920 to 1936. He had been educated outside the South, with a B. A. from the University of Toronto and a Ph. D. from Johns Hopkins.

Moffatt, Dr. James (1870-1944)

A prominent Scottish theologian and church historian, Moffatt is best known for his modern translations of the Old and New Testaments, which appeared as the complete Moffatt Bible in 1926. From 1915 to 1927, he was professor of church history at the United Free Church College in Glasgow. He became Washburn Professor of Church History at Union Theological Seminary in New York City in the fall of 1927, and remained there until his retirement in 1939. Moffatt was obviously culling his library in preparation for his move to New York City when he offered books to Wilson Lyon and Frank Gray during their visit in the summer of 1927.

Murphree, Dennis (1886-1949)

Elected lieutenant governor of Mississippi in 1923, Dennis Murphree became governor when Governor Henry L. Whitfield died in office on March 18, 1927. Murphree continued to support Whitfield's efforts to reduce spending and fund Mississippi state government on a "pay as you go" basis. He spent most of his first months in the governor's office dealing with the catastrophic consequences of the great Mississippi flood of 1927. His time in office, however, was brief, since Theodore Bilbo successfully won the second Democratic primary and was elected governor in the fall of 1927. Murphree's subsequent bids for the governorship were unsuccessful in 1935 and 1943. However, he was elected lieutenant governor both in 1931 and 1939, assisting Mississippi governors who guided the state through the Great Depression.

"A new man from South Dakota": Clayton Bion Craig (1904-1978)

A graduate of the University of South Dakota, Clayton Craig was in residence at Pembroke College (1926-29), receiving a P. P. E. B. A. (3rd Cl.) in 1929. After a brief stint in teaching and business in New York City and Cincinnati, he devoted the rest of his professional life to the affairs of the Christian Science Church in Boston and Cincinnati.

"The new Rhodes scholar from Tennessee": Edgar Elliot Beaty (1904-1975)

A native of Okalona, Mississippi, Edgar Beaty graduated from the University of the South in Sewanee, Tennessee, and then was selected as a Rhodes Scholar from Tennessee. Beaty was in residence at Pembroke College (1926-29). He received a jurisprudence B. A. (3rd Cl.) in 1929. After practicing law in Okalona for three years, he served as an attorney and manager with the Federal Land Bank in New Orleans (1932-50) and as an attorney and counselor for the United States Navy (1950-72).

"An old Mississippi Rhodes scholar": William Luther Finger (1897-1991)

A graduate of the University of Mississippi, William Finger was in residence at St. John's College (1916-21), with absences for military service in World War I. He received a B. A. in history (shortened). From 1927 to 1933, he was an assistant commercial attaché in the United States Foreign Commerce Service attached to the U.S. Embassy in Paris.

Rhoads, Owen Brooke "Dusty" (1902-1987)

A graduate of Haverford College, Owen Rhoads (always referred to by Wilson Lyon as "Dusty") was in residence at New College (1925-28) after being elected as a Rhodes Scholar from Pennsylvania. He received a B. A. in jurisprudence (2nd Cl.) in 1927 and practiced law in Philadelphia throughout his professional career.

"Rhodes scholar from Connecticut": John Cecil Rushworth Whiteley (1904-1959)

A graduate of West Philadelphia High School and Wesleyan University in Middletown, Connecticut, Whiteley was in residence at Wadham College (1925-27), receiving a B. A. in history (3rd Cl.) in 1927.

After working for National City Bank of New York in both Paris and New York, he spent the remainder of his professional career in managerial positions with Scott Paper in Pennsylvania, Brunswick Pulp and Paper Company in Georgia, Marinette Paper Company in Wisconsin, and Ford International, Incorp. in New York City, where he was manager of the Operations Credit Department at the time of his death.

Robinson, Thomas Hoben (1903-1993)

A Canadian from Gibson, New Brunswick, Thomas Robinson graduated from Acadia University and was appointed a Rhodes Scholar from Nova Scotia. He was in residence at St. John's College (1925-28), receiving a B. Litt. degree in history in 1928. He and Wilson Lyon became acquainted during their first months in Oxford, and shared "digs" together in town during their third year at St. John's. Robinson taught first sociology and then economics at Colgate University in Hamilton, New York from 1928 to 1942. It was he who learned of the opening in the Department of History that led to Wilson Lyon's job at Colgate in the fall of 1929. In 1936, he received a Ph. D. in economics from the University of Chicago. Returning to Canada in 1942, he became assistant director of National Selective Service at the Department of Labor in Ottawa. In 1943 he moved to Montreal where he served as manager of industrial relations for the Canadian International Paper Company for twenty-five years.

The Lyons and the Robinsons and their young families lived across the street from each other in Hamilton, New York, during the years that Lyon taught at Colgate.

Ryder, Lady Frances (1888-1965)

The daughter of the 5th Earl of Harrowby, Lady Frances Ryder grew up in an affluent family. During World War I, her mother opened their London home to military personnel from Commonwealth Nations who were on leave. Lady Frances Ryder continued this tradition after the war, formally organizing the Dominions Fellowship Trust, which received funding from the Rhodes Trust since it offered hospitality to Rhodes Scholars during term breaks.

Sams, Robert Shields (1905-1969)

A native of Georgia, Bob Sams was a classmate of Paul Havens at Princeton. He was elected a Rhodes Scholar from Georgia in 1925 and was in residence at Merton College 1925-27, receiving a B. A. in jurisprudence (3rd Cl.) in 1928. He spent his professional life in Atlanta where he practiced law from 1928 until his death in 1969.

Skewes, James Henry (1888-1958)

Born in Cornwall, England, James Skewes was brought to the United States in 1891 by his parents. In 1922 he became editor of *The Meridian Star*. He also was an owner of the *Laurel Leader-Call* for over twenty years, as well as being associated in ownership with newspapers in New Mexico, Colorado and Missouri. Active in the affairs of Meridian and the state throughout his professional life, he served as president of the Mississippi Press Association during part of the time that Wilson Lyon studied abroad.

Smith, Murray (1909-2007)

Wilson Lyon's first cousin, Murray Smith, was born in Collins, Mississippi, and educated in schools there and in Wiggins, where the family moved in the summer of 1925. He received a B. S. from Mississippi State in 1932. Following army service in World War II, he returned to Mississippi, working initially as an aviation forecaster at the Jackson airport. In 1955 he was transferred to New Orleans, where he continued as an aviation forecaster until his retirement in 1972. In 1971, he was named "outstanding line forecaster". His love of tennis, to which Wilson Lyon introduced him in the summer of 1924, continued throughout his life; he and his wife, Willie Mae, played in countless senior tennis tournaments after his retirement.

"My supervisor": R. B. Mowat (?-1941)

R. B. Mowat was a tutor in history at Corpus Christi College at Oxford University at the time he supervised Wilson Lyon's B. Litt. thesis research. His book *The History of European Diplomacy 1815-1914* made him particularly well versed in the field covered by Lyon's thesis topic. It also qualified him to help direct Lyon's research to areas that would allow him to make an original contribution to the study of Napoleon and Louisiana. In 1928, Mowat left Oxford after being appointed professor of history at Bristol University. He was returning to Britain, after lecturing in the United States for the Carnegie Trust when he was killed in a military plane crash in Prestwick, Scotland.

"My supervisors": R. B. Mowat and Robert McNutt McElroy (1872-1959)

McElroy was Haimsworth Professor in American History at Oxford University at the time he advised Wilson Lyon to write his B. Litt. thesis on "The Sale of Louisiana to the United States". The actual writing of the thesis was supervised by R. B. Mowat. McElroy came to Oxford after teaching at Princeton University from 1898 to 1916. During the 1920s and 1930s he taught at Cambridge University and other universities in the United Kingdom as well as at Oxford.

Swearingen, Mack Buckley (1902-1969)

A graduate of Jackson High School and Millsaps College, Mack Swearingen was elected a Rhodes Scholar from Mississippi in 1924, the year that Wilson Lyon interviewed for the scholarship for the first time. He was in residence at Exeter College (1924-27) and received a B. A. degree in history (3rd Cl.) in 1927.

Returning to the United States, he received a Ph. D. in history at the University of Chicago in 1932. During his professional career, he taught at his alma mater, and Marshall College, Tulane University, Georgia State College for Women, Elmira College, and Lake Erie College, Ohio.

Thatcher, Lloyd E. (L. E.)

Thatcher was professor of biology at Ole Miss, whom Wilson Lyon met in Paris in early September, 1926. Girault Jones remembered him as "a skilled organist and an Episcopalian" who helped revitalize the life of the Episcopal church in Oxford. Thatcher, who had only a B. A. degree from Ole Miss, was one of sixteen Ole Miss faculty members who lost their jobs in 1930 during a major political purge of college and university faculties throughout the state that was initiated by Chancellor Powers, with the encouragement of Governor Bilbo. His lack of a Ph. D. was possibly a major factor in his dismissal.

Vice-chancellor: Francis William Pember (1862-1954)

Pember was vice chancellor of Oxford University (1926-1928). The vice chancellor is the senior officer and administrative head of the university. Pember matriculated from Balliol College, Oxford in 1880 and was admitted to the bar at Lincoln's Inn in 1889.

Wilson, Josephine Yongue (1849-1948)

The mother of Wilson Lyon's mother, she was born in Selma, Alabama, moved to Mississippi, and married Thomas Eugene Wilson at the end of the Civil War. They had eight children. Their home was located at Garlandville, Mississippi. Grandmother Wilson was a wonderful homemaker, who loved flowers. She remained alert and active until shortly before the time of her death.

Wylie, Sir Francis James (1865-1952)

Wylie was a lecturer, fellow, and tutor in classics at Brasenose College in Oxford in 1903 when he was named as the first resident agent in Oxford for the Rhodes Trust, a post he held until 1931. He was responsible for the administration of the scholarship program and welcomed the first Rhodes Scholars to Oxford a year before Wilson Lyon was born. As Oxford secretary for the Rhodes Trust, he was deeply involved in the planning and construction of Rhodes House, which became his home and the headquarters for the Rhodes Scholarship program after it opened in May of 1929. The warmth of his relationships with Rhodes Scholars is made clear by Wilson Lyon's references to having tea with him at his home at 9 Park Road.

REFERENCES

Carter, Hodding. *Man and the River: the Mississippi.* Chicago, New York, San Francisco: Rand McNally and Company, 1970.

Civil War Pension Records. Elijah W. Lyon File. National Archives. Washington, D.C.

Heidelberg Centennial 1884-1984: A Travel Through Heidelberg Heritage, 1984.

Hendrick, Burton Jesse. *The Life and Letters of Walter Hines Page.* Garden City: Doubleday, Page and Company, 1925.

High School Report to State Accrediting Commission, 1927-28. Mississippi Department of Archives and History, Jackson, Mississippi.

Jasper County (Mississippi) News, 3 January 1924-27 December 1928. Mississippi Department of Archives and History, Jackson, Mississippi.

Jasper County WPA File. Mississippi Department of Archives and History, Jackson, Mississippi.

Jones, Girault. Personal reflections on Wilson Lyon as an Ole Miss undergraduate. J. D. Williams Library, University of Mississippi, Oxford, Mississippi.

Jordan, Cecil "Boots". *The Story of Jones County Agricultural High School 1911-1957.* Jones County Junior College, 2001.

Kenny, Anthony, ed. *The History of the Rhodes Trust, 1902-1999.* Oxford: Oxford University Press, 2001.

Lyon, E. Wilson. *The Education of a Mississippian.* Personal papers of Elizabeth Lyon Webb.

_____. Letters from abroad to the Lyon family and Girault Jones, 1925-1928. J. D. Williams Library, University of Mississippi, Oxford, Mississippi.

_____. *Louisiana in French Diplomacy, 1759-1804.* Norman: University of Oklahoma Press, 1934.

_____. *The Man who Sold Louisiana, The Career of François Barbé-Marbois.* Norman: University of Oklahoma Press, 1942.

Lyon, E. Wilson Papers. Personal and professional writings. Honnold/Mudd Library, Special Collections of The Libraries of the Claremont Colleges, Claremont, California.

McLemore, Richard Aubrey. *A History of Mississippi.* 2 vols. Hattiesburg: University and College Press of Mississippi, 1973.

McMillen, Neil. *Dark Journey: Black Mississippians in the Age of Jim Crow.* Urbana: Illinois, 1989.

Mississippi Power and Light Company, Economic Research Department. *Mississippi Statistical Summary of Population 1800-1980.* Bay Springs, Paulding, Ellisville, and Jackson, February, 1983. Mississippi Department of Archives and History, Jackson, Mississippi.

The Mississippian. 21 September 1923-24 May 1924. Bound volume. J. D. Williams Library, University of Mississippi, Oxford, Mississippi.

Ole Miss Commencement Week Program 1925, E. Wilson Lyon Papers, Honnold/Mudd Library, Special Collections of The Libraries of the Claremont Colleges, Claremont, California. Box 1, File 17.

A Register of Rhodes Scholars, 1903-1981. Oxford: The Alden Press, 1981.

The Rhodes Trust. *Rhodes Scholarships, Memorandum, United States of America, 1924.* London. Office of the American Secretary of the Rhodes Trust, Vienna, Virginia.

Rotberg, Robert L. *The Founder. Cecil Rhodes and the Pursuit of Power.* Oxford: Oxford University Press, 1988.

Sansing, David G. *The University of Mississippi: A Sesquicentennial History.* Jackson: University Press of Mississippi, 1999.

Smith, Murray Wilson. *Murray and Willie Mae: Their Life Story.* Raleigh, North Carolina: Self-published, 2007.

State of Mississippi, Department of Education. *Biennial Report and Recommendation of the State Superintendent of Public Education to the Legislature of Mississippi for the Scholastic Years 1927-28 and 1928-29.* Mississippi Department of Archives and History, Jackson, Mississippi.

Wilson, Thomas Eugene, Personal account of Civil War service. E. Wilson Lyon Papers, Honnold/Mudd Library, Special Collections of The Libraries of the Claremont Colleges, Claremont, California. Box 1, File 9.